T0302538

TRADITIONAL BRICKWORK

Construction, Repair and Maintenance

TRADITIONAL BRICKWORK

Construction, Repair and Maintenance

TERRENCE LEE

THE CROWOOD PRESS

First published in 2022 by
The Crowood Press Ltd
Ramsbury, Marlborough
Wiltshire SN8 2HR

enquiries@crowood.com

www.crowood.com

© Terrence Lee 2022

All rights reserved. No part of this publication may be reproduced or transmitted in any form or by any means, electronic or mechanical, including photocopy, recording, or any information storage and retrieval system, without permission in writing from the publishers.

British Library Cataloguing-in-Publication Data
A catalogue record for this book is available from the British Library.

ISBN 978 0 7198 4141 5

Cover design: Blue Sunflower Creative

Frontispiece: Tattershall Castle by I. Greenshed

Acknowledgements
The author acknowledges those who have provided help and assistance, including N. Charrington of Layer Marney, East Malling Trust and staff at Bradbourne House, Peter Minter for his assistance in Chapter 2, and all those on whose property I have worked and who have allowed me to take the photos of it – A. Ellis; P. Graham; J. Hoole; P. Kanas; N. Narramore; A. Richards; M. Standage; G. Whitfield; W. Zuk.

Typeset by Simon and Sons
Printed and bound in India by Replika Press Pvt. Ltd.

Contents

This book is about the construction, repair and maintenance of buildings constructed from one of the most versatile building materials yet created – the brick. Wrought from the topmost clays or brick earth, bricks were manufactured in a way that remained essentially unchanged from the twelfth century until industrialization in the nineteenth century when much deeper, harder clays began to be exploited.

Only twice during the long pre-industrial period of brick manufacture covered in this book, did English brickwork reach levels of sublime skill unrivalled in Europe. Yet the repair of this brickwork was as ingrained a tradition as the construction of brickwork itself, a fact observed by Batty Langley (1696–1751), a commentator and architect who observed that '*decay is the life blood of the trade*'.

The intention in this book is not to try to elevate lime mortar-based traditional brickwork skills over those of modern conventional cement-built brickwork on a building site, any more than it is to place lime as a binder over cement in terms of their importance to construction. On the contrary, the aim is to regard them as two sides of the same coin, each equally important in its own realm; well-constructed new build on one hand and traditional brickwork conservation on the other, in the hope that the practitioners of each elevate their skills to a craft through the love and care that they put into it.

Whilst there are interchangeable skills in modern cement-based brickwork and traditional work, many would agree that the skills needed in the use of lime (the interpretation and approach to the myriad of variables in features, qualities and natures of brickwork found across seven centuries of historic brick buildings) requires a different and more varied set of skills. Yet, in undertaking the conservation and restoration of traditional brickwork, my own experience has shown that there should be a balance struck between maintaining tradition and efficiency, and economy of practice so that the skills can be adopted and executed by the modern skilled bricklayer who wishes to learn and bring the skills to site without being shackled too much by the past.

The knowledge and skills included in this book are based on personal experience of working on and studying a diverse range of traditional and historic brick buildings in different parts of the country. I have attempted to base the chapters on the knowledge which I have gained and found to be useful in my own journey within the brickwork craft, and in brickwork conservation in particular.

I have examined the background to the use of brickwork in England, its manufacture and spread, and provided examples of some brick buildings in different parts of the country and particularly those of the southern counties and West Midlands. I have investigated the identification and vulnerability of traditional handmade brick and set out an approach to its assessment and physical examination, as well as tools, materials and aspects of knowledge and principles to both inform and execute repairs. Finally, I have provided examples of some problems which can be encountered when using lime mortars and their maintenance.

Whilst I state from the outset that it is not possible to learn such skills from a book alone, it is hoped nonetheless that it will provide inspiration and information for bricklayers who want to enter the heritage arena, homeowners who are also the custodians of traditional properties and building professionals and enthusiasts alike who wish to understand more about some of the techniques which can be used in the conservation of traditional brickwork.

Chapter One

The Use of Traditional Brick to the End of the Eighteenth Century

Bricks have been used in an unbaked form for perhaps 10,000 years. The searing heat of the desert regions in which they were made baked them sufficiently hard for use in construction. From around 3500 BC, some civilizations such as the Assyrian and Babylonian Empires of Mesopotamia used baked bricks to great effect achieving an extremely high standard fired bricks, often lavishly decorated with coloured enamels, and laid on beds of naturally occurring pitch.

The Romans became consummate manufacturers of tiles and bricks, or *tegula,* both unbaked *crudus* or baked *coctus.* The large increase in population in Rome and other Roman cities by the late Republic (509–27BC) required buildings to be built taller and with baked bricks that were required for this purpose. The Romans possessed the technological skill required to do this and were able to exploit clay deposits to make bricks during their occupation of the British Isles.

Roman bricks, or *tegulae,* were in fact more like thick tiles than bricks as we know them today. They belonged to different size orders measured in multiples of palms of the hand and were serrated so that they could be broken into triangular shaped pieces. This facilitated their use in wall systems, such as *opus testaceum,* in which the bricks provided either a brick facing and/or one or more bonding courses for walls made with either a masonry rubble, or lime, concrete filling. Because Roman bricks have been found in Britain in this form, one could be forgiven for thinking that the Romans left brickmaking as part of their considerable legacy following their departure from the British Isles in 450 AD, but this was not the case.

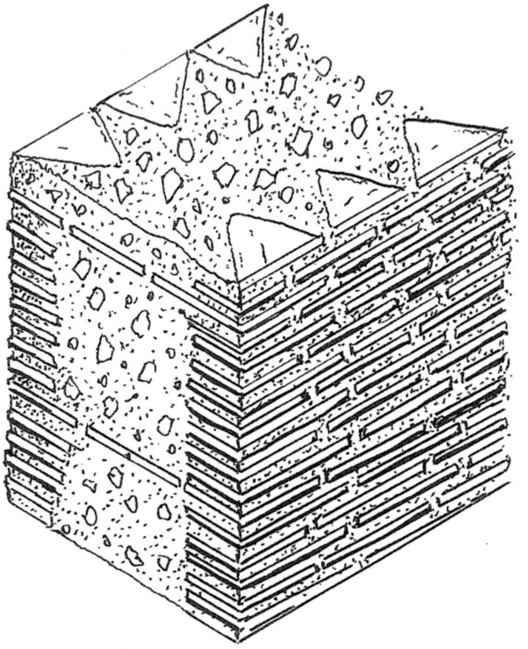

Roman bricks were often used as facings or bonding courses with an infill of lime concrete.

Roman bricks continued to be used in Medieval walling as bonding courses in a lime and rubble wall. Reclaimed brick would have been used wherever it could be found.

Saxon and Norman Brick

When the Romans left Britain in the mid-fifth century, brickmaking of any scale appeared to lapse as there is little knowledge of any such production in this period. This comes as little surprise since the Saxon people who arrived in Britain, and pushed the native Britons westwards, were a timber-working people in a land where timber was still the most accessible construction material, particularly for ordinary people. By the seventh century, the Christianized Saxons carried out considerable salvaging of Roman bricks which can today be found in some of their early churches. Following the Norman invasion and conquest from 1066, stone masonry was used for such churches, too, but only after the Normans had fully established their conquest of England did the skills of masonry become adopted by the Saxons. Whilst there is little available archaeological evidence of Saxon brick manufacture, it is likely that their economic links with Europe and Christian pilgrimages to Rome must have made a deep impression on them, and that their experimentation with brick production was a likely consequence.

Medieval

Norman domination of England led to the gradual replacement of temporary timber fortresses with stone masonry structures, as well as the construction of cathedrals and castles. But the usefulness and versatility of brick was recognized as thousands of bricks were imported as part of the construction of the Tower of London in the late 1070s. In the twelfth century, brickmaking skills were reintroduced to England from the continent where there was already a tradition of brickmaking, the word brick derived from the French *brique*. Examples of early bricks can be found at St Nicholas Church in Essex and large numbers of Roman bricks continued to be used – when they were available – at places such as at St Botolph's Priory. The artery of goods, ideas and skills was the Hanseatic League, a Northern European trading block which had ports in England, and which provided an important conduit via her eastern counties. The introduction of brickmaking skills in England can probably be attributed to craftsmen and brickmakers from Flanders, possibly Flemish immigrants fleeing war or religious persecution and who settled in the eastern regions of England around Hanseatic ports such as Norwich or Hull. The use of brick at this juncture was fashionable and expensive and used exclusively by royalty, nobility, the Church and seminaries of learning. Methods of brickmaking and bricklaying were gradually assimilated by the English with the first brickworks set up in the Hanseatic port of Hull by the end of thirteenth century.

Reasons for the Spread of Brick in England

The prime mover of the introduction of brick in twelfth-century Medieval England was a growing population and prosperity of the country, largely as a result of the wool trade which set in train the introduction of brickmaking and brickwork to England, and which was to transform the built environment. The skills of both manufacture and use of brick were imported from ideas emanating from continental Europe, primarily from Flemish immigrants who were hired for their skills. The skills that were introduced were assimilated into the eastern and south-eastern counties of England where there was comparatively little standing timber and negligible building stone, but where there was an abundance of good brick earths and clays beneath their feet.

Brick was far cheaper to manufacture than it was to extract and shape a piece of stone of the same size and could be deliberately manufactured to a durable hardness and to a size convenient for use. It was also very versatile and could easily integrate into, or be used in conjunction with, other materials such as stone or flint to form composite walling, or with timber. The abundance of good brick clay in some regions enabled clay to be won and bricks to be manufactured close to, if not on, the site of construction making it highly convenient and far more economical. From a practical viewpoint, it was found to be less draughty than wattle and daub when built between timber frames, both storing heat and insulating against sound. It was also fireproof – a crucial factor in a built environment which consisted, for most of the population, of timber-framed buildings whose panels were infilled with wattle and daub, whose floors were covered with rushes and whose rooms were lit with tallow candles. It is no coincidence that because of the threat of fire, it would be the chimney stacks of lesser houses that were among the first elements to be constructed of brick in the fifteenth century.

A significant factor in our understanding of the spread of brick in England was the nature and condition of transport links. As late as the eighteenth century, there were barely any roads as such, but very often simple mud tracks which would have been treacherous, if not impassable, during the winter, and would involve the loading and offloading of carts to enable them to travel up steeper inclines, not to mention the potential for brigandage and robbery. Bricks, on the other hand, could be made and used wherever good clay was found and often near to where the building was intended to be built. This factor only began to change with the advent of canals in the late eighteenth century.

Brick already had a long tradition of use in the Netherlands, Germany and Poland, and where brickmaking had continued to develop after the decline and fall of the Western Roman Empire. Now English royalty, nobility and the Church could demonstrate their largesse in a fashionable material that, quite apart from all the practical benefits as a fireproof material, could be either cut and shaped on the spot by the use of a brick axe, scutch hammer or the edge of a trowel, or deliberately moulded and fired into desired shapes for architectural enrichments or for decorative finishes and then finished in situ. It could be colour washed both to unify and add lustre to walling or arranged in patterns using contrasting brick colours and glazes, with the jointing painted or struck to form shadow and symmetry.

At first, many thousands of bricks were imported for use in high status properties and ecclesiastical buildings. By the thirteenth century, England's eastern Hanseatic ports such as Hull, founded in 1290, not only provided a conduit for the importation of brick but in 1303 also became the first English town to have its own brickmaking facility. Because fine clay

St Nicholas Church, the Capella ante Portas of Coggeshall Abbey. Bricks here measure 330mm × 152mm × 51mm within its walls. These 'great bricks' date from the end of the twelfth century and are perhaps among the oldest Medieval bricks to be found in the country. (Photo: John Armagh)

Remains of St Botolph's Priory, Colchester, Essex. Roman bricks continued to be salvaged and used where they could be found, such as in St. Botolph's Priory, dating to the late twelfth century where large quantities were used. (Photo: John Armagh)

deposits were found to be abundant, particularly in Eastern England where good stone was scarce, it was only a matter of time before enterprising craftsmen – driven by the needs of the nobility and of the Church – began to make them in England.

Medieval Brickwork

Medieval brickwork focused on the desires of royalty, nobility and the Church to construct palaces and castles as status symbols and power projection in England and Europe. Ordinary people continued to live in timber-framed houses, with few lesser houses being built entirely of brick until the eighteenth century. Before the skills of brickwork and brickmaking were adopted in England and assimilated into working practice, brickmakers and bricklayers were often hired from the continent and commissioned to produced work of a very decorative nature including intricate coloured patterning of the exterior, moulded work and coloured joints and walls. Medieval brickwork tends to be generally irregular in composition, not least because of the wide irregularities of the bricks used but also perhaps due to the inexperience of indigenous bricklayers.

Photograph of Tattershall Castle, Lincolnshire 1434–35. The skills of brickwork were seized upon by English nobility during the Medieval era. (Photo: I Greenshed)

Medieval brickwork, though characterful, can tend to be nuanced in appearance and can include such idiosyncrasies as the use of random sized cuts of brick in the wall and an inconsistent bonding arrangement on successive courses. Inconsistencies in brick length affected the arrangement or bonding of the brickwork leading to 'straight joints' in which one perpendicular joint appeared directly over another (inexcusable in modern brickwork) in a run of brickwork where a consistent overlap or bond could not be achieved.

Yet another factor in the reason for the irregularities of brickwork in this period (and to an extent in later work, too), was the fact that English brick working was in its infancy and the skills had not developed or been fully assimilated from their continental cousins. It was not yet subject to the principles or rules of bonding which bricklayers would in time apply to their work, and which would be developed over the centuries and make the work more pleasing to the eye. Medieval masons who were used to working with stone appear to have treated the bricks rather like random stone masonry, in which the requirement for bonding was perhaps less stringent. Perhaps they were also driven by the need to minimize wastage of the precious commodity of brick, and to use any cut that could be put in the wall.

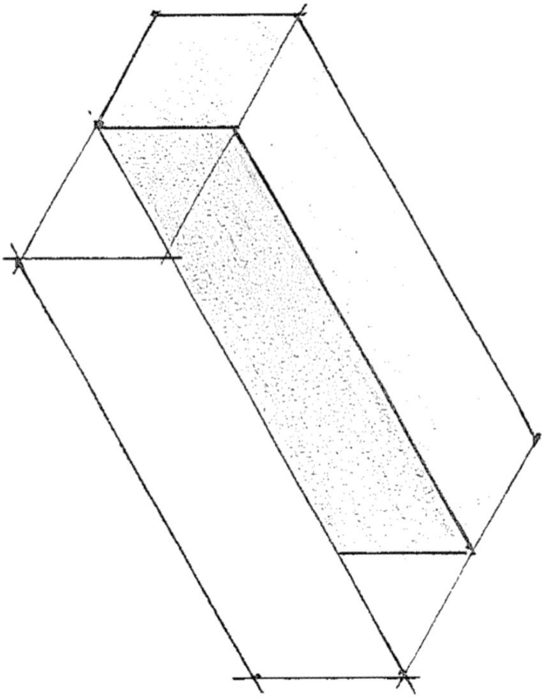

A queen closer is a full half a brick lengthways, whilst a closer is half a queen closer and used to produce ¼ bond.

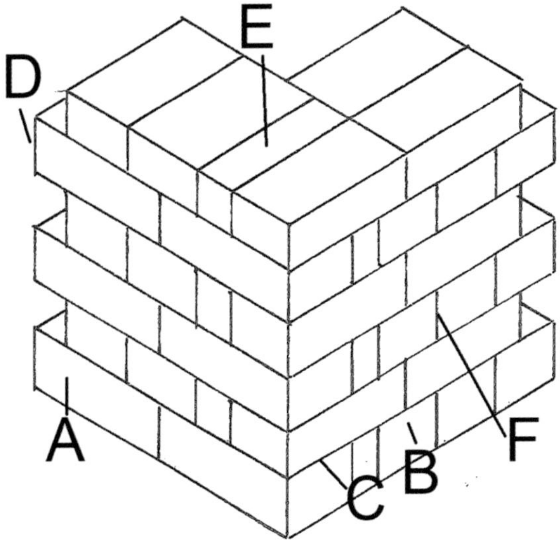

English bond quoin indicating brick craft terminology. A ¼ bond, or lap, is achieved by use of a queen closer of approximately ¼ brick in size inserted after the quoin header. Note that when the wall changes direction, the bond changes. A=stretcher; B=header; C=bed joint; D=toothing; E=queen closer; F=perpendicular joint.

Two bonds of this era were English bond and English cross bond. These are the strongest of brickwork bonds and consist of alternate courses of headers and stretchers. Of these, English bond could be considered more austere visually. This bond gives the greatest strength (over appearance) of all bonds because of the number of headers projecting into the wall. It was a bond which perhaps provided medieval bricklayers, who had been used to working with stone masonry, assurance of strength.

English cross bond was very similar to English bond, except that a header is inserted beside the first stretcher on alternate stretcher courses making them visually less monotonous and more pleasing to the eye than English bond. It enables patterns to be incorporated into the brickwork by using selected coloured bricks yet is as strong as English bond. Medieval brickwork was of substantial thickness which, when measured in multiples of brick length, could be several bricks thick. This was considered necessary

English cross bond is an optimum bond because it creates the stepping effect to enable the use of patterning whilst still as strong as English bond. Note the bonding arrangement at the quoin in which a header is placed after the stretcher on alternate stretcher courses.

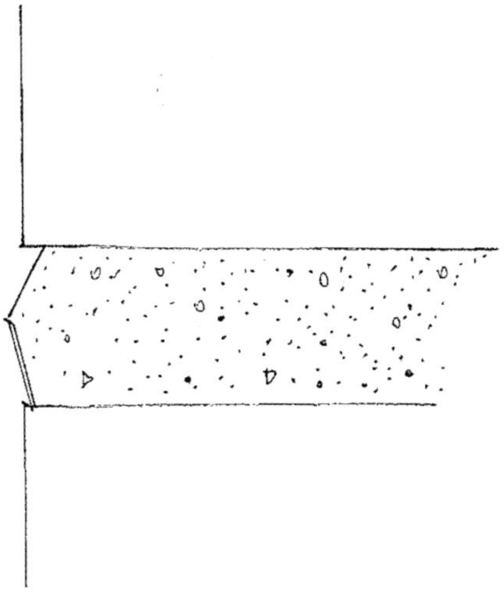

A profile of a double struck joint. The point of the joint was rarely as sharp as this one shown, but the shadow cast by the lower angle could be particularly effective.

to support the huge timbers, or bressummers, used in construction of floors and roofs of the palatial buildings constructed during the period.

Pattern in the brickwork was a common feature of the grand medieval brick houses and castles of the nobility and royalty. The patterns were arranged in all manner of shapes including saltires, crosses, diamonds, etc. They were produced by using bricks that had been fired to a dark blue or grey colour due to being closer to the heat source in the clamp. They were chosen to be laid in specific places on each course of bricks to achieve the desired pattern. Salt glazes could be painted on the ends of bricks to increase the number of these dark headers.

Joints were often thicker on bed and perpendicular joints to compensate for differences in brick thickness, sometimes as much as 25mm thick, and were used to bring the brickwork courses up to gauge where required and to offset the irregularities of Medieval brick. Medieval joints were given different profiles such as a double struck profile which, in effect, separated the thick joint in two thereby reducing the impact of such a thick joint. They could also be painted in different colours to create shadow and contrast. The mortar used was lime putty which was relatively soft compared to the hydraulic limes used in later centuries. Brickwork was often colour washed using pigments to achieve a consistent colour and which would make subsequent patterning and jointing stand out to great effect. For this purpose, natural earth ochres were imported from the continent just as they still are today.

Brick Sizes

Medieval brick sizes varied considerably, some known as great bricks could measure as much as 250mm × 127mm × 50mm, the width being slightly more than the 100–105mm which has been consistent throughout the history of brick development. Such large bricks would have been cumbersome and inconvenient to use and would in effect be treated as masonry blocks.

Brickwork in the Sixteenth Century

Background

The Tudor Period saw an increase prosperity and wealth in the nation based on the wool trade and new opportunities for building farms and country houses on new tracts of land by the gentry that had been recently seized from the Church during the Dissolution of the Monasteries. Henry VIII encouraged the construction of stylish properties by wealthy landowners from lands seized from the church by the Crown. The use of brick, now highly fashionable and more accessible, became high status, not only in the south and east of the country but also now spread into the West Midlands. Consequently, brickwork began to be seen as a craft to be undertaken in the same league as stone masonry. It was fashionable with key figures of royalty, the nobility and the Church who chose brick for their substantial palaces. The skills of the bricklayers reached new heights of excellence too, and this period is notable for decoration and use of colour. This can be seen in fine examples of patterned brickwork at Layer Marney Tower in which the clever use of bonding enabled diverse patterns to be created. Although in general there was at least a partial reliance on commissioning continental craftsmen and brickmakers, the skills of brickwork were now being assimilated by English bricklayers.

Layer Marney Tower in Essex (*c.*1520) is an exquisite example of brickwork and terracotta with sublime patterning and moulded brickwork, including label moulding, over the windows. (Photo by kind permission of N. Charrington)

Tudor Approach to Brickwork

Tudor brickwork was characterized by red brick, elaborate gate houses, vivid decoration and stone features, particularly around openings. Moulded brick was popular because it could be used to replicate masonry features, such as for label moulds, but perhaps more famously in chimneys. The chimney stack was one of the first manifestations of brick for many people as coal burning, which was becoming more prevalent, made the removal of smoke and fumes imperative. For those that could afford one, chimney stacks became a major focal point. Appearing in the sixteenth century, the degree of decoration reached in chimney decoration was epitomized in buildings such as Hampton Court Palace which was built in the early sixteenth century with later additions which continued to be incorporated into high end brickwork construction centuries later. These highly ornate twisted chimneys were constructed by manufacturing moulded bricks into specific shapes and then rubbing them in situ to a final finish. Elsewhere, use of the brick axe to cut a brick into shapes to be finished it in situ was a common feature of this era.

Brickwork Bonds and Joints

English bond, or English cross bond, continued to be used, because the latter provided the means to insert elaborate decoration in the form of patterned brickwork or diapers using grey flared headers of the bricks. A myriad of patterns was used, including diamonds, saltires, zig zags and crosses, in particular diaper patterns formed by coloured headers, but many other patterns too. Binder-rich mortar joints were still relatively thick compared to later eras. The joints often double struck which reduced the visual impact of the jointing on an elevation by half by dividing the joint and creating shadow.

Brickwork and Timber Frames

Timber framing was a method of construction in England for many centuries, and most of those buildings that survive were built in the sixteenth and seventeenth centuries. When brick became available, it became fashionable to have the panels of these buildings bricked up in a method known as brick noggin, which improved resistance to fire and was less draughty than the original wattle and daub that had been used for millennia. Sometimes, the timber frame was constructed on a brick plinth to form a hard-wearing and fireproof base for the building.

Brick noggin is sometimes found to be a ½ brick thick (approximately 100mm) which explains why stretcher bond was often used in this situation. Brick noggin is sometimes found to have been built against an inner core of rougher brick infill which was plastered on the inside. Sometimes, two skins of brick are tied together by the occasional header brick or occasionally simply a ½ brick thick wall. In 1605, James I banned the use of timber to build houses and although one reason was the threat of fire, he may have also been concerned that timber stocks should be retained for construction of naval ships.

Brickwork in the Seventeenth Century

Background

Although brick was still considered a material reserved for wealthier people, its use in the construction of chimneys and infilling between timbers had spread rapidly. Meanwhile, influences and ideas of the Enlightenment in Continental Europe, which had already been active for years, manifested themselves in England led by Inigo Jones (1573–1652). His knowledge of architecture of the Classical Roman and Greek periods led to architecture as a new profession, and inspired those that could afford them to incorporate these features into their new houses.

Brick noggin in a timber-framed house. Brick can place stresses on timbers when used in this way. However, given the size of timbers involved some examples have stood for centuries.

The prime mover for the spread and development of brickwork in this century was the Rebuilding Act of 1667 governing construction which appeared in the period after the Great Fire of London in 1666. A part of this was the prohibition of the construction of timber-framed buildings completely and minimizing its use in other elements of façade construction, and incorporating methods intended to prevent the spread of fire within the brickwork itself. This pivotal event changed the nature of building and the rapidity of the spread of brickwork which forever changed the built landscape, first in the cities – beginning with London – but then eventually creeping slowly into the countryside where timber-framed houses began to take on coats of brick as their owners upgraded them with this new and fashionable material. Many bricklayers came to London during this period to help with reconstruction. Known as 'foreigners', they helped to spread bricklaying skills further afield into the rural counties. Whilst the threat of fire presented the practical reason to rebuilding in brick, it also lent itself to the style adopted by those that could afford to build the new classism whose ideas were borrowed from the continent, in particular Italy, and which was introduced into England by Sir Christopher Wren (1632–1723).

A brick façade in Rye, East Sussex (c.1623), with a distinct Renaissance feel and straight out of an artisan's pattern book, here incorporating classical elements including panels, 'streight' arches above the windows, pediments, pilasters and moulded brickwork with a plinth at the base. The bond here is English, still common at this time as a façade bond.

Brick Quality and Size

The seventeenth century saw technological advancement in brick manufacture which improved the quality of bricks, together with ideas and styles influenced largely by the Netherlands. They still had a very rustic quality, though, particularly in the first quarter of the century. Brick sizes vary between different qualities of brick and, whilst they might be consistent within

Patterned brickwork of 1607, a continuation of the style of the previous centuries, here used in conjunction with stone quoins. The brickwork appears to be English cross bond, yet is still quite random in the use of ½ and ¾ bats, a factor which no doubt aided the forming of the patterns made with flared headers.

These rustic bricks belong to the building shown above and are very rustic in appearance, resembling those of earlier centuries. The original light mortar can be seen underneath, whilst the modern cement pointing placed over the top of it is dark grey in colour.

A high level of skills shown here both in brickmaking and laying. Moulded brickwork at the pediments and cornicing, and gauged indented arches above the openings creating shadow and contrast. The bond used here is English bond.

An axed brickwork semi-circular arch. Here the brick voussoirs are cut to a templet but made from the facing brick rather than a rubber used in gauged work.

An example of a brick plinth built on sandstone footing, *c.* late 1600s, in Ellesmere, Shropshire. Note the difference in brick quality of the brick and brickwork of the lower plinth and the facing brickwork above it. The finer red facing bricks measure 230mm x 105mm x 60mm, whilst those of the plinth are 235mm x 105mm x 63mm but with considerable variation.

one building, they might differ from another of the same period.

Foundations, Plinths and Footings

Buildings did not have foundations as we recognize them today, but instead might have had brick footings. Footings may have consisted of several courses of brickwork below ground level and were built from bricks that would not pass for the best facing work, but which were no less durable and were very suitable for this purpose. A similarly hard yet less visually attractive brick might have been used to form a plinth under the façade of a house, whilst some country houses were built on large masonry blocks seated directly on the earth and which provided a stable platform on which to build the brickwork. Lesser houses sometimes had a footing consisting of brick on edge laid directly on the earth. Damp proof courses (DPCs) were unknown and did not begin to appear until the nineteenth century.

Anatomy of a Seventeenth-Century Country House Wall

Later in the seventeenth century, it became fashionable to transform earlier timber-framed buildings into

Brick on edge footing laid directly onto soil. Foundations were practically unknown in early domestic brick buildings.

brick ones and imitate ideas and fashions emanating from London as far as budgets would allow. To do this, the method used was often to fill in the timber frame and build a skin around it of facing bricks. Quite often, this outer skin was not tied into the inner brickwork, so whilst a building may have had walls nominally two bricks thick or more, the outer wall could be of a skin of brickwork approximately 100mm in thickness.

The infilling of the timber frame of the original building was done with relatively poor-quality underfired bricks, or semmels, and in no particular bond. Random sized pieces of brick have also been used in this backing brickwork and these do not conform to the gauge height (brick and joint) to that of the outer skin. An avoidance of waste of materials was probably a major consideration in the construction.

Brickwork Bonds

English bond continued to be used in the seventeenth century due to its strength, but Flemish bond was up and coming, and first appeared in its truest form in the Dutch House in Kew, Surrey in 1631. The Dutch House was one of a cluster of important brick buildings built during the reign of Charles I, known as the Artisan Mannerist, which alludes to the whim of the artisan bricklayer in constructing brickwork features for their clients from pattern books influenced by designs from the continent. Artisan is a word that today is more often linked with certain types of traditionally made bread or beer, but even as recently as the 1980s it was a term used when referring to City and Guilds craft disciplines.

The external skin of this Shropshire country house constructed during the late seventeenth century looks, from the outside, like a solid wall in Flemish bond but is in fact only ½ a brick (100mm) thick. The bricks used for the outer skin are of a good-quality facing brick with good arrises and are consistent in colour.

From the mid-seventeenth century, Flemish bond became the bond of choice in brickwork until the beginning of the twentieth century. It was considered more attractive to look at than the austere English bond. Whilst weaker than English bond (it has internal straight joints), it was more economical because it enabled poorer-quality bricks to be used behind the front or face bricks, thus reducing costs. The Dutch House also demonstrates the first instance of gauged work in England. The term *gauge* simply means 'measure' and it suggests the degree of accuracy in preparation, setting out and execution of this sublime skill. Using soft bricks, known by practitioners of this art as

Front view of Kew Palace, in Kew Gardens, London. Formerly called the Dutch House, it was a residence of King George III and Queen Charlotte of Mecklenburg-Strelitz. The Dutch House demonstrates a first in the skills of the brickwork craft during this period. It is the earliest building in England where pure Flemish bond was used, in which alternate headers and stretchers are used on the same course. (Albertistvan CC BY SA 2.5)

'rubbers,' gauged brickwork can be constructed using extremely fine joints which are as narrow as 1.5mm. At the Dutch House, it has been used to construct the Ionic and Corinthian capitals either side of the front door. In some cases, gauged work during this period could appear more clunky and less refined than in the eighteenth century, but it was none the less used to great effect. Colour washing continued to be used to unify the brickwork of premier building façades.

Colour washing on late seventeenth-century brickwork, Montgomery, Wales.

Pointing and Jointing

Double struck joints were still used on Jacobean brickwork to divide joints (to provide shadow) which were still relatively wide due to the nature of the bricks. Another method was to strike the centre of the joint with a line produced by running a tool with a thin bladed profile over a straight edge. The effect of this was to divide the wide joint and to avert the eye away from the rougher edges of the rustic brick.

Brickwork in the Eighteenth Century

Background

For most of the eighteenth century, the Georgian Dynasty reigned, and their architecture was centred on those of the Classical Roman and Greek eras whose civilizations were revered for their grandeur, power, sobriety and order. Well-connected English travellers were inspired by the ruins of these civilizations

Ruled jointing on a form of Flemish bond brickwork, sixteenth-century, Cockshutt, Shropshire. The mortar used here is lime rich and was doughy and fatty in consistency to enable a neat and relatively deep profile like this.

A profile of a modern yet appropriate double struck joint in Canterbury, Kent, with a more rounded, rather than pointed, centre profile. The joint is achieved by running a trowel along the top and bottom arrises.

and brought back ideas to England where they were quickly absorbed into building practice. The architectural basis of the ideal building was considered to be the Roman temple, but the philosophy of construction of this long era, encompassed three key principles of refinement, good taste and craftsmanship.

By adopting an approach like this, buildings of all types and sizes during this era achieved a greater degree of standardization than perhaps at any other point in history. Whilst on the one hand, a sublime quality of brickwork was achieved on the finest buildings, even the humblest of houses could show evidence of the bricklayer's skill even if only a nod to the classical features. Although many grand country houses were constructed by the wealthy, the English townhouse was, and still is, perhaps the most ubiquitous landmark of this philosophy and can be found in many towns and villages of England. This century is notable, too, for the deceptions employed to make building materials look more refined (and thus more expensive). In brickwork, a notable example of this approach was tuck pointing which gave the impression that the building was constructed in gauged brickwork.

Sometimes corners were cut in the construction of brickwork to save time and money, and this was manifested in the use of bonding timbers inserted into the inner walls. These were intended to help to tie the brickwork together, to bring brickwork to level or simply to save on bricks used. Then, as now, there were bricklayers of different levels of skill and aptitude, some working continually on more mundane works, others on high craft enrichments.

Garden Wall Bonds

Garden wall bonds, such as English and Flemish, generally consist of three to five courses of stretchers to one course of the core bond (headers or alternate headers and stretchers respectively). Often used for the rear and sides of buildings, garden wall bonds required fewer headers and enabled poorer quality, though no less durable, bricks to be used. It is a feature of this era that the fronts of buildings were often constructed by bricklayers using a finer brick than the sides and rear.

The radical building planning laws and fire prevention, which were initiated in the seventeenth century, continued into the eighteenth century. It was found that a new system of rating buildings by floor space and value could help reduce costs by adopting a largely symmetrical and less flamboyant style of brickwork façade, which often consisted of a flat slab of brick masonry with vertical linear window openings and

Town house *c*.1700, Church Stretton, Shropshire. Still drawing on fashions from the previous century, it has stone quoins and enrichments and gauged brickwork arches. This building would have been extremely fashionable in a rural county at this point in history.

Bradbourne House, East Malling, Kent. Modernized in the Adam style in 1774, this exquisite building epitomizes the Georgian building philosophy in symmetry, order and craftsmanship and encompasses numerous brickwork features beloved by them. (Photo by kind permission of East Malling Trust)

Garden wall bonds consist of three to five courses of stretchers to one course of the core bond. Here, English garden wall bond with four courses of stretchers to one of headers.

Bonding timbers inserted into internal walls and could be prone to decay in damp conditions.

Flemish garden wall bond here with stretchers to one course of Flemish bond.

Monk bond is similar to Flemish bond but has two stretchers to each header on every course.

The epitome of Georgian town house design displayed on houses at Bedford Square, London. Note the symmetrical layout, gauged arches above the windows and brick and Coadstone around the entrances.

central decorative doorways, arches over the windows and culminated with a brick parapet at the top to conceal the roof. Generally, the eighteenth century saw the introduction of some pivotal technological improvements to the finished brick (*see* Traditional Brick Manufacture from the Twelfth to the Eighteenth Century) and hence to the appearance of finished brickwork.

Quality and Size of Bricks

Technological improvements and standardization, good-quality brick clays and a reduction

The 'bricks' on this Queen Anne style property in Tenterden, Kent, appear in places to stand proud from one another as if poorly laid. In fact, they are mathematical tiles hung on battens and designed to look like bricks, a practice common in towns of the southeast of England. Note the Queen Anne arch with badly damaged voussoirs.

in costs in brick production saw better-quality bricks being made and brick being used to construct houses at different social levels. Lesser-quality bricks continued to be used for the sides and rears of buildings and for utilitarian structures. During this period, brick sizes were coincidentally very similar to the size of the modern metric brick, but this changed with the advent of the brick tax in 1784, at which point bricks reached sizes that would equate in size to later Victorian imperial bricks.

Foundations and Footings

Buildings of this era were often constructed with a brick footing of several courses, sometimes on a foundation of crushed and rammed rubble or clinker, and sometimes directly onto the sub soil or constructed in a trench using a hard, durable brick. Partition walls, in particular, are often found to have been built directly onto soil. Walls were generally thicker at the base to provide stability, perhaps two bricks thick or more and diminishing to one brick thick at the parapet.

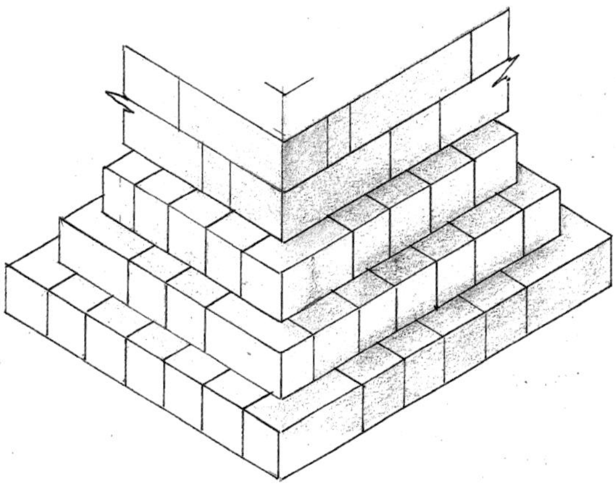

A typical footing found below ground level at the base of a wall from the eighteenth century onwards. Note the use of header bricks to provide strength in construction.

Brickwork Bonds

As with previous centuries, it was a matter of pure economics to use the best quality bricks on the fronts of buildings and the second-class, but no less durable, bricks on the backs and sides. Flemish bond was the bond of choice for this century because it was seen as pleasing to the eye. For a time, header bond was also highly regarded and favourable on brick façades because it provided a complex mesh of jointing which was pleasing to the eye, and was an extremely strong bond on account of the number of header brick laid transversely on the wall. Here too, bricks were sometimes snapped to give the appearance of header bond but without the full depth of brick. Garden wall bonds were common on the sides and rears of houses, and utilitarian rough-ringed arches were often used over openings on these elevations. Internally, brickwork bonds could be quite random on the basis that it was expected to be plastered.

Flemish bond is visually more pleasing than other bonds and was the bond of choice for face work until late in the nineteenth and early twentieth centuries. The bond enabled fewer facing bricks to be used by inserting an inferior-quality brick behind the face stretcher.

Colour and Contrast

Colour was used in eighteenth-century brickwork to great effect and was a key component of the Restoration era and of Georgian brickwork finish. Colour and contrast could be achieved in different ways and on all classes of property. For example, different hues of brick were often built around openings and above window heads, or used to differentiate block bonding on corners of buildings or in the form of darker flared header bricks. Such facings were often accentuated and enriched by using the centuries-old tradition of colour washing called ruddle (which was used to mark the backs of sheep) using natural pigment, with a medium of glue size, to provide lustre and definition. Contrasts were achieved simply by the use of bricks of different colours, textures and qualities or by forming chequerboard patterns.

During the middle of the century, there was some opposition by some prominent architects and commentators to the use of red bricks, and colours which were more akin to the colours of stone were advocated. Colours such as browns and dirty yellows, which resembled stone, were popular as were blue and grey bricks as these were believed to have been made from the best brick earths.

An example of different brickwork contrasts from Faversham in Kent. Here, yellow stocks contrast with red window dressings whilst gauged brickwork in the form of flat arches, pilasters, cornicing and platt band provide the enrichment. It is probable that the façade would have been tuck pointed, too. Note the appearance of sagging in these flat arches.

A brick façade with contrasting flared blue headers and red stretchers in Flemish bond in Wem, Shropshire. Note the broken bond to the right of the window consisting of two headers occurring on alternate courses which avoids an unsightly run of three stretchers and allows for a header and closer at the reveal.

Yellow Stock Bricks

A certain type of brick, ubiquitous in London and other parts of the South East, is known in housebuilding as the 'London stock'. Although yellow in colour, they were strangely referred to as grey stocks perhaps as a result of the bricks being manufactured by mixing lime with fuel ash and other such substances. The best

Contrasting cream stretchers and blue headers in Flemish bond, Wem, Shropshire.

A flared header commonly used to create colour contrast and pattern. Note the contrasting yellow mortar typical of the south of England.

Contrasting grey headers with cherry red window dressings around the openings, Hampshire.

Blue grey headers in a house in Canterbury, Kent. The close mesh produced by header bond was found very appealing, whilst the blue bricks make a pleasant contrast with the red window dressings and quoin. Note the modern cement pointing below the window.

Queen Anne style house with contrasting header and stretchers in a house in Tenterden, Kent, used to great effect to create a chequer pattern.

Brown, earthy coloured brick, and brown mortar (perhaps used to imitate stone masonry) used in conjunction with stone quoin in Canterbury, Kent.

Contrasting colours of yellow stock facing bricks with red block bonded facings. The stocks used here have the small flecks of black which is caused by the internal fuel used in their production.

examples of these yellow bricks are known as *malms* from the brick earth from which they were made which had a high, naturally occurring lime content and produced the familiar yellow colour. The material to make these fine quality bricks ran out in the mid-nineteenth century, at which point chalk had to be brought in and added to the clay to produce them. Yellow stocks come in a variety of hues of yellow and buff, and often have black particles on the surface which are as a result of the use of internal fuel in the bricks.

Pointing and Jointing Finishes

Jointing in brickwork is a term which refers to the bricklayer's finishing the joints as work proceeds by striking, inverting or dividing them with a neat linear compression, or creating a visually pleasing line at the lower arris of the brick. Pointing in contrast is carried out after the brickwork has been constructed and often on top of the bed joints whilst they had not fully hardened. Mortar joints made a significant visual impact on a façade of between 25 and 30 per cent of the wall surface. Jointing or pointing the brickwork, therefore, adds symmetry and order to brickwork, either drawing the eye from rougher quality bricks or completely disguising the bricks and joints to make them look finer.

Fine-quality malm bricks used in the construction of deep faced gauged arches and semi-circular arches set in chequer patterned brickwork, Hampshire.

Tuck Pointing

Tuck pointing began to appear in the mid-eighteenth century as a deception to give the impression that the building was a much more expensive proposition. The application of finer details and quality then, as now, depends on the money available to carry out the work with gauged work being the most expensive form of brickwork available. In essence, this entailed the disguising of the existing brickwork, first by unifying of the surface by colour washing it. Then, the joints were filled with a pigmented mortar or *stopping* to cover up the rough edges of the bricks which matched to the brick colour and then applying a straight bead of contrasting lime putty which would appear as a perfectly symmetrical mortar beds and joints. In time, this method became the finish of choice for all premier façade and in the nineteenth century was even used on utilitarian buildings during the Victorian era such as water towers, pumping stations and below railway bridges.

Traditional Reasons for Failure of Tuck Pointing

Then as now, tuck pointing sometimes failed due to poor workmanship, incorrect methods, materials and costs. Today it can be found sometimes largely intact, sometimes with barely any remaining or with vestiges of the original colour wash on the bricks and minimal putty ribbon visible. Tuck pointing may have failed not long after it was applied for several reasons.

White tuck pointing on blackened stock bricks in London. The perpendicular putty ribbons are vertically plumb whilst the horizontals are equally spaced.

Sometimes, to save time, coloured stopping was not inserted to the correct depth, if at all, and the putty ribbon had been applied over a normal bed joint that had been coloured. Occasionally, the stopping had not been *housed,* which means a narrow compression made centrally to the joints to receive the putty, or had been laid directly over brick causing it to drop off relatively quickly. Tuck pointing is an aesthetic rather than a structural joint and is vulnerable if applied incorrectly or with the wrong materials and methods. Yet whilst historic tuck pointing could fail through poor workmanship or method, it is also vulnerable from the effects of environmental conditions, atmospheric

In this late nineteenth-century example from Tenterden, in Kent, the vulnerability of tuck pointing is evident. The putty bead has been laid over the top of the bricks in many instances as a result of the setting out of the work but much of it has fallen away. Note the dark stopping used and brick smiles in the brick faces.

Tuck pointing applied directly over the bricks of an arch in Wem, Shropshire. Note the difference between the actual brick positions and the setting out of the putty ribbon.

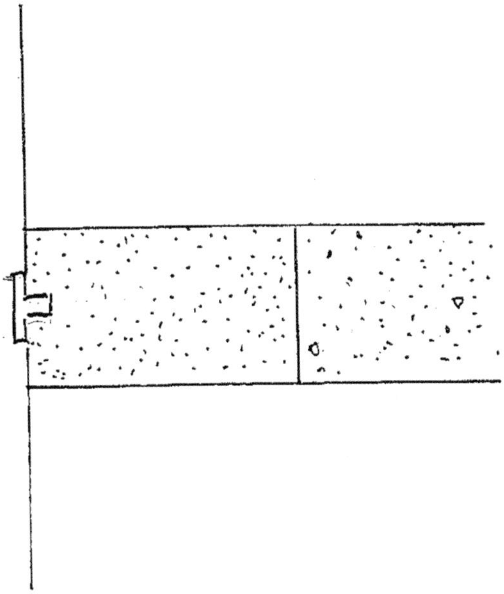

Profile of tuck pointing showing the lime putty 'tucked' into a housing or groove in the backing mortar, at a point when both will fuse together and the putty sits proud of the brickwork.

In this example from Shropshire, the bed joint has been coated with a colour wash as a substitute for inserting stopping. The ribbon was applied directly onto it, possibly with no incision or 'housing' for it to be tucked into and may have resulted in its failure. Interestingly, the edges of the headers have all been bevelled by hand.

pollution, chemical damage (salts) and to decay because of modern interventions such as hard cement pointing.

Penny Rolled or Ruled Jointing

More commonly during the seventeenth and eighteenth centuries, joints were treated in a far less elaborate way than tuck pointing, but where craftsman's touch was still apparent. One example is a joint variously termed penny rolled, penny ha'penny or ruled joint in which an impression is made central to the bed and the perpendicular joints. This joint could be regarded as a deception because its neat, ruled lines draw the eye from the rougher edges of the bricks, whilst providing symmetry to the brickwork. It is important to note that often on speculative builds, teams of pointers would point up a building after the walls had been constructed using a thin veneer of lime – a rich, fine mortar – over that of the still green (not fully hard) brickwork joints. This is possible because the putty used was moisture retentive (so stays soft for longer) and would still be green enough to form a bond between the two, provided the timing was right.

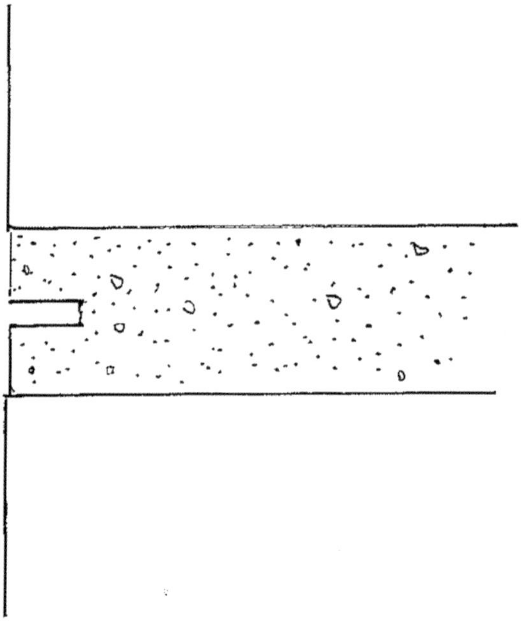

Profile of a ruled joint showing the central compression of between 1mm and 2mm, this one with a flat profile.

A lime rich mortar has been laid over the bed joints but has crazed after it was carried out, something that if executed today would not be a desirable outcome.

A fine example of penny rolled or ruled jointing *c*.1770 illustrating how this simple device can add symmetry to walling and distract the eye from brick quality whilst providing shadow effect. The width of the compression is 2mm – the profile often found to be dictated by the thickness of the joint. Note, the vertical compressions do not cross the horizontal ones.

Overhand Struck Joint

Another type of eighteenth-century jointing is the struck joint or, as it was also known, overhand struck joint, which consists of an inverted joint

A fine example of a panel of ruled jointing shown here with a 1mm profile on lime mortar joints with well made, woodfired bricks contrasting with red facing bricks at Bradbourne House, East Malling, Kent. (Photo by kind permission of East Malling Trust)

The struck joint is inverted or angled inwards (A). The joint is ruled at the invert to draw the eye away from the unevenness of the brick blow (B) by effectively dividing the joint (C).

This original example of eighteenth-century penny-rolled jointing in Wem, Shropshire, was spared the fate of the rest of the façade (which has been cement pointed) by the erection of a small porch the outline of which is still visible but has since been removed.

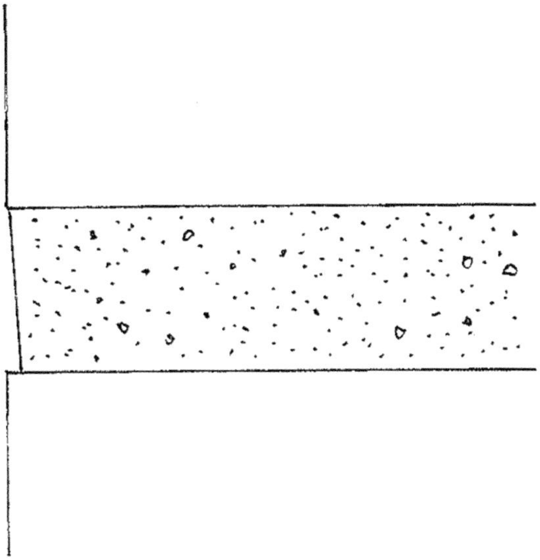

Profile of the overhand struck joint. Today, this type of joint would not be specified by architects because the ledge produced at the bottom of the joint might retain moisture which could freeze during winter and cause damage to brick arrises.

An example of an overhand struck joint on an eighteenth-century façade. The joint has been cut using a Frenchman at the point at which the joint is inverted.

which created a ledge of 1–2mm on the arris of the brick beneath it, and then struck again along the top edge of the joint. Whilst it is sometimes stated that joint was used internally only, there is abundant evidence of it on the side and rear elevations of Georgian buildings and sometimes on the front, too. Struck joints might show evidence of another

An example of a late nineteenth-century overhand struck joint. Note the fine line at the top of the joint executed using a Frenchman and the ledge formed at the bottom of a trowel blade width. The angle on the perpendicular joint is inverted from right to left, the opposite way to weather struck and cut pointing.

device, sometimes ruled, sometimes lightly incised using a Frenchman tool.

Weather Struck and Cut Joint

The weather struck and cut joint is a joint of the mid to late nineteenth century and was not used prior to this. It lends itself to larger, well-formed bricks with sharp arrises and narrow joints beloved by the Victorians and Edwardians. Today, a version of this joint finish is often seen applied to buildings of all historical eras – not only historically inappropriate but often poorly applied – overhanging onto bricks, and either untrimmed or trimmed without the use of a straight edge.

Inappropriate cement mortar weather struck on Georgian era brickwork.

Window Openings

A major change in construction habits emerged in the eighteenth century, with a view to fire prevention, regarding window openings, via two key Building Acts. From 1709, wooden sash window boxes were required to be set back 4 inches (100mm) into the opening in an attempt to prevent fire windows igniting (which can happen in an extremely hot

Although this window is a replacement and not original, it has been installed virtually flush with the brickwork as it would have been before the Acts (to reduce the risk of fire) were introduced. There appears to be no rebate. Note the gauged and moulded bricks to the platt band above the window.

Example of a post-1774 Build Act opening showing the brick rebate against which the sash box was positioned.

The sash box is set behind a rebate in this photo. Note the use of white painted render on the window reveals to reflect light.

A selection of gauged brickwork enrichments of sublime quality at Bradbourne House, East Malling, Kent. The bricklayers who built these were at the very top of their profession. (Photo by kind permission of East Malling Trust)

atmosphere). In 1774, the timber was also required to be hidden behind a brick rebate of 4 inches.

Gauged Brickwork

Gauged brickwork enrichments are features constructed with much finer quality bricks than even the best facing bricks, and with very narrow joints. The skills required to construct gauged brickwork are at the pinnacle of the bricklayer's craft. Such features were used to enrich the façades of premier houses on the principle floors, but gauged camber arches

Deep red gauged ashlar work with 3mm joints and contrasting reds at Bradbourne House, East Malling, Kent. Note the imperfections in the faces of the red gauged bricks. These are the result of small inclusions exposed when the brick is cut. (Photo by kind permission of East Malling Trust)

Gauged camber arch in good condition despite the fact that the brickwork around it has been heavily cement pointed.

A Queen Anne arch requires two striking points to construct it. One for the flat arch element either side and one for the semi-circular part.

were often installed on even the smallest town and country houses and are ubiquitous in England's villages, towns and cities. Gauged brickwork, or red masonry, delighted the observer because of its fine jointing and precise cut of brick which resembled the finest masonry ashlar work. Gauged brickwork enrichments including hoods, pilasters, mouldings, aprons, elliptical bullseyes and panels demonstrate the skill of the craftsman in executing this work in which no expense was spared.

It required a sound knowledge of drawing and geometry in order to cut the brick into the desired shape, in addition to exceptional fine craft skills at each stage of the process which enabled joints as narrow as 1mm, and rarely as wide as 3mm, to be achieved. Although gauged work was constructed in the seventeenth century, it appeared to reach a level of sublime quality during the eighteenth century. Gauged arches can be found of various qualities in both their execution and materials used, but all are particularly vulnerable to the use of modern materials and a lack of knowledge then and now (*see* Vulnerability of Traditional Brick). Gauged brickwork was constructed from a special kind of brick called a rubber which could be rubbed on a stone to create extremely accurate and thin joints.

The bricks were made from clay that might have been washed several times to remove inclusions and

A fine set of gauged camber arches in Rye, West Sussex. The bricked-up windows could be 'Pitt's' Windows', named after the British Prime Minister, who applied taxes on windows to help pay for the American War of Independence, or it could be used to provide symmetry to the elevation.

enabled the brick to be cut in adjustable wooden boxes (cutting box) using a bow saw.

Not all gauged arches that date from the eighteenth century are fine examples. Poor attempts to lengthen the voussoirs, in order to use offcuts of brick and minimize waste to extend the face height of the arch, are sometimes visible by the presence of seemingly unaligned, angled joints which may appear out of place, but which originally would have been blinded out by pigmented mortar and/or brick dust. False joints were scored horizontally in the faces of specific bricks to form the correct 'bond', i.e., Flemish, and these were filled with lime

Gauged brickwork with decoration that would have been carved and finished using files and pumice stones.

Gauged arch *c.*1680s across a window frame with several slipped voussoirs in Faversham, Kent.

putty, which having fallen out over the centuries, has caused them to be revealed. In a reversal of the extension of the bricks at the extrados of the arch, this practice avoided having to use small cuts to form the closers in the bond.

Whereas, in most of the previous century, arches were built straight across the window heads (hence the old term 'streight arch)', which provided their main means of support, arches in the Georgian era were built with a slight camber. The need for a camber, or rise, in the arch was because of the practical repercussions of the Building Acts of 1774 (*see* above), which meant that the arch could no longer be built across the top of the window frame but had to be self-supporting.

A tuck pointed gauged arch of yellow stocks in London.

This arch in Much Wenlock, Shropshire, had been tuck pointed with the putty ribbons still just visible. The Dutch joints designed to extend the brick cuts at the extrados were not well camouflaged in this instance. Note the cement repair in the top centre of the arch.

The camber also served to remove the optical illusion of the arch sagging in the centre. From a practical perspective, the camber made the construction of the arch more complicated because the soffit bevel of each brick had to be cut according to the line of the camber (*see* Gauged Brickwork Arch Construction). Although the wedge-shaped voussoirs provided some tensile strength, and this self-support was improved slightly with the addition of a camber, arches were not tied into the brickwork above or behind them, and generally a timber lintel positioned behind the arch supported the brickwork above, though occasionally a relieving arch was used to do this, too.

An example of a relieving arch used to support the inner mass of brickwork over an opening. This one consists of a single band rough ringed arch built above a timber lintel.

Problems with Eighteenth-Century Brickwork

The use of Flemish bond in brickwork enabled the bricklayer to cut the bricks into two half bats and use them in two places in the wall, eking out the facing bricks whilst cutting costs considerably though at the risk of losing the structural integrity in the walling. Sometimes, entire façades can be found constructed in this way during conservation work and are often found bowing in places. The consequence of this cost-cutting measure was the forming of separate skins of brickwork which were not tied through inside the wall by full header bricks. This could be compounded by difference in the gauge, or the course heights of the better-quality facing bricks and the rougher place bricks used inside the wall which made tying through impossible, and potentially created a dangerous weakness in the façade of the building.

As before, bonding timbers continued to be used. They were, and still are, vulnerable to the effects of moisture and could cause structural problems in the worst scenario.

Circular Work

Anatomy of a Georgian Circular Bay

A view inside a Georgian era construction can reveal interesting insights into construction methodology of the time. Snapped header bricks were often used to facilitate the construction of curved walling as it is easier to make the bricks turn through a curve that way. As a result, the header bricks could not form a full, one-brick depth of walling, resulting in an outer skin independent of the remainder of the brickwork. Such a method could make the structure vulnerable to weaknesses designed into a building, such as tall windows above one another on consecutive floors.

Constructing circular work involves the use of a trammel to lay the bricks around the circumference. To enable bricks to be laid in circular or curved work and, in order to maintain tight perpendicular joints,

Snapped headers have dropped out of position in this Georgian circular brickwork.

In the same section of walling here, shown supported by scaffolding, the detachment of the outer brickwork can be seen, and the timber window heads. Note, the modern cement constructed repair to the right of the picture.

A curved gauged arch with 100mm soffit and 2mm joints; this one supported by a hoop iron band visible just above the window.

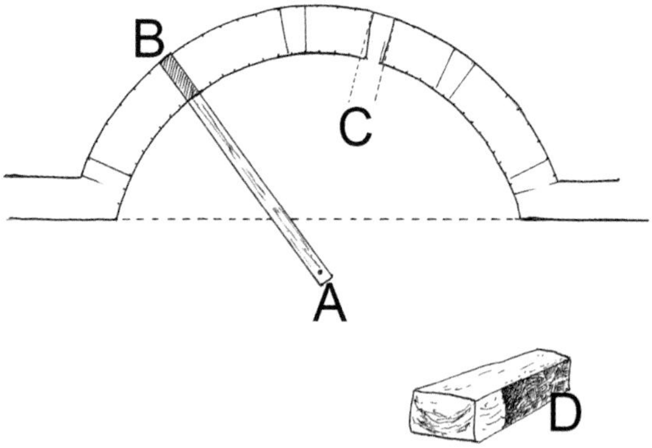

The trammel is positioned where required and a flat length timber fixed on a length of steel reinforcement (A). The end of the timber forms the outer curve of the wall (B). The bricks are set out around the curve dry (C) but bricks may require to be trimmed to ensure that they work around the curve successfully (D).

the sides of the bricks can be trimmed off so that the bricks are narrower at their rear. As has previously been seen, the use of header bricks can facilitate this but potentially with the loss of some strength through the wall.

Chapter Two

Traditional Brick Manufacture from the Twelfth to the Eighteenth Century

The basic process of brickmaking in what is known as the soft mud process remained essentially unchanged for the next five centuries. Although there were technological advancements in the manufacturing process which made the practice more efficient and cost effective, it did not mean that all brickmakers adopted such innovations, or indeed processes, at once and techniques varied from region to region resulting in bricks which varied widely in quality and form.

A London bed, eocene clay deposit in the south of England. (Photo by kind permission of P. Minter)

Winning the Clay

Brickmakers were able to make use of an abundance of easily accessible surface Pliocene clay deposits or brick earths, found where there was a scarcity of stone at riverbanks or where there had been once stands of timber, particularly in the East of England. These surface deposits were the sole source of clay for brickmaking up until the Elizabethan period and continued to be exploited by brickmakers into the nineteenth century. Brickmaking was a seasonal occupation consisting of five main stages. The clay was 'won' in autumn with enough obtained to last throughout the brickmaking season. Next, it was spread out and weathered during the winter to allow the frost to help break down the clay. It was turned periodically to facilitate and, at this point, any stones and biological matter were removed when found. The clay was puddled into a pliable mass using the feet of humans or horses and covered to protect it from the elements to ensure that the body of clay would be cohesive when fired. Pummelling the clay in this way served to temper it and was intended to enable stones and organic matter to be removed by hand, but was not entirely effective. The addition of water made the clay more workable before it could be moulded into bricks in spring. Once moulded, the bricks were dried outside until they could be handled, then fired.

Brickmaking could take place in one of three ways. Bricks could, for example, be made on the property of an estate where the staff and servants could be employed to make them, perhaps in efforts to reduce costs. Similarly, estate workers might be used to lay the bricks, and this is perhaps borne out by poor quality of brickwork that can sometimes be found in boundary walls and outbuildings. Bricks were also made by itinerant brickmakers, often whole families, setting up brick yards to manufacture the bricks and clamps to fire them as close as possible to where a building was to be built. Finally, there were permanent brick yards set up as commercial enterprises where there were abundant clay deposits, of which

Here, clay is heaped into a bed having been thoroughly soaked for use the following day. (Photo by kind permission of P. Minter)

A place brick from Shropshire found in the buried footings of a building. This misshapen nature of this brick suggests it was formed on the ground by hand, possibly without the use of a mould. It measures 250mm × 116mm × 60mm. Note the blackened core, an indication of clamp firing and a rapid rise in temperature during firing.

the earliest was founded in 1290 in Hull on the eastern seaboard of England. The diversity of forms of manufacture, techniques and processes prompted monarchs throughout the ages to introduce edicts to standardize the size and form of bricks, and the extent of their success is visible in the shear diversity of quality and form of the bricks that can be found when investigating and working on England's historic and traditional buildings.

Brickmaking would have been a hard and robust life for those involved, yet whilst conditions of work would have been unenviable from a modern perspective, there was a living to be made. Brickmaking incorporated a structure of jobs at the top of which was the moulder, and with each member of the group having a specific job, such as breaking the bricks out of the mould and taking them for drying. The brickmaker was responsible for seeing the production through from start to finish, starting with sourcing suitable clay deposits which was a skill in its own right. In a family enterprise, all members old enough to contribute had their own job, and young children used to tread the clay with their feet.

Moulding Bricks on the Ground

Initially, bricks were made directly on the ground, perhaps formed into a brick shape by hand, and then by spreading out the clay and cutting it into brick portions using a wooden frame rather like a kitchen pastry cutter. Another method employed was to use wooden handheld paddles to form the bricks roughly into shape, or even simply by hand. Methods such as these can still be found in parts of Southeast Asia. The obvious inconsistency of these methods created bricks that were highly nuanced in form.

Bench Moulding of Bricks

The moulding bench made its appearance in England in the fifteenth century and must have been recognized by brickmakers as a welcome departure from the backbreaking ground manufacture method and made it easy to develop a hierarchy of brickmaking skills, whilst making the manufacturing process more efficient. It was, after all, in the interests of the brickmaking team to be as efficient as possible since they were manufacturing bricks on a piece work basis, with a well-organized team producing up to 5,000 in a full working day. The pliable clay was thrown into a bottomless mould directly onto the bench which was liberally doused with water to facilitate its removal.

A wooden mould used in traditional brickmaking today. Moulds were often made of beech wood but from the nineteenth century were often lined with steel to form bricks far more consistent in form. (Photo by kind permission of P. Minter)

Clay destined to be used for making rubber bricks for gauged brickwork. (Photo by kind permission of P. Minter)

A brick moulder cuts the frog from a half round coping brick. (Photo by kind permission of P. Minter)

Slop Moulding

Early moulds were quite shallow to enable them to be filled with clay more effectively, and this factor can account for the relative thinness of medieval bricks as deeper moulds prevented the clay form reaching the corners of the mould properly. The timber mould was lubricated using water, in a method known as slop moulding, making the process of moulding wet and slimy in nature as the name suggests. One disadvantage of slop moulding was that when the brick was fired, the clay shrank from the edges often resulting in bricks with rounded corners and edges which was exacerbated the deeper the moulds used.

The top of the mould was then struck flush to remove excess clay by using a bow shaped device called a strike, and the brick turned out on to a flat piece of timber board to be taken out to dry. The bricks needed to develop a skin to enable them to be dry enough to be handled and stacked for firing, and this process could take up to six weeks. They were laid directly on the ground before being spaced further apart to allow air to circulate around them and to turn them over. Getting the brick out of the mould often required pushing down on the brick with the fingers, which partially accounts for the prints of brickmakers that can sometimes be found on such bricks. The method of drying on the ground accounts for the imprints of flora and fauna found on them.

Sand or Pallet Moulding

Water had been used for centuries as the agent to release the bricks from the mould, often resulting in rounded edges as discussed above. The introduction, in the seventeenth century, of the use of sand for this purpose made the process much more efficient. Sand was dusted both inside the mould and on the exterior of the still green brick, and now instead of the brick being turned out wet from the mould as it had been previously, it was turned out onto a small pallet which was then placed on a hack barrow and conveniently taken out for drying for up to a month. Sand moulding enabled the bricks to be dried on their edges on hacks (covered platforms) straight away rather than having to be laid on the ground to become dry enough to be able to be handled first. This was a time and cost saving factor in production, and further improved the quality of the brick. It also gave the brick a rough glazed surface of different hues, as the sand melted at high temperatures.

A frogged brick.

Improvements in the Mixing and Tempering of Clay

Previously, the removal of stones, pebbles and other undesirable items was done by hand. As with other aspects of brick manufacture, the increase in demand led to the introduction of new innovations. Late in the seventeenth century, the pug mill appeared. This enabled the brick manufacture process to be refined further and coincided with the exploitation of deeper clays of the Eocene layer rather than the topmost brick earths. The horse-powered pug mill consisted of a cylindrical container with blades pointing inwards on the inside, which stirred up the material as it was inserted and also enabled the better separation of stones from the clay. These factors combined to reduced labour costs and simplified the addition of other materials like sand and ash to the clay mixture before it was put in the mill. This resulted in a more efficient method of forming a pliable, consistent mass and enabled the production of more materiel with which to mould comparatively better-quality bricks.

The Frog

In the late seventeenth century, an innovation called the frog began to appear in brick manufacture. The frog is the indentation or hollow that is a characteristic of modern bricks today. The frog was formed by the insertion of a raised piece of wood called a 'kick' onto the stockboard which was in turn was secured to the moulding bench, over which was fitted the wooden moulding frame. Its purpose was to force the clay into the corners of the mould when it was thrown in forming well-formed and thicker bricks. The reason for the use of the word 'frog' is uncertain. It may for example, take its name from the part of a horse's hoof associated with the horse powered pug mill.

In addition to improving brick form, the frog would have several other benefits to brick production and use. The frog facilitated handling by the bricklayer and functioned as a means to better bond the brick into the wall. Later, during the industrial era, it enabled the brick manufacturer to have their name stamped inside the frog and reduced the amount of clay needed for each brick thus reducing costs. Traditional handmade bricks often have no frog, which appears to suggest that the introduction of this device was not universally taken up by brickmakers or known to them.

Traditional Firing of Bricks

Until the advent of downdraft kilns in the early nineteenth century, two types of methods of firing were

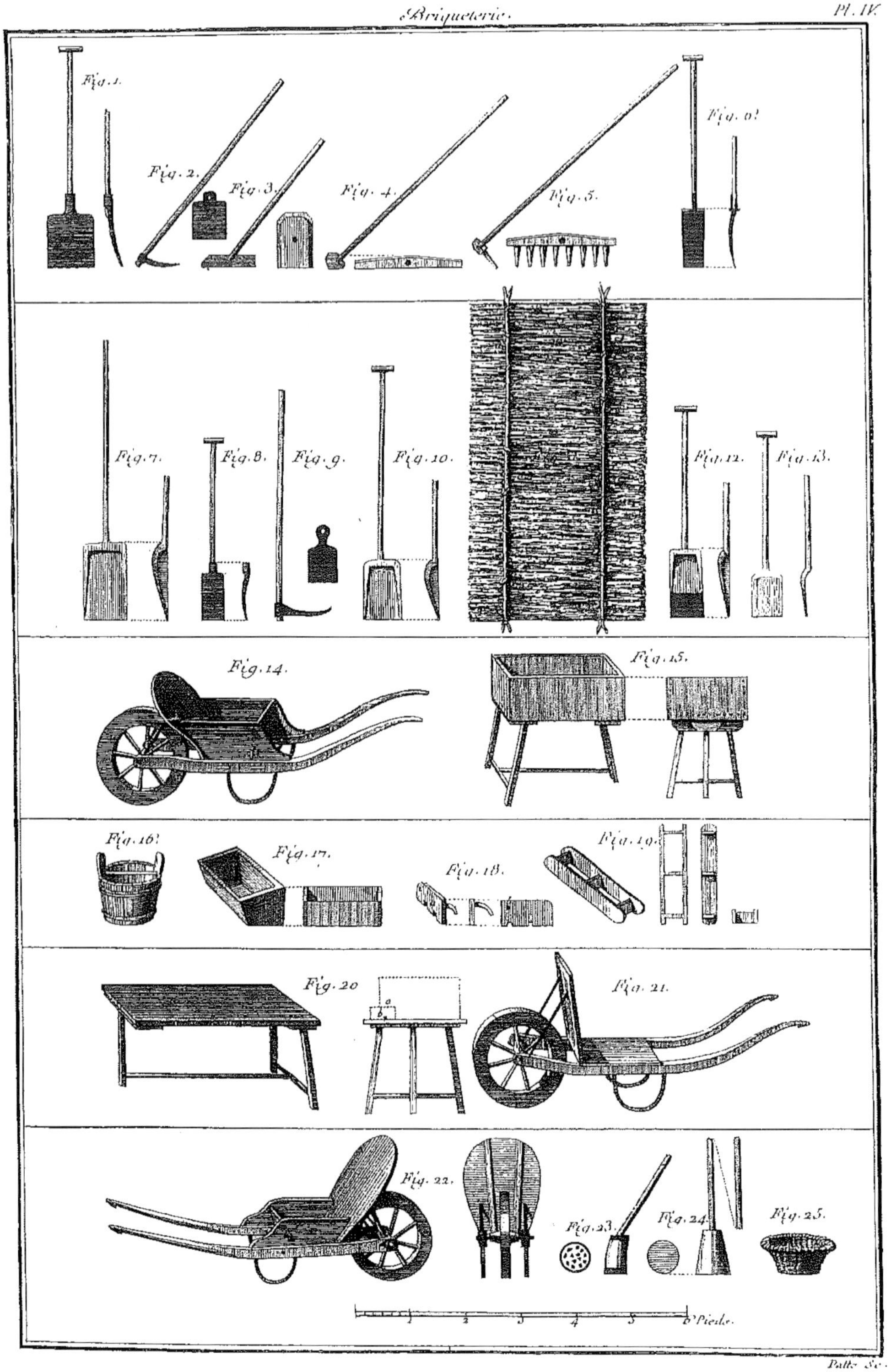

A detailed study of brickmakers tools including those for winning and preparing clay, moulding bricks and transporting them for drying. The wicker implement on the second row from the top is a wind break. (From *L'art du tuillier et du briquetier,* 1763, courtesy of Thames & Hudson)

employed in traditional bricks manufacture. One method was the clamp and another was a simple kiln construction called an updraft kiln, both of which will be dealt with here. For both, successful brickmaking relied on passed-down skills of the brickmaker, an ample supply of brick earth or clay and a copious supply of fuel, either wood or coal, with which to fire it. Until the advent of the canals in the 1700s, the poor condition of transport links and the cost of moving materials must have been an important factor in keeping the sourcing of materials and brickmaking confined as local to the site of the building work as possible.

Clamp Firing

Firing usually started in mid-spring and continued throughout summer when better weather was more likely. If rain was anticipated, it would probably have been unwise to attempt to fire especially in winter. A clamp was a temporary method of firing the bricks, consisting of as many as 150,000 unfired bricks stacked up on alternating layers of combustible material. The outer layers of the clamp, formed by bricks that were often poor-quality and underfired from previous firings. The floor was made from bricks placed on their edges and spaced apart to allow for the passage of air. Evidence suggests that the clamps were rendered over with mud, with the aim of keeping in heat and gases, and perhaps providing some protection from the rain.

Fire channels were built through the base of the clamp, which allowed oxygen to circulate through the material. Fuel, such as such as hedge cuttings, furze and any other forms of timber (though not construction grade timber, which was far too valuable) that could be sourced from managed coppicing of woodland trees, were used to fire the bricks. Where it could be obtained, outcrop coal was used even during the Medieval period, but wood in various forms was then more common. It is likely that the demands on fuel for burning seriously inhibited the expansion of brickmaking until the exploitation of coal for this purpose, and once the means of obtaining coal more efficiently was conceived. Once lit, the clamp fired the bricks reaching temperatures of between 900–1100°C before burning itself out, taking two or three weeks, and for the larger clamps up to three months. There was no control over the rate of burning, nor of the quality of the finished product, and there ensued a sorting of the bricks to grade them for use.

Updraft Kiln Firing

Contemporaneous with clamp firing, but confined more to the sites of permanent brickworks, updraught kilns were a more efficient way of firing at a time of increasing demand and growing population. These consisted of, in the most simplistic of forms, two parallel walls up to 3m in height and approximately 6m in length with arched fire ports or grates made in each side and usually a door to enable access to stack the bricks. The bricks were stacked inside on a suspended floor of brick which enabled heat and gases to circulate around the stacked bricks and tiles, whose proximity to one another often left tell-tale markings on them. The open roof was plugged with turf and mud to minimize the loss of heat (though not entirely successfully). On the simpler structure types, the ends of these parallel walls were sealed up with unfired bricks and the whole edifice often rendered over, like the clamp, with mud or turf. The permanent structures consisted of a walled enclosure with grates as before, but also incorporating a door to enable access to stack the bricks.

The two-week burn occurred in two phases; an initial and then fiercer heat allowing for the staged heating and firing of the brick load. The increased use of coal made this more efficient in labour and fuel. The growing scarcity of timber and increased use of coal, particularly after the first Industrial Revolution, undoubtedly played a part in the spread

Although this image is of French clamp construction, it gives a good indication of the scale of a typical clamp structure, with some 500,000 bricks being fired here. Note the fire channels at the bottom and the activities of the men atop the clamp, one of whom appears to be daubing the outside with clay or mud to help prevent the leaking of gases. (From *L'art du tuillier et du briquetier*, 1763, courtesy of Thames & Hudson)

and expansion of brick production, even before industrialization of the manufacturing process occurred. Even with a supply of timber from managed woodlands and hedges, England was facing a growing scarcity of available timber at a time when the expansion of naval and commercial ship building had an increased requirement for timber. Like the brick clamp, however, the bricks had to be sorted out into different qualities once the fire had burned out.

Internal Fuel in Bricks

It was discovered that adding ash from domestic refuse to the clay for brickmaking, acted as an

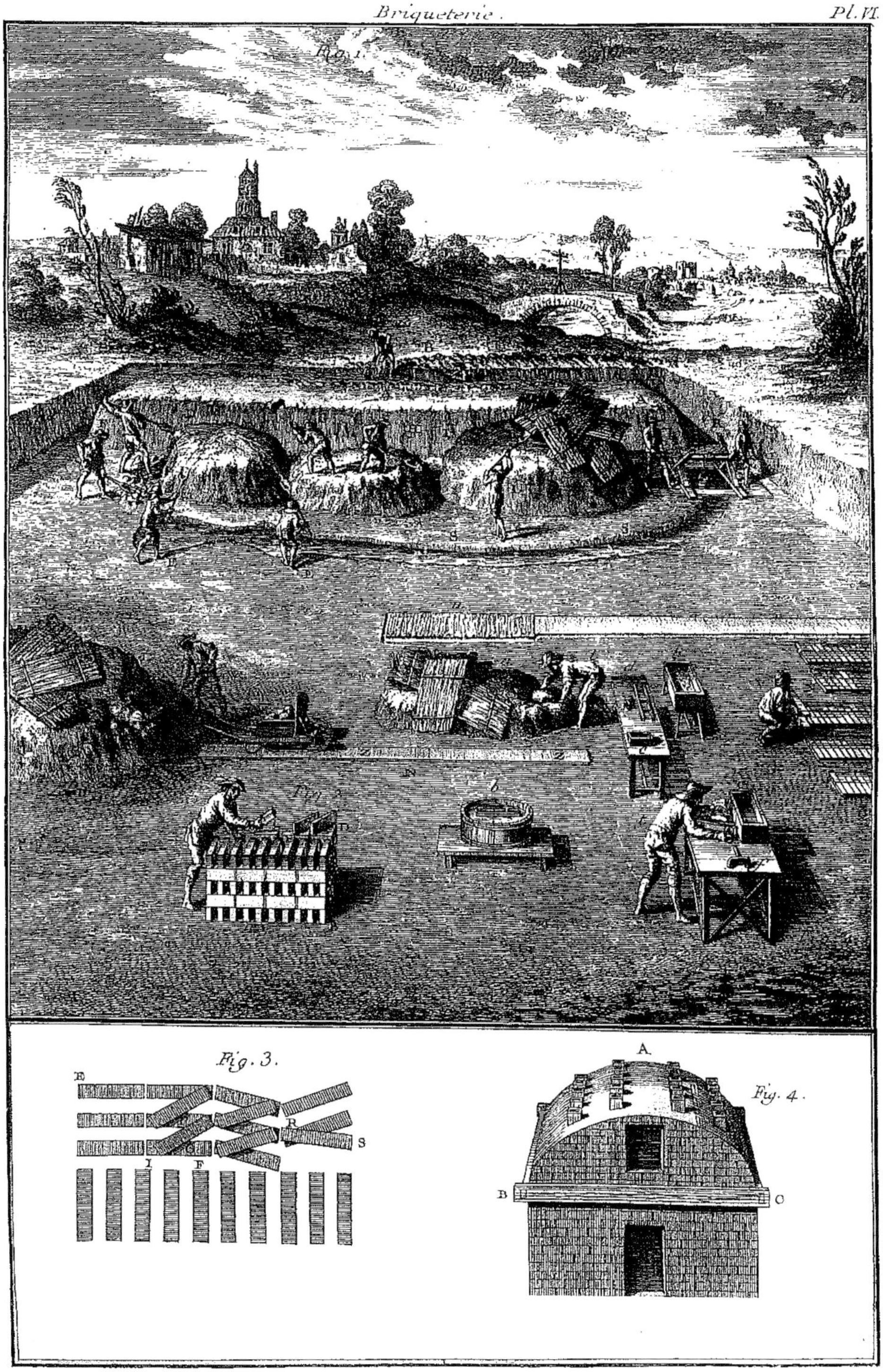

An illustration of works associated with brickmaking and a more permanent solidly constructed updraft kiln. Note the flue chambers under a suspended floor and the roofless design. (From *L'art du tuillier et du briquetier*, 1763, courtesy of Thames & Hudson)

internal fuel, effectively burning the brick from the inside. It is likely that this practice is as old as brick-making in England, but this increased in the decades following the Great Fire of London in 1666, after which the fields around London had been covered with ash deposits which heavily infused the soil. The addition of an internal fuel could not only reduce the costs of firing considerably, but also reduced the amount of clay required in each brick. Unfortunately, this reached a point at which the beneficial component was being increasingly replaced by an overabundance of other non-combustible materials, such as sand, which negated the properties of the internal fuel and resulted in a weak, inferior brick (*see* Vulnerability of Traditional Brick). Less scrupulous brickmakers saw this as an opportunity to reduce their costs, but the practice eventually led to poor-quality bricks. Although the practice was at one point banned in an area around London, the usefulness of the internal fuel meant that the ban was lifted by royal decree, provided that its use met specific laid down proportions.

Chapter Three

Characteristics of Traditional Brick

Traditional handmade bricks can differ widely in appearance. This variation is apparent in bricks from century to century, region to region and building to building in colour, form, texture and general quality. Quite apart from the variables of human skill and application in the making of bricks, this variation can differ depending on the use of technologies and the prevailing socio-economic factors of the region. Technologies – such as the use steel-lined moulds, the insertion of the frog in the manufacture, the horse powered pugmill, the fundamental change from slop to sand moulding and the method of firing – were not adopted simultaneously by all brickmakers at one convenient point in time in all the traditional brick regions of England. Consequently, when identifying and questioning the quality of the bricks of a given historic building, knowledge of this range and the causes for this variation, can help to form the basis of our understanding of them.

Parts of a brick: stretcher face (A), header face (B), margin (C), frog (D), arris (E). Bricks are identified in a wall by the size of the exposed face, the longest being the stretcher and the shortest the header.

The choice of bricks used in traditional brickwork construction was influenced by what was available from a firing, and the owners of the most expensive buildings (or those that acted for them) took the best bricks for their buildings. The choice of brick used in each building was influenced by a number of factors. Fashion and architectural style and the Building Acts emanating from London, for example, influenced the manner in which they were used, but even such factors and styles varied from place-to-place, perhaps not reaching the comparatively remote counties for years because of the difficulties in transportation. The financial situation of a property owner often dictated the extent to which fashions and construction details were applied to their building. Finally, both manufacture and the architectural use of brick varied according to the mindset, philosophy and geopolitical and socio-economic climate of a given historical era.

It is rare for there to be absolutely no suggested date of a traditional handmade brick building because of the availability of maps, historical records and documents and research that may have been undertaken. It is possible for there to be confusion over the dating, perhaps because of brick size or form or the way the brickwork was constructed. This can be because of the presence of brickwork alterations carried out over the centuries, which may differ from the majority of brickwork, and when bricks of different qualities, sizes and with different jointing finishes have been employed using the skills associated with a given era.

Brick Sizes

Identifying the date of traditional bricks simply by size alone is notoriously difficult, if not impossible, because of the limited success of standardization measures at different points in history. It is common for brick sizes to be associated with specific historical eras, i.e., the narrower they are, the older they are, etc., but this is not necessarily the case. Several factors influenced the gradual process of standardization of the traditional manufactured brick, leading to the standard metric size of 215mm × 100mm × 65mm available today. These were the gradual improvements in manufacture by using simple but effective brickmaking technologies as discussed above. The ability of the bricklayer to hold and manipulate the brick comfortably and with efficiency was also key, the ideal size being approximately twice as long as it is wide. A bricklayer should be able to hold a brick comfortably in one hand without having to put it down whilst applying mortar to the wall. Another factor was the gradual development of bonding which led to a more efficient building practice. As any bricklayer knows, bonding becomes more difficult to achieve the greater the variation in length of brick size. Finally, changes in fashion and taxation, as a result of geo-political events, played their part, too. Historical examples of interchanging brick sizes include the Medieval Great brick, brick tax bricks from 1784 and those of the Arts and Crafts era from the turn of the nineteenth century, which sometimes reverted to brick thicknesses as narrow as 50mm.

With or without a building date, the size of a brick should not be the first consideration. Instead, the empirical knowledge gained through understanding of the raw material and visual observation of the brick and its characteristics – texture, quality of form, colour, patina and that of the brickwork – location (on the building) of the elevation, joint finish, bond, architectural style and use of colours, are the most effective ways of building up an understanding for dating.

Examples of Brick Sizes

Standardization was attempted by monarchs as early as the Medieval era. Even as early as the reign of Edward IV, there were attempts at brick standardization with sizes of 228mm × 120mm × 55mm. Under the Tudors, sizes of 228mm × 114mm × 57mm have been identified. Sizes could be standard within one building but could differ between buildings of the same era, and there is often a great deal of variation. Gradually, monetary, technical, practical and aesthetic factors meant that by the reign of George III (1738–1820), bricks were of a size coincidently similar to modern metric sizes (2225mm × 102mm × 64mm).

Place brick, probably sixteenth-century, measuring 286mm × 115mm × 90mm.

Georgian era sand-moulded brick measuring 225mm × 100mm × 65mm.

Victorian machine-pressed brick identifiable by the stamped frog.

Modern perforated brick measuring 210mm x 100mm x 65mm.

The Brick Tax and Brick Size

In the last decades of the eighteenth century, whilst Britain already faced France in a global war, she suddenly found she had to deal with the American War of Independence (1784) and to help pay for this,

A brick measuring 245mm x 100mm x 90mm. The size might indicate a Brick Tax brick, but certainly its size would make handling difficult for the bricklayer.

construction materials, among other things, were taxed. Bricks, at this point in history, were far more standardized than in previous centuries and were approaching something like the modern metric brick in size. They were immediately seen as a good source of revenue and were taxed by the thousand. As a result, brickmakers began to increase the size of their bricks to circumnavigate this. The exchequer, being one step ahead, doubled the tax on bricks over 254mm × 127mm × 76mm in size and as a result some brickmakers made their bricks as large as possible within these parameters. This tax was only repealed in the mid-nineteenth century, giving an indication of its value to the exchequer.

Shape, Quality and Form

Bricks of all eras are recognizable by key features. The edges of the brick are called 'arrises' and are formed at the point at which two surfaces meet. In traditional bricks, these are often found to be rounded rather than sharp due to slop moulding method of manufacture and if they pre-date the use of the frog (*see* above). Handmade bricks will often be frogless, have rounded edges and may be slightly misshapen though this is certainly not always the case. Machine-manufactured bricks can be either pressed or machine extruded. The former may have evidence of the pressing, and the latter of evidence of the wires drag marks which cut the bricks into convenient pieces in the machine.

Brick Earth and Clay

Brick earths generally refer to the layers of loam-like material found just below the topsoil of the Pleistocene geological period, and are found particularly in eastern England and the Thames Valley. Since these were easily accessible, they were the only source of material for brickmaking up to and including the Elizabethan era, and their use continued into the

This panel of bricks dates from the late nineteenth century. They are machine pressed bricks and as a result have sharp, precise arrises and a uniform shape and size enabling much narrower mortar joint.

nineteenth century. Brick clays, in contrast, have been formed across different geological periods and over millions of years from the weathering of rocks, volcanic ash deposits and minerals varying from region to region and can be found both relatively near the surface and very deep.

Brick Colour

The almost limitless variety of colours of traditional brick is perhaps one of the facets of this material which make it so appealing to the eye. The colour of bricks can vary from region to region and from clay pit to clay pit, each of which may have a slightly different chemical composition. This is because clay, like rock, is found in layers formed millions of years ago and again, like rock, it is found in various colours such as grey, brown, red and occasionally blue. Consequently, there are innumerable colours and hues of bricks. Factors which determine colour include traces of iron in the clay when it oxidizes producing hematite (from the Greek word for blood) which influences the finished red colour of the brick and the more oxides there are, the redder the brick will be. Where there are no oxides present, or in the case bricks such as malms or London stock bricks, the high percentage of naturally occurring lime in the brick earth or the addition of extra lime, will create a yellow or buff colour. The presence of magnesium oxide will have a similar effect, whilst some clays such as the Gault clays found in the east of the country, will produce a brick that is very pale yellow to white in colour. Other clays, such as Staffordshire clay, will produce bricks of various hues of blue. Sand used as release agents, used in moulding bricks, could be influential to the colour of the fire skin of the brick as they fuse and change colour when exposed to high temperatures. In clamp firing, and to a large extent updraft kiln firing, the colours produced could not be influenced by the brickmaker because of the uncontrolled nature of the firings.

Flared headers such as this can be produced by the wood firing of bricks.

Kiss marks on these nineteenth-century bricks laid in Flemish bond in Broseley, Shropshire, give the walling a unique character. This type of marking is partially due to green unfired bricks or tiles being stacked against, or on top of, one another or against tiles fired at the same time.

The position of the bricks, and the unequal passage of gases and heat around the bricks, could influence the colour in spite of the nature of the clay. In the presence of oxygen, bricks turn red at about 900°C, but take on darker colours such as blues, greys and purples at higher temperatures. Therefore, those closest to the fire channels burned a blue and grey colour. Underfired bricks would have been used to build around the clamp or to close up the wickets of kilns or other such purposes. In contrast, with improvements in manufacture from the nineteenth century plus adjustable coal firing, bricks tended to have a far more uniform colour.

Fingerprints on a place brick dating from a sixteenth-century brick. Such impressions provide a glimpse of a centuries old activity captured in clay.

Brick Surface Markings and Impressions

Once fired, the brick is enveloped by a hard fire skin which protects the brick form the elements when it is laid. Other markings include the brickmakers smiles formed during the manufacture of sand moulded bricks. Markings on the bricks can be a result of the way they are stacked during firing with other of materials, such as the kiss marks of closely stacked tiles. Impressions were made on traditional brick in a number of ways: when they were laid out to dry on the ground they would be left with grass or straw impressions. Animal prints can sometimes be found, which happened whilst the bricks were laid out to dry, and

Detailed impressions, such as these grasses, indicate that this brick had been set upon the ground to dry prior to firing.

This brick with the brick makers smile produced by the use of sand in the moulding process. When laid, the smile should be laid smile upwards, as shown.

A stem and flower of a grass perfectly captured in clay. Note, the walling in which this brick belongs has been colour washed with red ochre pigment.

sometimes, the fingerprints of the brickmaker can be seen, formed as the clay is pushed into the mould.

Vitrification

Vitrification often occurred in wood-fired clamps and where bricks were near the fuel source but was also influenced by the mineral composition up of the clay. Vitrification is the reaction of materials such as lime and potash in the clay when fired at lower temperatures, and which act like a flux and help the material fuse together. Some fusion of this sort is necessary as a normal part of the firing process (*see* Vulnerability of Traditional Brick), but excessive heat can lead to the brick slumping. The result of this process is manifested by the appearance of bubbling of the brick surface.

After the bricks had been fired, bricks were sorted into qualities with the best ones set aside for face work whilst others, which might be no less durable, were used for the back and sides of a building, for filling inside thick walls or simply as material for crushing for foundations. Regionally, bricks were

Evidence of vitrification apparent in late eighteenth-century brick header, giving it an almost elastic appearance. Note the aggregate particles in the lime mortar which is still as good as the day these bricks were laid.

A badly warped brick found in the centre of a two-brick thick wall in an eighteenth-century house in Admaston, Shropshire.

given names which tended to reflect the nature of their malformation. An example of these being grizzles, clinkers, shuffs and burrs (*see* Vulnerability of Traditional Brick). Buildings for economic or utilitarian purposes, such as canal structures, were often built using lesser-quality bricks produced onsite from clay dug out of the canal.

Clamp firing was also an uncontrollable process in which temperatures could not be adjusted and varied significantly within the clamp, resulting in a mass of bricks with a wide variation of quality and in which temperature variation affected both the colour and form of the brick. The resulting bricks came in varying qualities with the best, or 'fronts', being selected for facing brickwork. Others that were well-fired but less well-formed were used for work at the back and sides of a property. Underfired ones, referred to as 'semels', were only semi-fired and consequently were not selected for face work, but instead were used for internal walls where they would not be seen, or even broken up as hardcore. Underfired bricks, perhaps poorly selected, can sometimes be identified on elevations during the assessment of brickwork.

Chapter Four

Knowledge and Skills for Traditional Brickwork Conservation

An image that epitomizes the divergence from traditional craft skills. On the left, unadulterated brickwork in lime mortar with penny rolled joints and on the right is cement weather pointing.

Articles and information dealing with brickwork, and building conservation in general, can be found relatively easily on the internet, including forums set up to discuss and debate specific conservation issues and practice. Some organizations and universities who deliver conservation degrees and diplomas also run their own continuing professional development (CPD). Conservation-accredited architects from the Institute of British Architects and surveyors from the Royal Institute of Chartered Surveyors are another source of professional advice and guidance about specific problems with a building.

For those who wish to change careers and learn brickwork skills, some colleges run night school courses which will teach the core skills of brickwork with experience gained through bricklaying on a modern construction site before migrating to brick conservation work. Some specialist skills relating to specific types of brickwork, such as the construction of gauged work, tuck pointing, historic pointing and jointing, brickwork conservation techniques and underpinning knowledge relating to traditional brick, are taught in seminaries of conservation, or privately by a small number of qualified, experienced and highly skilled individuals who are prepared to pass on their knowledge.

Sources for Self-Study

For modern-site brickwork skills and practice, National Vocational Qualification (NVQ) based test books can be found in bookshops. For traditional brickwork and brickwork conservation, it is useful to read a number of different genres. For example, books on brick history and architecture are useful to gain an understanding of the use of brick in the context of British architecture and its place among the main periods of English architecture. Textbooks and manuals written when lime was still used as the binder in mortars in brickwork and/or those written before the demise of the City and Guilds Craft and Advanced Certificate training, are especially useful to help to understand brickwork craft practice and applications. Then there are books written about the surveying and diagnosis of problems relating to historic buildings, and which have sections about the failure of materials, decay mechanisms and how to identify them. Last but not least, there are modern books written about brickwork which discuss not only the history of its use, but also the specialist repair and conservation of it.

Brickwork Conservation Philosophy

Buildings constructed in traditional and historic brickwork, whether listed or unlisted and of high significance or not, form part of our built cultural heritage. Their walls encapsulate centuries of wear, tare and patina formed over the centuries. They may have stood witness to hundreds of years of socio-economic and political change and bear the evidence of the work of generations of craftsmen and women. Work on such buildings should not be undertaken lightly, and to be prepared to do so means gaining an understanding of some key principles and adopting a certain approach to repair (with its own terminology) often referred to as the conservation philosophy. Some of these principles are set out below.

Authenticity

Authenticity can be compromised when repairs are carried out, even good ones, which erode the character of a building and diminish its value as an example of a building of a given historical period or era. To achieve authenticity, proven methods and techniques should be used to achieve a finish that matches the existing ones. These techniques can be derived from understanding the building construction, how things were done and what tools and materials were used, as well as the mindset and rationale of those that constructed the building centuries before.

An example of advanced brick decay on a seventeenth-century cottage in Shropshire. This would require careful consideration in terms of how, and to what extent, original material can be saved.

Breathability

The successful repair and/or construction of traditional brickwork relies on knowledge of how the materials and construction methods perform under different environmental conditions. 'Breathability' is a shorthand term, often used in conservation today, to describe how moisture can pass through and evaporate from a building due to the lime mortar, but capillarity is perhaps a more accurate term to describe this process.

Embodied Energy

This describes the labour and resources that went in to making, transporting, and laying the traditional brick (or any material) hundreds of years ago, and as such the aim would be to try and avoid replicating this effort and energy, by re-using materials thus reducing further resources and effort.

Conservation

This can be defined as conserving the brickwork now and for the future. It involves identifying, diagnosing and addressing the causes and symptoms of decay, arresting it and using carefully matched materials to make a stable, robust and durable repair using the correct skills whilst not detracting from the character of the building. Conservation, not restoration, of traditional brickwork should always be the primary aim when approaching repairs.

Listing

Many traditional buildings are not listed but should be treated with the same care and conscientiousness as those that are. Buildings are listed for different reasons and have what are sometimes known as 'values' which contribute to the significance and give them their listing status. These values may be architectural, for example, the style and brickwork features and perhaps the uniqueness of them. Values might be those of historical association, i.e., there is record of a famous person having stayed or visited, or something artistic, spiritual, religious and many more. Understanding the statutory protection of listed buildings, and the penalties for transgression, can protect both property owner and craftsman or woman. All too often, buildings are damaged, defaced or destroyed and the fabric irreparably lost because of a lack of awareness of the statutory protection or a brazen disregard for it.

There are three listing categories.

Grade I Listed Buildings:

Buildings that are of exceptional national interest, and often international, and constitute 2.5 per cent of listed buildings.

Grade II Listed Buildings:*

Buildings that are of more than special interest and constitute 5.8 per cent of listed buildings.

Grade II Listed Buildings:

Buildings that are of special interest and form 97.2 per cent of listed buildings.

Simply put, alterations and changes to listed buildings will generally require consent from the Local Authority in order to proceed. This is first and foremost the responsibility of the property owner, but the contractor and craftsman or woman is not devoid of responsibility and should not undertake works where this process has not been followed. Repairs do not normally require consent but even here, if a façade is changed in a way that alters or transforms it (for example, a full repoint – even if it is for the better) and changes the character of the building, this too will require at the very least alerting the conservation officer of the intention and receiving a written response before work proceeds as there may be objections to the work being undertaken. Buildings in conservation areas will generally require a dialogue with a conservation officer as even if a building is not listed, it is not an excuse to do any type of work.

Maintenance

This can be defined as preventing decay by regular care. In traditional brickwork, this refers to items such as minor pointing and repair of things which could directly affect the brickwork (*see* Maintenance of Traditional Brickwork).

Maximum Retention of Original Fabric

Only brick that is damaged beyond repair should be removed, and always with as little disruption to adjacent surfaces as possible. Where brick has to be removed, it should be safely stored and numbered with the aim of reusing as much of it as possible. For example, a brick with a damaged or partially eroded face could, once removed, be used to make other smaller cuts without resorting to using a new brick because, however well matched a new brick is, it isn't original material.

Minimal Intervention

In repairing traditional brickwork, the aim is to intervene only where required and not create work in order to avoid unnecessary damage or disruption. In short, if work does not need doing, don't do it.

This lime pointing is neither well-applied, nor an authentic joint finish. In addition to staining of the brick, the struck lines have been executed in a non-uniform, haphazard manner.

Parody of Traditional Finishes and Features

Parody could be described as an attempt by people to replicate a piece of traditional work, for example a joint style or an arch constructed without the knowledge of methods, to create authentic work, and which results in confusing one or more styles together in order to try and imitate it. It is usually the result of someone not possessing the skills or knowledge to execute historically accurate work, as a cost saving exercise, or both.

Responsibility to Buildings

Responsibility for what happens to a building belongs to the property owner who, in the case of a listed building, is simply a custodian of that building. The experienced craftsman or woman should own their craft and not treat the work merely as a commercial transaction, but instead treat it as something which confirms their aspiration to mastery of the work, and which ties them to the repair history of the building.

Restoration

This could be defined as taking a building back to a given point in history through physical and/or documentary evidence. Although restoration can have bad connotations in the context of old buildings, some buildings do reach a stage when it is applicable. Restoration could involve the large-scale integration of new

This wall consists of original seventeenth-century brickwork in English bond, to the right and bottom of picture. The red brickwork at the top left is new work in Flemish bond, built to make the wall functional yet conspicuously different from the original whose outline can be clearly identified to the right. As such, this is an example of conservation of an existing structure.

material such as handmade bricks, reconstruction of features, and potentially whole-scale repointing. Where existing materials are eroded to such an extent that they are considered beyond conserving, a demand for people with specialist brickwork craft skills can be generated, for example in the reconstruction of gauged brickwork enrichments or authentic jointing finishes, and this is good for encouraging and creating a demand for them. However, if wrongly interpreted, or carried out on a whim and not based on evidence of a given era (not to mention without proper knowledge and skills), restoration can cause catastrophic damage and disregard to, and loss of, original fabric which once lost can never be regained.

Repair

Making a repair in traditional brickwork is to arrest both the symptoms and causes of decay without altering or detracting from the character of the building and its features and damaging historic fabric. Repairs should entail putting something back like for like, and to fit in with adjacent brickwork without over embellishing it or conducting unnecessary work which could detract from its character.

Renovation

This is a term usually applied to a complete overhaul of a building, the very title of which could suggest the disassembly of original features in favour of modern ones.

Repair Philosophy

This is the planned strategy of repair based on information gleaned from the building as to how the work will be approached and will dictate the policies issued to the people working on it.

Significance

This can be described as a combination of values which make a building important and will be a

The removal of this modern intervention in a traditional brickwork garden wall is warranted because it is allowing water into the wall. Removing it and bonding a good matching brick into the surrounding walling will extend the life of this 200-year-old structure.

Blending in original bricks and selected replacements to make repairs.

A panel of conservation pointing. Note how the pointing has been worked around the eroded bricks to the narrowest neck of the joints. Here, the bar for brick replacement has been set high to avoid loss of original material.

determining factor in the listing grade that a building is given. Significance of features or elements when applied to the physical fabric of the building will often influence the priority of work on a listed building. The term 'significance' can apply equally to the most humble or the grandest of buildings, based on its history.

Specification

Specifications are generally written by architects and other building professionals, and set out the work for contractors in terms of a particular material that is to be used, where it can be acquired, and how exactly the work should be finished. Poorly written, unclear specifications can lead to unsuccessful conservation work.

Unwitting Vandalism

This can be described as action taken without malice but that, because of a lack of knowledge or skills in the area of work involved, often results in irreversible damage to the original fabric or an unsightly appearance to a brickwork feature. An example of this could be the grinding out of gauged brickwork joints when a house is being repointed in order to make them more 'watertight' by pointing with cement.

Traditional Materials

These are the materials used when the building was constructed. For vernacular brick buildings, this could mean materials found close to the place of construction, for example, clamp fired bricks or lime that had been brought by pack horse to the site where it was slaked to make mortar.

Chapter Five

Tools and Equipment

Brick Workshop

Working in traditional craft generally requires somewhere to store tools and materials safely. For some, a workshop, shed, garage, basement or some other space in which to store materials including pigment, powders, glue sizes and a range of accessories to prepare them is desirable. Here, it may be convenient to practice pointing skills, draw arches and other features, and to cut and rub bricks with which to construct arches. For the latter, this space may eventually become a necessity since, invariably, gauged arches are be brought to site ready prepared.

A multitude of tools and equipment would need to be assembled, including items for gauged brickwork which are not available to buy over the counter but must be made by a skilled joiner, all of which must be kept safe and secure. The workshop should be well-lit, have adequate shelving and power points, and be comfortable enough to be able to work in for prolonged periods. For example, rubbing bricks to make arches or practice some other skill at any time and be comfortable whilst doing so in an insulated building will enable work to carry on in the cold winter months. The size of the workshop is, of course, limited by economic and practical factors such as having the space available to install or erect one. It is useful to have working space to enable two people to work comfortably at the bench particularly for brick rubbing, squaring and other tasks.

An example of part of a workshop where jointing and pointing, training and practice can be carried out on a training panel. Note the tuck pointing tools on the right of the picture, arch construction equipment in the centre and pigments stored on the shelf above.

All bricklayers should have their own set of tools to which they have become well accustomed through practice onsite. Some tools used 100 years ago or more have been rendered obsolete by modern inventions and techniques which have improved the efficiency of bricklaying. That said, it is important to understand how and why they were used to

The work bench should be of solid construction and must not shake or move when rubbing bricks on the stone. Personal Protective Equipment (PPE) must be worn when working in this environment and accumulated dust must be removed at regular intervals. This brick dust can be stored and used as a pozzolan in mortar mixes (*see* Materials).

achieve the work that they did. Today, good quality bricklayers' tools, and supplementary ones which are adapted specifically for brickwork conservation, are readily available.

The conservation repair of traditional brickwork requires not only the tools most familiar to the bricklayer such as level, brick trowels, hammers and bolsters, but also supplementary tools and accessories useful to brickwork conservation in dealing with the wide range of tasks encountered when dealing with traditional brick buildings. For brickwork conservation, one key element is to be able to repoint neatly and effectively in lime mortar. To keep the work clean, this involves a range of homemade tools to fit the joint widths and fashioned from others to make them more usable. Power tools of various types are extremely useful in time saving for work onsite, such as mixers for mixing mortar, bench and portable saws for cutting bricks accurately to fit and form shapes, or specialist saws for the quick removal of defective bricks in a way undreamt of 200 years ago.

In addition to the construction, repair and repointing of brickwork, a more traditional range of tools and implements are those used for the construction of gauged brickwork. The bricklayer might be called upon to complete life size drawings, and then construct gauged brickwork enrichments such as arches or niches. Although it is important to understand and use traditional methods, even within this class of work there are elements of it that have been largely rendered obsolete by modern materials, particularly when time is a major consideration. Examples might include the use of acetate to make voussoir templets, or the use of a portable masonry saw which is ideal for cutting some natures of rubber bricks quickly and efficiently and which would only snap the wire of a traditional bow or frame saw.

Conservation and restoration of brickwork requires the bricklayer to be able to weigh out, mix and prepare pigments, washes and glue sizes and to recreate aggregates and for this a range of sieves, measuring implements and vessels is required.

Setting Out: Drawing, Measuring and Checking Accuracy

Accurate drawing and setting out is key to good quality brickwork, brick construction and repairs. Tools and accessories for this work range from simple steel squares to drawing implements and accessories.

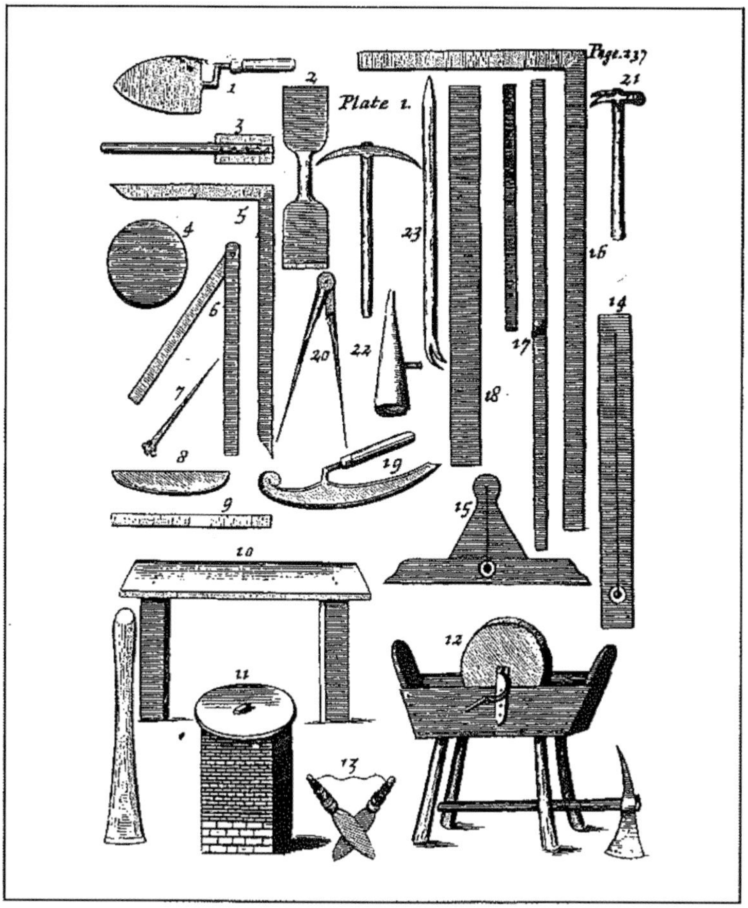

Traditional tools and equipment as laid out, drawn and described in Joseph Moxon's *Mechanick Exercises* (published between 1680 and 1703) whose publication reflected a growing interest in the 'mysteries' of craft work, and revealed secrets that had long been held close by the Bricklayers Guild. (Image courtesy of Thames & Hudson)

Drawing Set

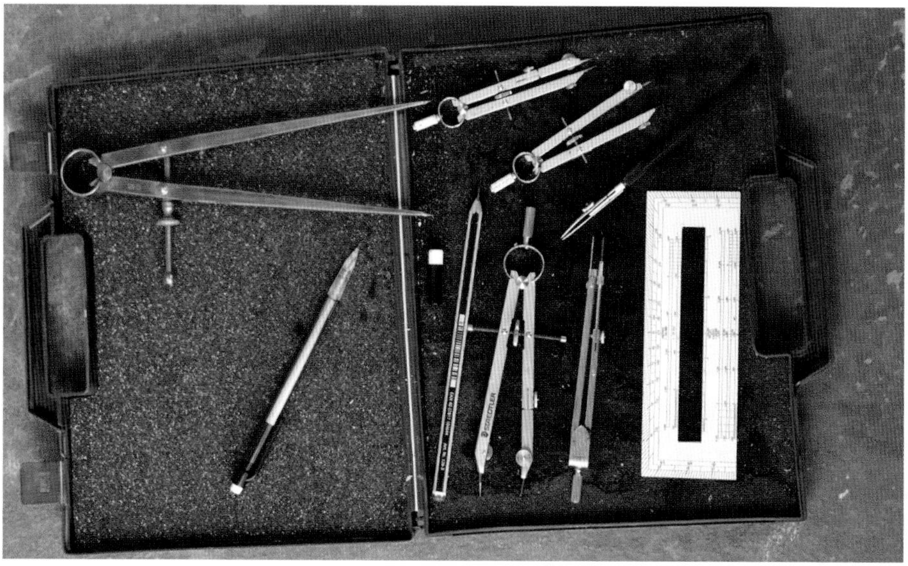

A drawing set contains instruments to draw brickwork detail, full sized arches and other enrichments.

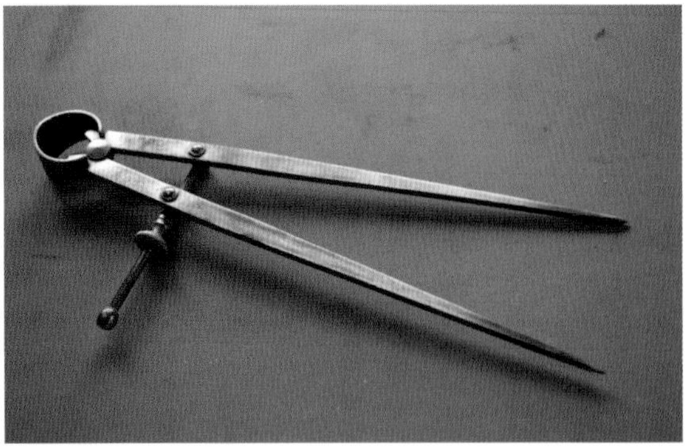

Sprung dividers with a knurled headed screw for fine adjustment.

Dividers

Dividers are used for marking out the positions of voussoirs when drawing and setting out arches, or any drawing where accurate measurement is required.

Set Squares and Scale Ruler

These are required to draw brickwork features and enrichment for reports, estimates and plans to scale, commonly in 1:20 or 1:50 and at angles including those needed for isometric projection, and common in construction drawing.

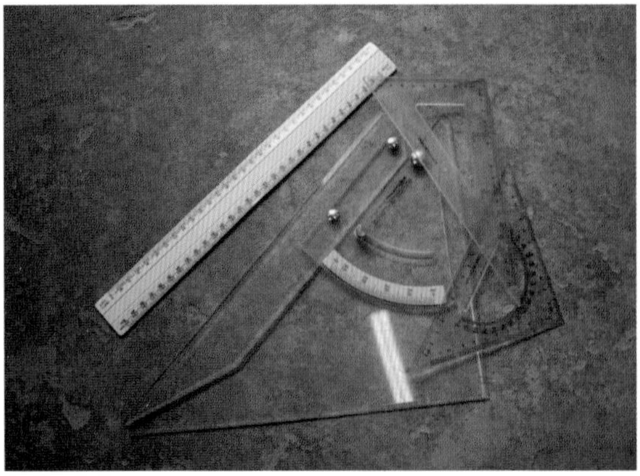

A group of instruments for producing angles and scale in drawing.

Spirit Levels

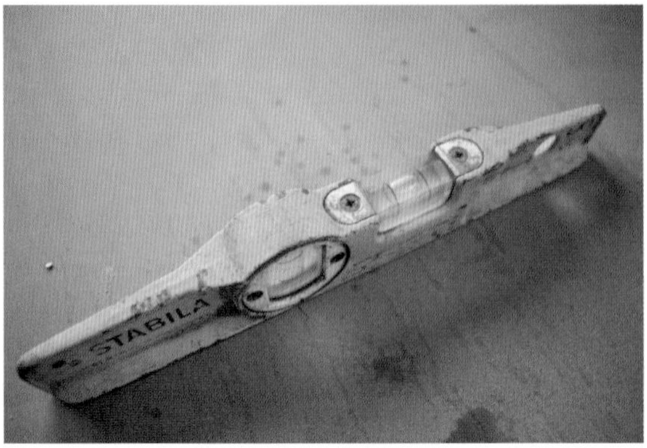

Boat level – a magnetic version is useful for working on a scaffold.

Whilst spirit levels are essential for checking brickwork construction, it is the eyes that are the primary tool.

Most bricklayers possess a range of spirit levels for checking the plumb and level of brickwork. The 1.2m level is a standard size for construction, though much longer ones are available.

Sliding Bevel

The bevel is used to mark angle cuts on brickwork and in setting out of angles, and is used for accurately marking angled brick cuts such as for the skewbacks for arches.

'T' square

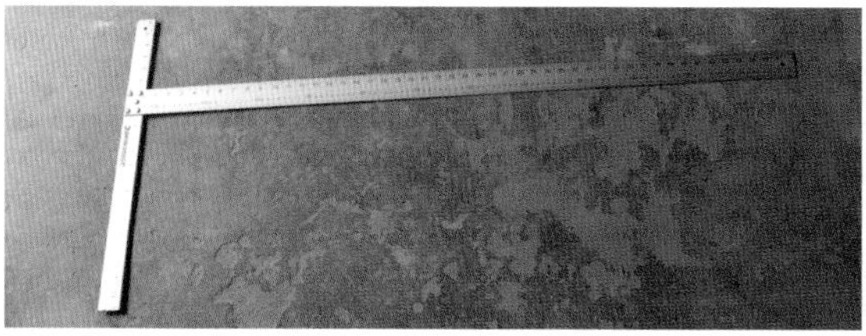

A 'T' square (above) can be used in conjunction with a drawing board or sheet of ply for ease in drawing horizontal lines and as a base line on which to set a set square to produce vertical lines.

A selection of steel squares including an engineer's square (top) convenient for the squaring of rubber bricks and setting out tasks.

Building and Engineering Squares

Steel squares have a variety of uses in brickwork including for setting out a 90° angles, for setting out a building, checking of square of quoins and piers during brickwork construction, and for squaring off rubber bricks during the construction of gauged brickwork.

Steel Building Square

A steel square used for setting out buildings and squaring piers and quoins. The outside measurements are typically 600mm × 400mm.

Pins and Corner Blocks

Pins are used in conjunction with builders' line to enable straight, accurate runs of brickwork to be laid. Corner blocks are an effective method of moving up lines quickly and conveniently.

Plumb Bob

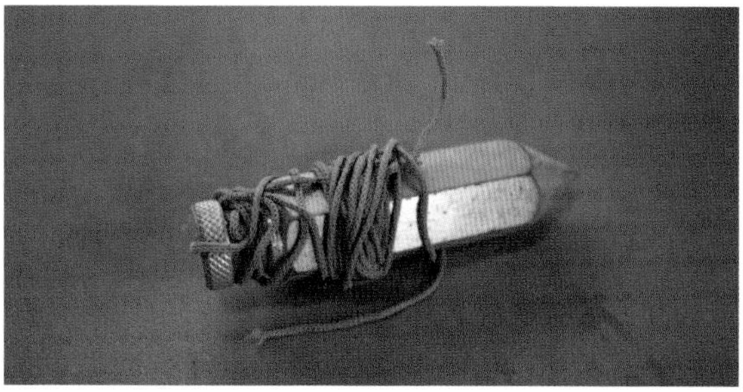

A plumb bob.

The plumb bob has been used in traditional levels for centuries for levelling and plumbing masonry and brickwork. The word 'plumb' is derived from the Latin word for lead, *plumbum*. Today, it can be used to ensure vertical alignment of brickwork joints, particularly when working from a multi-lift scaffolding when carrying out in tuck pointing.

Rulers and Tapes

Whilst a tape measure is indispensable for site work, when drawing arches for openings a 2m ruler is very useful for the accurate drawing of radiating lines from the striking point of a full-sized arch for a typical

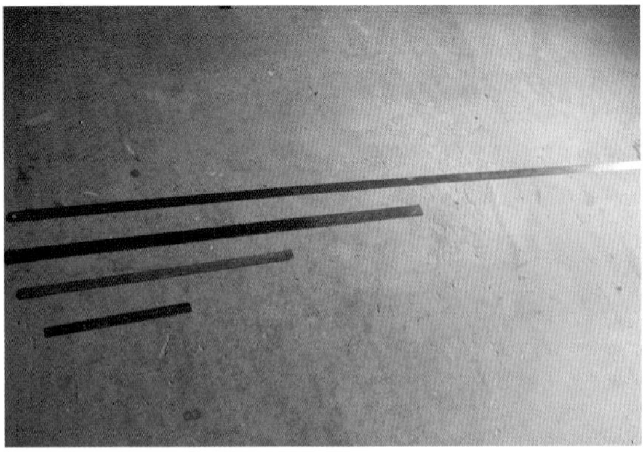

A selection of steel rulers used for drawing brickwork diagrams, enrichments and for setting out brickwork.

900mm opening through the voussoir positions. Shorter ones are used for drawing in detail, including joint lines on enrichments or for cutting acetate in combination with a Stanley or craft knife.

Keep tape measures in good condition by opening and lightly oiling the steel tape before closing.

Trammel Heads

Trammel heads are adjustable steel attachments; one to contain a pencil, the other a tapered point like a compass, attached to a length of seasoned straight timber for forming arcs and circles in geometry when drawing arches and enrichment designs of any size.

Trammel heads attached to a wooden rod or any length of rigid material.

A selection of pencils and fine permanent markers with leads less than 1mm in thickness.

Pencils

Pencils are used for drawing sketches, brickwork drawings, and full-size drawing of arches and enrichments, marking of bricks and of centres for the construction of arches. Standard carpenters' pencils can be useful onsite, but disposable retractable pencils are the most accurate for drawing because the leads are a constant thickness allowing for a higher degree of accuracy in drawing and setting out. For site use, they can be contained in a protective case or an aluminium tube. Fine permanent markers are useful for the marking of acetates to make templets for gauged brick pieces.

Cement Removal and Brick Cutting

Removal of inappropriate cement pointing forms a large component of the preparation of surfaces in brickwork conservation and often constitutes a major part of the job. The tools used to do this work must be robust yet light enough to carry out the work for long periods.

To remove cement mortar, a 2 ½ lb club hammer is capable of tackling most cement pointing encountered. Heavier club hammers may be difficult to use continually and could result in damage to the brickwork as well as repetitive injuries to the user.

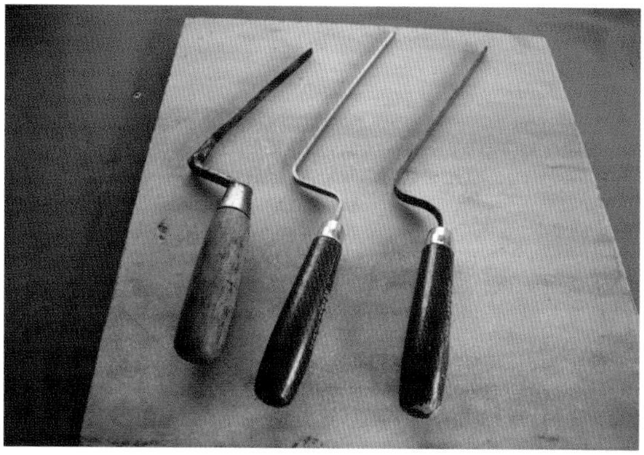

Jointers such as these two brand new ones can be cut down using a grinder to make them more convenient to handle otherwise they can tend to be too springy.

Jointers fashioned from finger trowels can be made to suit any joint width encountered. These finger trowels are often sold as 'tuck pointers' in builders' merchants, but tuck pointing is a term used in America for any form of repointing of brickwork. English tuckpointing is an entirely different skill (*see* Pointing and Jointing).

Tuck irons, or tuck pointers, are unusual looking items whose design dates back centuries. They are intended to be used with a timber straight edge to execute traditional forms of pointing such as ruled, tuck pointing or fine weather struck and cut pointing. They can also be used effectively for repointing arches with fine joints.

Tuck iron with 120mm long blade and flat profile used for applying putty ribbon in tuck pointing.

A range of 75mm tuck irons are used for applying perpendicular joints (or bed joints, if preferred) in tuck pointing and have different blade profiles, some being square in profile, others rounded. Shown here, a selection flat profiled irons ranging from 1mm (bottom) to 7mm (top).

Stubby tuck irons for executing tuck pointing in confined spaces and rounded or curved brickwork, such as moulded work.

Pointing hawks and boards (above) are used in conjunction with any of the aforementioned pointing and jointing tools, to carry pointing mortar. This example is made from plastic roof felt protector.

Small Tools (Plasterers' Leaf)

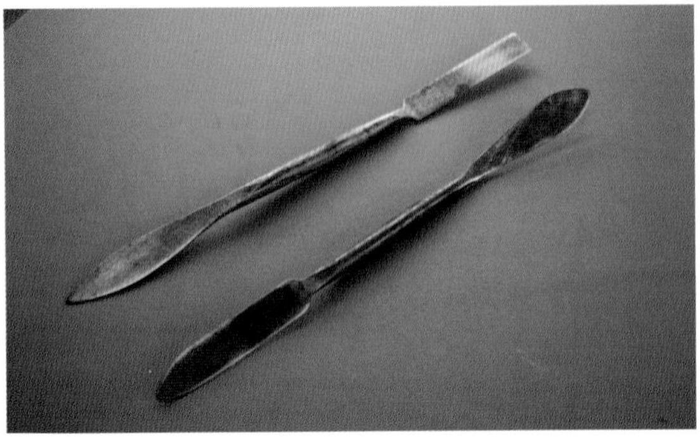

Small tools, traditionally used by plasterers, are invaluable for minor filling and numerous other jobs and come in a variety of blade sizes.

A set of traditional Frenchmen tools fashioned from a kitchen knife. The end of the blade is heated until cherry red, then cut at 30° angle either side of the tip leaving a small nib in the centre which is bent over to 90°. Both the angled edges and the nib are sharpened using a stone (pictured).

Decorators' Pallets

Purpose made decorators pallets can be used in conjunction with a small steel tool for minor filling or plastic repairs of brickwork.

Frenchmen

Protect the sharp tips of Frenchmen by wrapping in bubble wrap and fastening with elastic band during transit.

Frenchman Tool

No one appears to know exactly why these homemade tools are called 'Frenchmen', but their effectiveness in trimming the lime putty ribbon in tuck pointing is beyond dispute (*see* Tuck Pointing). Some prefer to use a craft knife for this purpose (*see* Pointing and Jointing) whilst others prefer the old-fashioned bone handled kitchen knife. Prefabricated Frenchmen tools are available from some tool manufacturers.

Straight Edges

Some traditional brickwork pointing finishes require a straight edge to produce an authentic joint. These include ruled, tuck pointing, and struck and cut joints which cannot be executed properly without one. Exceptions including double struck, flat, bagged jointing or modern conservation pointing. Straight edges should be of bevelled, seasoned softwood, or aluminium approximately 1.2m in length, with fabric or cork spacers or distance pieces on the back to allow mortar droppings to fall through when trimming certain joints (*see* Pointing and Jointing). Straight edges can be fitted with central handles on the rear though some prefer them without as they can be a hindrance.

A range of timber and aluminium straight edges. Cork or fabric spacers are attached to the back to provide a gap through which pointing debris can fall when putty ribbon joints are trimmed.

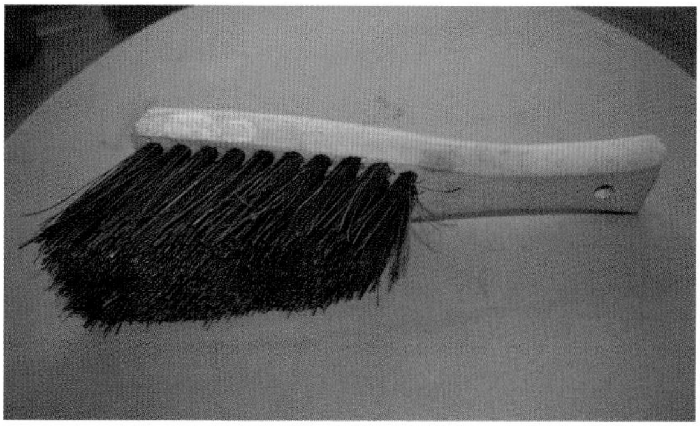

The churn brush can be used for providing a beaten texture to conservation pointing work but is not appropriate for most other traditional pointing finishes.

Brushes

The bricklayer will invariably carry a soft brush or broom head to brush off mortar debris from the work. When brushing brickwork, it is recommended to brush at a 45° angle to the work, so as not to drag or distort the surface of the work. In traditional brickwork, there are brushes for numerous types of work. These range from soft decorator's brushes which are useful to remove fine surface debris without damaging a recently applied jointing or pointing finishes, paint brushes used for applying colour wash or make up brushes for removing debris from the ribbon in tuck pointing. The ubiquitous churn brush is used for beating conservation pointing to provide a weathered finish slightly back from the arris of the brick, but has no place in the execution of other traditional joint finishes.

Soft brushes have a variety of uses in craft brickwork from lightly brushing completed work and removing the debris from certain pointing finishes such as tuck pointing.

> **Brushes**
>
> Keep the churn brush dry, clean and free of lime deposits and use a separate brush for the cleaning of walls, tools, etc., to prevent contamination of the 'finish' brush.

Gauged Brickwork – Tools and Accessories

The skilled traditional bricklayer might be in possession of a variety of traditional tools and accessories to carry out gauged brickwork. Whilst acquiring some of them can be expensive, they are a once in a lifetime investment.

Bow or Frame Saw

A traditional bricklayer will more than likely possess at least one frame or bow saw, constructed from beech wood by a good joiner for cutting rubber bricks in the

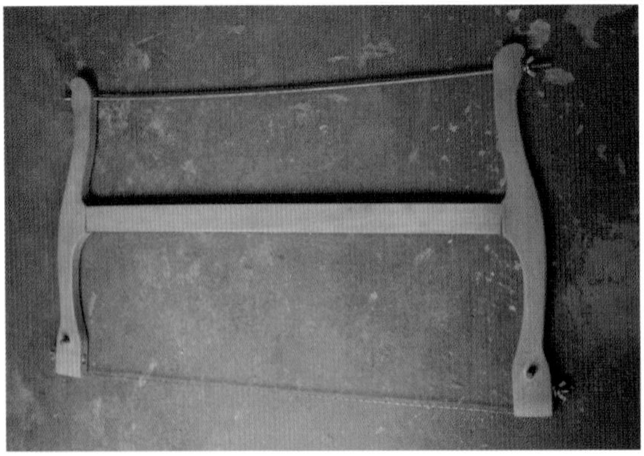

The frame or bow saw is traditionally made from beech and a wire blade with a tensioner of cord. This modern example has threaded bar tensioner and a blade of twisted MIG or welder's wire.

cutting workshop. The blade is made from welder's wire, or MIG wire, which when mechanically twisted will cut through suitable rubber bricks without 'wandering' in the way that a normal blade would. They do not cope well with some natures of rubber bricks which might contain large numbers of inclusions, for example flint blade tends to snap more regularly but are otherwise ideal for cutting shaped rubbers.

Rubbing Stone

The York stone or rubbing stone is used to rub down bricks for constructing brickwork enrichments in gauged work. It is usually made of flat, level stone approximately 470mm in diameter and about 75mm thick and can be purchased from some stone suppliers. When used in the workshop they should be levelled on a bed of lime mortar. An un-riven concrete paving slab can be a useful substitute in an emergency.

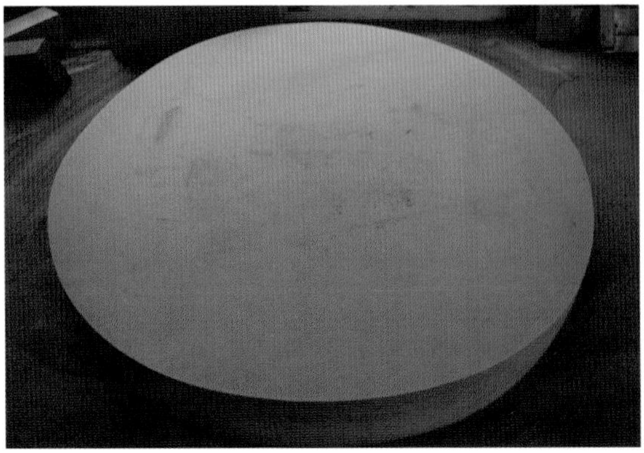

Rubber bricks are rubbed on the stone in a clockwise direction, checking the rubbed surface regularly using a steel square.

Rubbing stones

It can be useful to have two stones, one for use in the workshop and another for taking on to site for minor rubbing when constructing an arch or enrichment.

Bridge

As its name suggests, a simple homemade, wooden device which enables two bricks to be held tightly side by side in the cutting box for cutting with the bow saw.

Adjustable Reducing Box

The cutting box enables rubber bricks to be cut to shapes according to what the bricklayers need and are generally adjustable to aid this purpose. Other wooden moulds can be made to cut specific shapes of bricks. They are not available to buy off the shelf and would need to be made by a good joiner.

A reducing or cutting box with protective steel edging to protect the wood from the wire blade of the bow saw. The base of the box is adjustable to enable it to be adjusted to the required cut angle.

Carborundum Stone

Carborundum stones are fine grained stones sold as either flat oblong blocks or in other shapes to rub brick and masonry or finish carved brickwork in situ.

A carborundum stone.

Files and Rasps

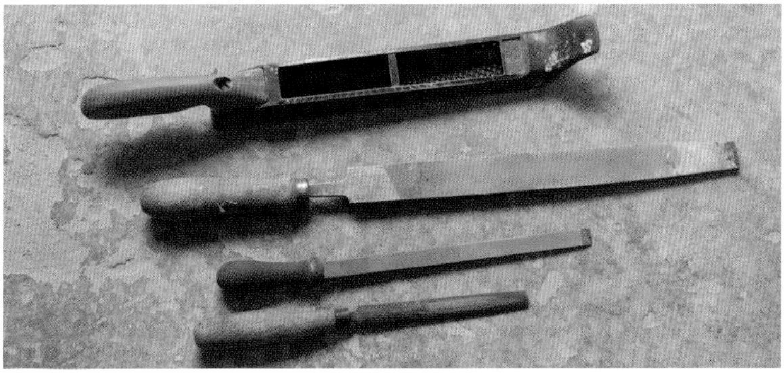

Files are useful to shape and reduce bricks whilst in the cutting box, for finishing moulded or carved work in situ and for other such fine adjustments.

Engineer files of different sizes can be purchased cheaply at car boot sales.

Engineers Steel Square

A small steel square is ideal for squaring rubber bricks as it is easy to handle. This blade on this example measures 153mm.

DPC

Certain types of Damp Proof Course (DPC) material happen to be 1mm thick and as such are very useful for setting out arches to ensure the correct joint spacings.

Some types of DPC are 1mm thick making them useful for forming dry joints or spacers when arranging a gauged arch or enrichment on a bench.

Portable Timber Arch Bench

An arch bench should be of sturdy construction with carrying handles. When constructing an arch, the arch drawing – minus the radiating lines – can be taped to the top of a bench and the arch voussoir placed on it, each in their correct position so they can be easily identified and picked up for laying in the correct order (*see* Gauged Brickwork Arch Construction). The bench can also be used for seating a rubbing stone in a temporary site workshop.

Scribe

A tool used for scoring a brick prior to cutting that can be bought specifically from a good masons' suppliers.

Seamstress Twine

Seamstress thread is much finer than the types of line used in brickwork (though far less strong) and is useful for running gauged work to line or setting out the positions of arch voussoirs.

Fishing Line

Fishing line (below) is very strong and difficult to break accidentally, as well as fine and therefore very good for laying gauged brickwork and for setting out and checking the positions of voussoir, particularly where very fine joints are required.

Seamstress twine is finer than builder's line and will break more easily when stretched.

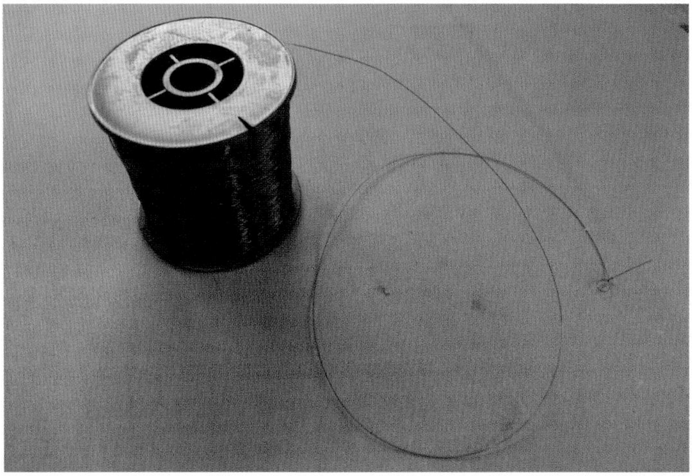

Fishing line is a useful method of creating a very fine line to lay ashlar gauged work to.

Cutting of Acetates

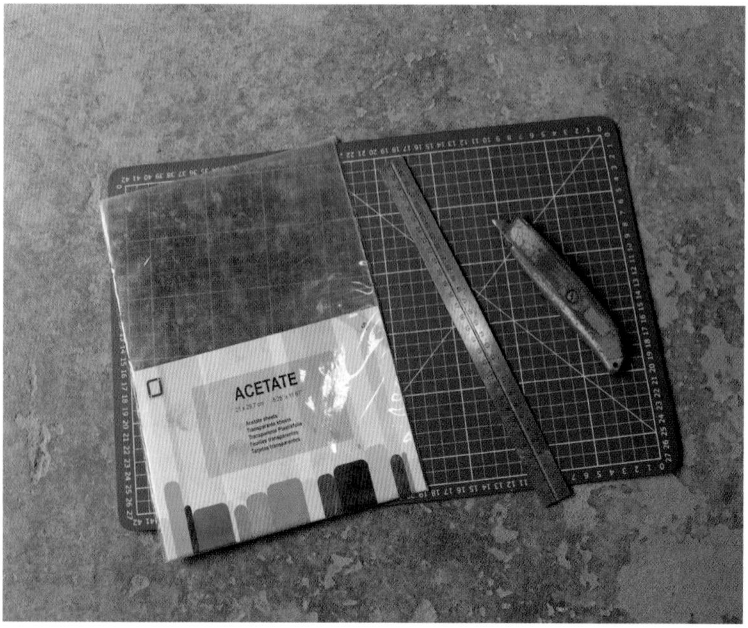

Acetates for making templets for gauged work can be cut on a cutting mat with a steel ruler and carpet knife. White paper can be used under the acetate so that it can be seen easily on the mat.

Power Tools

The use of power tools on traditional and historic buildings is a controversial subject, not least because of the potential damage that that can be done to historic fabric by using them. Many people in conservation circles do now accept that a power tool in the right hands can be an extremely useful addition to the craftsman or woman's arsenal, and some bricklayers are using small disc cutters to collapse hard cement joints with some reputable written sources now supporting this view. Understandably, some heritage conservation organizations are dubious, if not implacable, in their opposition to the use of grinders, understandably, as they may have experienced bad workmanship or damage to their heritage assets by the use of such machines and cannot afford to take the risk of their use. There are some points to make about their use. Firstly, the bricklayer needs to be prepared to carry out work solely by hand if the situation demands, as it quite often does, and to do so they need to be properly equipped with quality hand tools. Secondly, trials using small grinders should be carried out to satisfy the architect or property owner before their use on a project to assess the impact, method and result of the work. Thirdly, the user needs to be experienced and trained in the use of the tool, and aware of the context of the building, and thus the implications, and not prone to lapses in concentration. Finally, that there will be a cost implication for carrying out *all* works by hand.

Other power tools are available on the market including reciprocating saws with plunge type blades which allow the removal of bricks extremely quickly and with no damage to adjacent brickwork and can rake back joints ready for pointing very efficiently. In the wrong hands, the sharp tungsten-tipped blades can leave marks on the face of the brick if the blades are not directed into the joint with care, and it can produce quite a lot of dust which will coat the adjacent brickwork if not contained and controlled as stipulated by the manufacturer. As with all machine tools, it is often the misuse of the tool rather than the tool itself which is the cause of a problem. Note that saws of this type will not always cut through hard cement mortar effectively, so this would still

A type of reciprocating saw with elongated blades that is sometimes used to remove bricks. To remove a brick by hand can take as long as 40 minutes but with a reciprocating saw as little as 3 minutes. They should be used by an experienced operator and only if judged to be appropriate for the building.

need to be first removed by hand. Reciprocating saws can be fitted with an assortment of blades for other tasks, such as cutting the roots of trees and shrubs and raking out mortar joints.

Electric Whisks

When smaller batches of mortar are required, too small in size to warrant the setting up and use of a mixer, a mortar whisk is a good investment. A standard cement mixer has to be cleaned however little mix is made in it and, of this, some will inevitably be left around the drum. A mortar whisk can be used in conjunction with a plastic or rubber tub, and ensures thorough mixing therefore saving time and effort, including for hot mixing.

Whisks of various sizes can have different uses, the larger ones for mixing mortar mixes for laying and pointing. Smaller ones can be used with a battery-operated tool to mix up solutions and glue sizes.

A whisk appropriate for the mixing of pigment solutions and glue sizes.

Whisks

Clean whisk blades thoroughly after use to prevent contamination of mortars by dried debris from previous mixes.

Electric Hammer Drill

This tool is useful for weakening and drilling out of bad repairs whose materials do not have to be salvaged and can be broken out with impunity. It is also useful for drilling into cement joints to weaken them prior to their removal by hand, and for the insertion of stainless fixings. Battery-operated tools are useful for work on scaffolds.

Portable Masonry Chop or Clipper Saw

Portable or table-mounted masonry chop saws are an excellent investment where the repetitive cutting of brick on site is required and will produce an excellent straight and clean cut. It will make short work of rubber bricks if they are of the type which have too many inclusions to allow efficient cutting with a frame saw. The user must be trained and wear correct PPE appropriate to the machine.

Buckets and Containers

Sealable tubs for mixing and storing mortars and aggregates, for batching materials, colour washing and a host of other jobs are essential for lime mortar work. Those used for the gauging and batching of materials should be kept as clean as possible, whilst those used to make and mix colour washes and pigments should be set aside for that purpose alone so as not to corrupt other mortar mixes.

Spray Bottles and Accessories

The wetting of brickwork and fine mist spraying is essential in repairs and construction in lime mortars. For small areas and minor repairs, pressurized spray bottles are usefully sized relative to the work being carried out. Generally, hoses with adjustable heads are the best for enabling a constant supply of directed water on a much bigger scale onsite.

Steel Shovel

A good steel shovel is essential for the bricklayer. They should be well maintained and kept clean to avoid the accumulation of lime.

An adjustable hose wand has several settings to allow varying moisture application on lime work including a fine mist spray.

Steel shovel.

Steel shovels

Clean steel shovels to prevent build-up of materials using water, a brush and a piece of brick.

Sieves and Riddles

Sieves and riddles are used for the sieving or punching through of dry aggregates and when combining ochres with aggregates when making pointing and building mortars and pigmented plastic repair mortar.

Measuring Cups and Spoons

Spoons and receptacles for accurate measuring of materials such as ochres and powders.

Miscellaneous Items

Through site experience, it is found that a variety of items are useful in the repair of traditional brickwork. For example, a small piece of rubber brick, used like a pencil eraser, is useful for cleaning off minor lime stains from softer red bricks as the work proceeds. The rough side of a standard washing up scouring pad can be used to flick off lime debris. Timber lath can be used to form scrapers for etching mortar joints to form texture, and for ironing out hairline cracks from newly applied joints or transferring marks from drawings to arch formers. Drags to remove lime mortar can be fashioned from steel with hooked ends for this purpose. Small brushes, such as make up brushes, can be used to touch up brickwork using colour wash solution.

Miscellaneous items used in tuck pointing and brick repairs. Such items are accumulated from experience of working with a variety of brickwork conservation materials

Chapter Six

Materials

The wide range of traditional materials available provides a broad pallet of colours and texture with which to build, repair or nourish and beautify traditional brickwork. Handmade wood-fired bricks come in a multiple of hues, with no two being the same, to blend in with the original work or can be used to create the contrasts discussed in an earlier chapter. A myriad of different aggregates, when used with different forms of building limes, present different colours and textures which can appear different in varying degrees of shade and light. Pigments can be used in washes to touch up and enhance stained and tired brickwork and to mix with mortars to create an illusion either in tuck pointing, filling dummy joints, 'extending' bricks and plastic repairs. Identifying these materials, understanding the natures and performance, their advantages, disadvantages, and limitations is crucial to executing good quality, authentic and robust repairs to traditional brickwork and this knowledge, once gained, becomes an indispensable addition to the bricklayer's repertoire.

Aggregates

Aggregates provide strength, durability and structure to the mortar joint. When choosing an aggregate for lime pointing, the aggregate should be no greater in size than ⅓ of the height of the joint. Even if the original mortar is not sent away for laboratory analysis, a sample of the mortar can be taken, crushed, and sieved to ascertain the size and colour of the aggregates used and matched to what is actually seen. Authenticity in colour and texture is important for the pointing and repair mortar to blend in. To achieve this, it is worth expanding the search for the appropriate aggregates. Aggregates found as local to the building as possible should be considered first, but it is possible that the colour still might not match the original mortar. For example, in Shropshire, red and red/brown aggregates are quarried, yet there are many traditional buildings with yellow/buff mortars. This could be because old seams of rocks were quarried out, and the aggregate colours are no longer produced, or that certain types of rocks had strata of more than one colour, or perhaps even that they were brought in from different regions. Collecting a range of local aggregates and making labelled samples is a useful method of building up a colour pallet. In this way, a knowledge of which sands can be used to make different colours, for example, mixtures of yellow and red sands create buff colours.

When a mortar has been used on a job, the ratios of aggregates to lime can be recorded in a notebook, together with the colour achieved when set, and can then be referred to at a later date for other jobs as required. Aggregates are much easier to use if they are dry as it is then possible to ascertain the water component of a mix more easily (except when using mature lime putties which require no extra moisture). Dry aggregates can also be sieved, and this is useful because dry sieving enables the sand component of a mix to be created from a variety of aggregates more easily. Onsite, on a hot day, bags of aggregate which are invariably still wet inside when purchased, can be opened and the aggregate spread out on a plastic sheet to dry. Then, when completely dry, they can be stored in labelled, clean sealable buckets until needed.

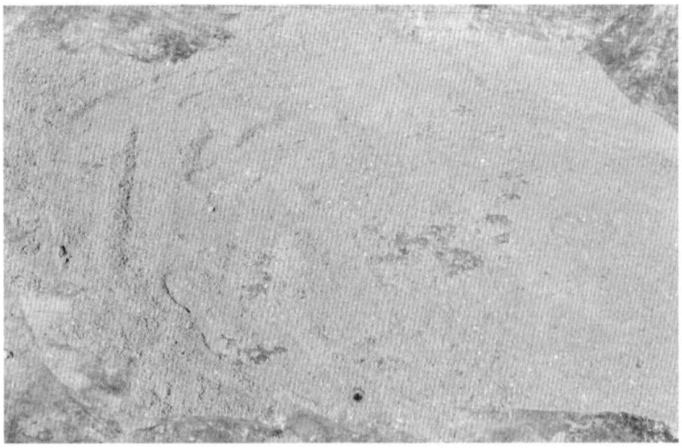

Aggregates laid out to dry in the sun on a plastic sheet.

> ## Aggregates
>
> When storing aggregates, indicate on the tub the colour, size and where the aggregate was purchased.

Sieving aggregates for use in mortar mixes. A set of sieves, ranging from 6mm down to 2mm, is a useful addition to the traditional bricklayer's panoply. On a bigger scale, a riddle can be set up to allow greater quantities of aggregates to be sieved at one time (*see* Tools and Equipment).

Some secondary sources describe a lime mortar mix as consisting of one part lime to three parts sharp sand. Sharp sand alone can be far too gritty for mortar pointing where a particular historic finish is required, and not all sharp sands are standardized and therefore do not all have the same size particles. The three parts of aggregate can in fact be made up of a number of different aggregates needed to form the colour and texture required and is achieved by examining the contents of the sample. Mortar used to point a premier Georgian façade, for example, might be very fine indeed. Historically, lime pointing was often carried out over the top of the bed joints whilst they were still relatively green, and done by teams of pointers with a mix that was often much finer and more binder rich than the bedding mortar (*see* Pointing and Jointing).

Kiln Dried Sand

Kiln dried sand can be used to make mortars for laying gauged brickwork, or to add to other aggregates to make mortars for building or pointing, but note that although the particles are only up to 1.5mm in size, it is still too large to make suitable tuck pointing putty.

Bricks

Some people believe any brick that looks old is appropriate for repairs to any traditional property. In fact, sourcing the wrong type of brick for a traditional brickwork conservation project can have serious implications for the building. When selecting bricks for the

Kiln dried sand can be purchased from most builder's merchants.

repair and construction of traditional brickwork, they should, where possible, be sourced from traditional brick manufacturers who specialize in using traditional techniques and methods of manufacture appropriate to a given era, and who can provide bricks which are compatible with – and can be integrated into – a historic repair yet with appropriate frost resistance (*see* Vulnerability of Traditional Brick).

It is wise to begin brick searches for conservation projects in a timely fashion to avoid having to make last minute decisions on which brick to use. Note that Georgian and Victorian buildings were often built using a place grade (but no less durable) brick on the sides and back of a property, so it is important to source bricks suitable for differing elevations of the same property and which match in colour, texture and size.

An imperial sized brick measuring 225mm x 77mm x 111mm from brick manufacturer, H. G. Mathews.

Brick (Rubbers)

Rubber bricks are those made from very good quality clays and which, in the main, have few internal inclusions used for the finest brickwork enrichments. They can be cut using a bow saw or clipper saw which can then be rubbed on a York stone to enable accurate joints ranging from 1mm to 3mm in thickness and are used create gauged work and other enrichments. Rubber bricks are generally made from very fine-quality brick clays, usually washed several times to remove inclusions (the small fragments of flint and pebbles found naturally in brick clays). Gauged work is in a class of its own due to the time, quality and finish of the work, and therefore gauged or rubber bricks can be quite expensive depending on the quality of rubber used, and considerably more if they have been pre-prepared by the manufacturer for specific work.

Some grades of rubbers have small inclusions in them which makes cutting with a bow saw difficult, since when the saw wire encounters an inclusion (such as a piece of flint) the wire blade will snap, and this might happen fairly regularly. Despite this,

An example of a 230mm x 100mm x 60mm facing brick; this particular example being from Lambs Bricks and of a size often found to be appropriate to the Restoration era (1660–1685). Note the sandy texture and brick smiles.

An example of a full-sized rubber brick measuring 240mm x 82mm x 190mm. Note the narrow and deep frog. The markings on the brick indicate the fact that the brick clay has been washed and the also shows the company that produced it, in this case Bulmer Brick & Tile.

A cross section of a rubber brick which, in this case, has many small internal inclusions.

they have their place in the repair of gauged arches of earlier eras of buildings when the process of manufacture was perhaps less refined.

Superior quality rubber bricks have few or no inclusions at all and cut beautifully with the bow saw or, if they are harder, with a clipper saw, and produce very sharp arrises and extremely high-quality work.

An example of a pre-squared block for constructing gauged work. Note the sharpness of the arrises. Pre-squared rubbers can save much time and effort in squaring the brick.

Brick Dust

Brick dust collected from gauged rubbing work can be stored and used as a pozzolanic additive in mortar mixes or used as one ingredient in plastic repair mixes. It cannot be used to form colour washes, or used to make stopping for tuck pointing.

Brick dust texture. Note, it should not be confused with natural earth pigments and cannot be used to colour mortars in the same way.

Marble dust can be purchased form leading art shops as a fine powder.

Marble Dust

Marble dust can be used to add sheen and brightness to putty ribbon in tuck pointing.

Glues

Glues can be used as a medium in colour washes and for adding (as a glue) to pigmented plastic repairs instead of fresh water. Rabbit skin glue has been used for centuries for many applications, and is available from leading art suppliers. It can be made into a solution of the consistency of wallpaper paste for addition to colour wash recipes as well as pigmented plastic repairs.

Rabbit skin glue crystals look a little like demerara sugar. When made up into a solution, it can be stored in 5-gallon plastic containers and used when required. A capful of disinfectant can be added to a mix to remove the smell.

Alum

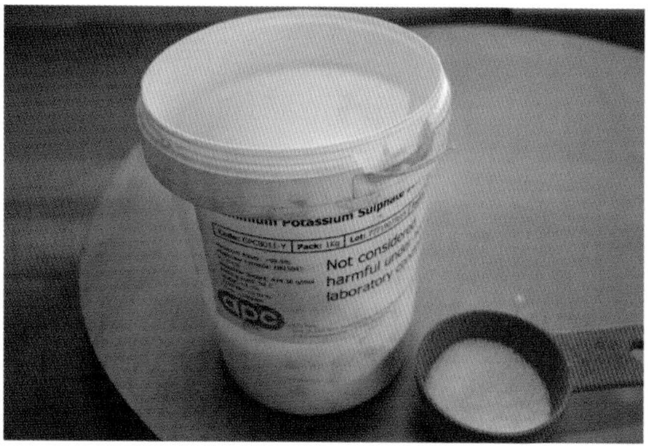

Aluminium potassium sulphate is a mordant used as a fixative in the preparation of colour washes.

A colourwash solution formed from rabbit skin glue solution, alum and red ochre.

A bale of oakum tar hemp. This material was traditionally used in the repair of boats but can be very effective when forming joints between brick and timber.

Oakum tar hemp can be twisted into a rope or braid for insertion as a seal between brick and timber.

Hemp (Oakum Tar Hemp)

Oakum tar hemp is a breathable and flexible material which can be used to seal between timber windows and brickwork (*see* Brickwork Repairs) and was traditionally used for the decks of boats. The hemp is infused with Stockholm tar, which is the resin of the pine tree. It has a natural smell and leaves an oily but not unpleasant residue. It can be bought as a bale, usually in a sealed plastic bag.

Hessian

Hessian can be used to cover and protect newly built or repaired brickwork. It comes either in rolls

New hessian tends to have a temporary 'waterproof' capacity and should ideally be fully submerged in water for a period until thoroughly soaked prior to use. It can then be hung over the scaffold until needed, by which time the excess moisture would have dripped out.

approximately 40m long, or in sheets or as sacks. Once fully wetted, hessian is effective for keeping wall surfaces damp and preventing the rapid drying of the mortar, provided that enough layers have been used. It is useful to cover hessian layers with an impermeable material to prevent moisture loss. When using hydraulic limes, any material that can hold moisture or prevents its evaporation from the wall surface is equally useful, and this could include carpet or underlay, or blankets or scaffold coverings (*see* Protection of Traditional Brickwork).

LIME MORTARS FOR BUILDING AND REPAIRS

There have been numerous publications on lime (*see* Bibliography), its history of use and manufacture, but it is inevitable in a book about traditional brickwork that the mortar used in its construction would be discussed, as it is this traditional component that is integral to brickwork repairs throughout the period that this book covers and beyond. Here, an overview will be provided of limes that can be purchased today, their use onsite, natures, characteristics, availability, disadvantages and limitations. The practical implications in applying them will also be discussed in this chapter.

A good mortar for brickwork should be workable and, for most bricklayers and masons, its workability implies that it possesses several properties. It should be fatty enough to be easily manipulated on a spot board into trowel-sized portions for transferring onto the walling being constructed, and to retain its shape and form when lifted by a jointer for pointing. The mortar should be suitably water retentive to make it spreadable, and not be crumbly or 'short' when spread. It should form a full regular bed which, regardless of the texture and porosity of the brick, fills up all irregularities as it is spread. In the process of laying, when the bricks are pushed down with the fingers, the mortar should provide enough suction to form an adhesive and cohesive bond between the bricks or stone masonry to both the bed and perpendicular joints. A mortar should also be durable to make it weather resistant and prevent water penetration, and so that many years would elapse before repointing was required. For traditional brickwork, conservation-minded bricklayers and masons find such properties can be found in certain lime mortars.

Differences between Cement and Lime Mortars

In England, lime has been used in mortars in traditional building for centuries. Even in the first quarter of the twentieth century, lime was still considered a viable building mortar in a technical college syllabus in modern brickwork until its use virtually died out in the 1950s, lest in the context of cement-lime mortars, the use of which largely disappeared in favour of plasticizer additives after the 1970s and 1980s.

The end of the First World War had ushered in a fundamental change, not only in the method of constructing houses from solid walling to cavity walling which, soon after this event, became the standard way of building, but in the innovation of building materials. Factory produced bricks were already common, and had been since the mid-nineteenth century, but the addition of concrete blocks, concrete lintels and reinforced concrete floors enabled massed housing and, crucially, quicker housing to be constructed. These changes coincided with the huge loss of life resulting in the death of craftsmen, including many thousands of bricklayers. As a result, cement mortars were (and still are) seen as being key to the more rapid increase in housing construction and as much more cost effective not requiring the aftercare that lime mortars require.

Cement is made by heating a mixture of chalk and lime at extremely high temperatures to produce a material that sets much quicker than lime and has fundamentally different characteristics. It is hard and brittle and as a result is prone to hairline cracking when movement occurs in the traditional building, often allowing the ingress of moisture, and can make a poor bond with porous bricks, with the potential for water ingress. Cement mortars are likely to continue to be a feature of modern construction, but their use in repairing and pointing softer traditional brickwork in historic and traditional buildings should be strenuously avoided.

Whilst it is intended that cement mortars provide an effective barrier in preventing moisture ingress in modern cavity wall construction, through their rigidity and hardness, lime mortars allow capillarity to allow the movement of moisture out of the building through traditional lime-built walls. They also remain flexible until fully carbonated and allow for movement and natural settlement and even, to a certain extent, for the self-healing of hairline cracking in the mortar. Despite the excellent bonding properties of lime mortars, their comparative softness allows for the disassembly of damaged original brickwork and the salvaging of bricks, something difficult if not impossible in cement construction. Lime mortars are sacrificial and are designed to protect the edges of the bricks and thus provide an indication of when the brickwork should be repointed.

With these comparisons in mind, the real problems have been (and still are) caused when cement mortar, believed to be impervious and resistant to moisture, is used in repairing traditional and historic buildings that were originally built using lime mortar. In this scenario, the worst characteristics of a cement mortar – hardness, brittleness and inflexibility – are amplified and more often than not set the scene for other agents of decay to cause physical decay of traditional brick (*see* Vulnerability of Traditional Brick).

It was once widely accepted that bagged hydraulic building limes were of great advantage, not only because of the perceived benefits to the building, which there surely were compared to very hard cement mortars that had been used since the 1950s, but also for their versatility and ease of use, particularly for builders that were converting from using cement to bagged powdered limes. In fact, Natural Hydraulic Lime (NHL) 3.5 appeared to be the default material for most occasions of general repairs and pointing. Today, different types of building limes can be purchased and used for different buildings and structures, on a case-by-case and like-for-like basis, depending on factors such as the historical era and context of the building and the type and nature of the work. For many brick buildings from the Medieval period to the eighteenth century, the period covered by this book, slaked lime rich mixes were the norm and today, these and mature putty-based mortars for specific work, are often considered the best option for repairs. In all cases, thorough research is necessary to ensure that the correct type of lime is being used for the building being repaired. Laboratory testing of lime samples removed during a brickwork assessment will identify the elements and composition of a lime mortar, whilst the conservation-minded and trained craftsman or woman will need to know their materials and understand in what circumstances the different types of limes are appropriate and how to use them. Lime for building is readily available these days. Builder's merchants tend to sell the moderately hydraulic NHL 3.5, whilst specialist lime manufacturers and heritage stockists will supply limes of all types.

Hydraulic Limes

Hydraulic limes are those which, as their name suggests, can set under water and continue to harden as they set. They contain varying amounts of impurities and clay particles which, when mixed with water, create a chemical reaction forming a set. Hydraulic limes are available in powdered material in 25kg bags in either a white or off-white colour, and packaged in three ways: feebly hydraulic lime (NHL 2) which has less than 12 per cent impurities and when mixed is perhaps the 'fattiest' of the hydraulic limes, moderately hydraulic lime (NHL 3.5) which has up to 18 per cent impurities and eminently hydraulic lime (NHL 5) which has up to 25 per cent impurities. Hydraulic limes are particularly good for work that is constantly immersed in water, such as in canals

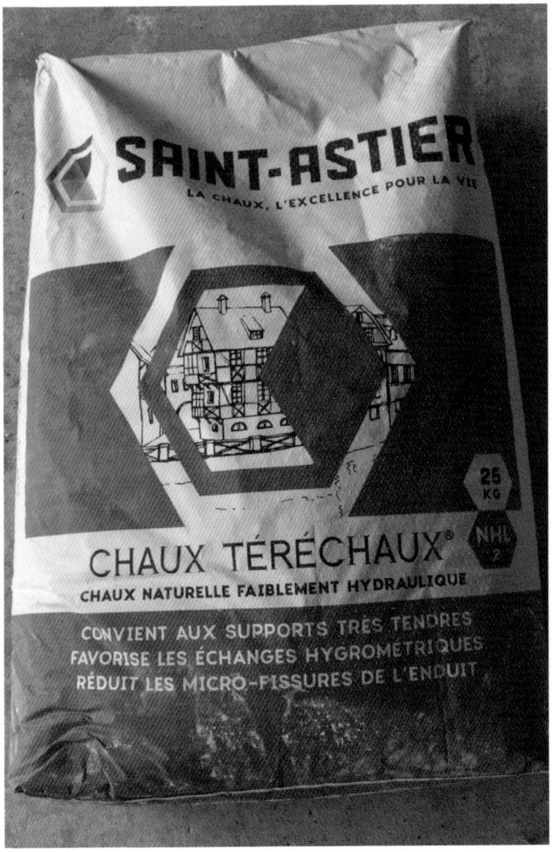

A 25kg bag of natural hydraulic lime (NHL 2).

or in works below ground, or where there are high levels of exposure, or perhaps in later Victorian and Edwardian buildings.

Air or Putty Limes

Non-hydraulic limes, or fat limes, are produced form 95 per cent pure sources of calcium carbonate and their set is slow and gradual as a result of contact with the atmosphere, hence the other name by which they are referred – air limes. Lime is manufactured by the burning of limestone or calcium carbonate ($CaCO_3$) in a kiln. During the burning, carbon dioxide (CO_2) is driven off and the resulting material is known as quicklime or calcium oxide (CaO). Slaking occurs when water is added to this quicklime and there is a violent exothermic reaction in which the quick lime boils and spits until initially all of the larger pieces of it have broken down, but yet will continue to slake thereafter, until a putty is formed. The resulting material, or putty, has a texture not unlike cream cheese with a milky liquid sitting on top known as milk of lime, calcium hydroxide ($Ca(OH)_2$). The maturity of a putty is measured from the point of initial slaking, when it is then stored in an airtight container. The longer that period, the more the moisture would have worked on breaking down even the smallest particles of lime, hence mature putty. Lime putty is available in plastic tubs or 25kg sacks, commonly labelled as matured for a minimum period of four months. The maturity of the putty indicates the extent to which any particles of lime would have slaked down, forming a thick cream-like material, and consequently the longer it has matured the better. To make a mortar with this material requires the addition of a suitable aggregate in proportion and the lime is normally moist enough not to have to add water to it.

Advantages of Using Putty Limes

In general terms it is the present orthodoxy in conservation circles to consider using softer limes whenever possible as these have many advantages over their hydraulic cousins. Significantly, they are softer than the bricks they are used in conjunction with, protecting the brick edges but also acting as a sacrificial material acting as an indicator of when maintenance is required.

Mature lime putty is moisture retentive, has excellent suction particularly for the laying of bricks, and are guaranteed to be much softer than the bricks which they are used in conjunction with, although lime putty mortars may require the addition of a natural pozzolan. From a practical point of view, air limes offer possibilities in craft repairs which are not necessarily facilitated by using hydraulic limes which have a quicker set and which are less moisture retentive, whilst at the same time demanding extensive on-going hydration to set properly. For example, when executing some historic jointing finishes, lime rich mortars with high moisture retentivity enable finishes such as 'penny struck' jointing which requires a neat, crisp compression to be made in the joint (*see* Pointing and Jointing). Note that sacks or containers of premixed putty mortars purchased today can

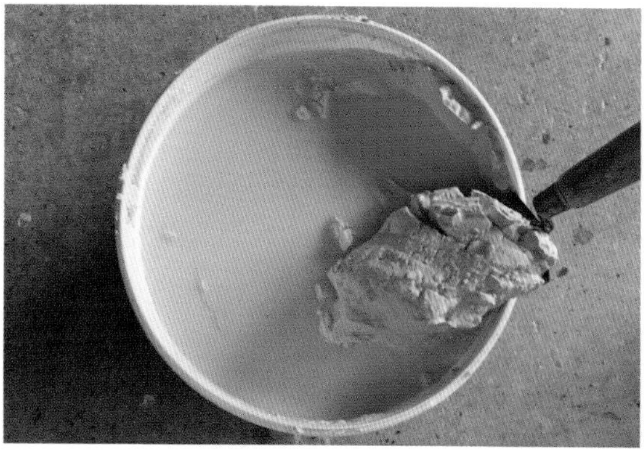

An open tub of lime putty showing the water of lime which prevents the putty being exposed to oxygen. The material has a consistency of cream cheese and is better for being stored to mature.

contain some moisture. To reduce the moisture, it can be spread onto a scaffold board. All lime mortars and putty mortars appear to benefit from having been mixed up at least twenty-four hours prior to their use as they become fattier.

A tub of mature lime putty. The lids should be kept sealed when not being used.

Availability of Lime Putty

Mature lime putty is a very versatile material and can be easily obtained in either tubs or 25kg plastic sacks. For larger construction jobs, the sacks are perhaps more cost effective. The tubs are easy to store, and once empty they have numerous uses for the storage of various materials such as powders and aggregates.

Premixed Lime Putty Mortar

Lime putty mortars can be obtained premixed with aggregates selected by a manufacturer to offer a palette of colours to match those commonly encountered and for selection by the purchaser. Premixed mortars are available with aggregates of different grades to suit different joint thicknesses. Joints under 10mm might require a premixed lime mortar often sold as 'fine' with an aggregate not exceeding 2mm in size. Wider joints may require a coarser, premixed mortar though

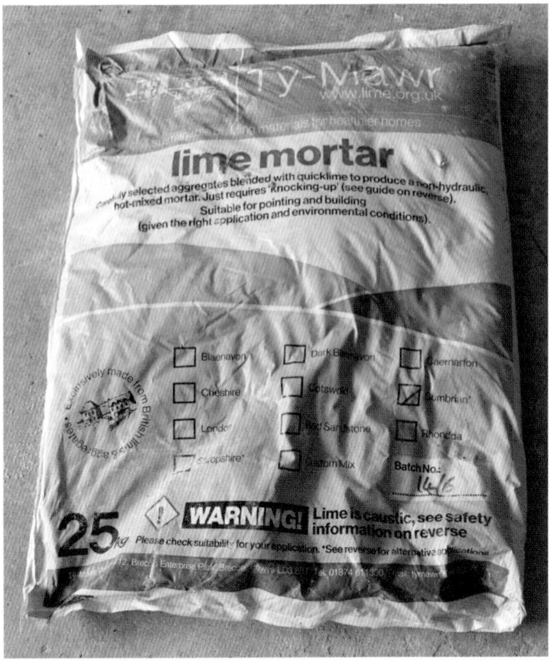

Premixed lime putty in a 25kg sack. Handling and storage of these must be done with care to avoid splitting and piercing the sacks, remembering that the product should be kept airtight until it is used.

it should be considered that no aggregate should be more than one-third the height of the joint.

Sometimes, premixed lime putty in sacks can appear quite stiff, particularly those at the bottom of a pallet due to the weight on top of them which compresses the material. Lime putty can be easily knocked up to release the moisture contained within it in a tub, on a board or using a roller mixer, mortar whisk or other forms of mixer depending on the scale of the work. There should be no requirement to add water to it, but sometimes, in the case of the example given above, a very small amount of water may be needed to prime using an electric whisk to make it lively again. For pointing, putty should ideally be used as stiff as practicable because the more moisture in it, the more shrinkage cracking may occur with rapid evaporation (*see* Pointing and Jointing). That said, it also needs to be of practical workability for laying bricks in an efficient way and if it is too stiff, this will be slower. Some feel that laying bricks and pointing is far more satisfying when using putty mortars, as opposed to hydraulic ones, as they are buttery, provide better suction with the brick and are more moisture retentive. Moreover, due to their 'fattiness' for pointing using mortars with larger aggregate sizes, they can be picked up and carried on the narrowest of jointing irons.

Hydrated Lime

The type of lime that was, and still is, commonly available in the builder's merchant was hydrated lime and, until the advent of liquid plasticizers, was used as one of the components of a composite mortar (compo) of cement, aggregate and lime as a plasticizer. This is simply dried lime putty, a material from which molecular moisture has been driven off in the kiln. It can be mixed with water (hydrated) to form a putty a day or two before use, gauged for the mix before water is added.

Hot Lime Mixing

Hot lime mixing is an increasingly popular method of producing a putty by undertaking the slaking of quicklime onsite and, once understood, is an easy and effective way of making lime mortars. In addition to being highly capillary active, hot limes can provide the characteristic white lime fleck of traditional lime mortars and are very lime rich because of the expansion that occurs during slaking. Hot mixes are highly workable and water retentive, allowing optimal and durable bond with brick and masonry and, in fact, all substrates and are economic to produce and efficient in preparation.

Hot mixing is a method by which mortar of any character – from non-hydraulic to sufficiently hydraulic to set underwater (with pozzolanic addition) whilst preserving optimal workability and adhesiveness on any scale, either for small repointing work or brick work construction. The slaking of lime to make mortar is not the onerous and dangerous form

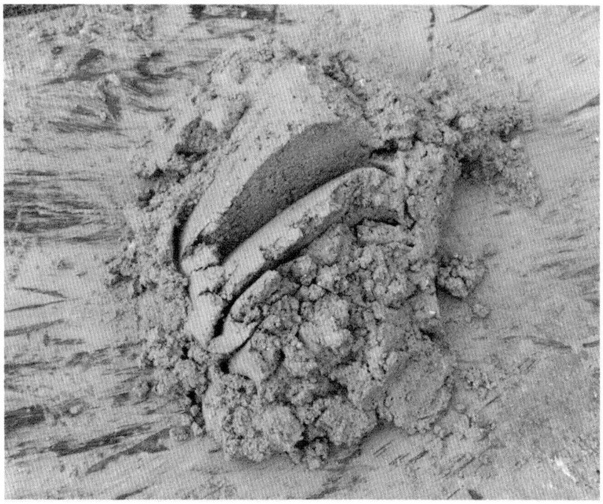

The ability to pick up mortar which retains its shape on a jointer of this size helps to illustrate the fattiness and moisture retentivity of a hot lime for pointing.

of producing mortars that it has sometimes been described as, and in fact is becoming more commonly used by craftsmen and women today who see this as important to the needs of the building, and who want to add this level of authenticity both to their mixing and the finished product. Hot lime mixes can be mixed in a mixer, on a concrete floor, on timber boarding or (on a small scale) in a vulcanized tub, metal dustbin or wheelbarrow, and are versatile, easy to use and authentic. In slaking lime, common sense safety measures must be taken such wearing full body protection (i.e. sleeves down, no shorts) and the wearing of gloves, mask and eye protection when mixing, as should be the case with the use of all forms of lime. With adequate precautions, hot lime mixes are easy to make.

Availability

Quicklime is available to buy at specialist building lime stockists in plastic tubs as a large granule (kibble), in 2mm to dust particles, or in a powdered form inside a plastic lining bag. It requires the addition of water and sand to form a mortar in a method often referred to as hot mix or hot mix lime.

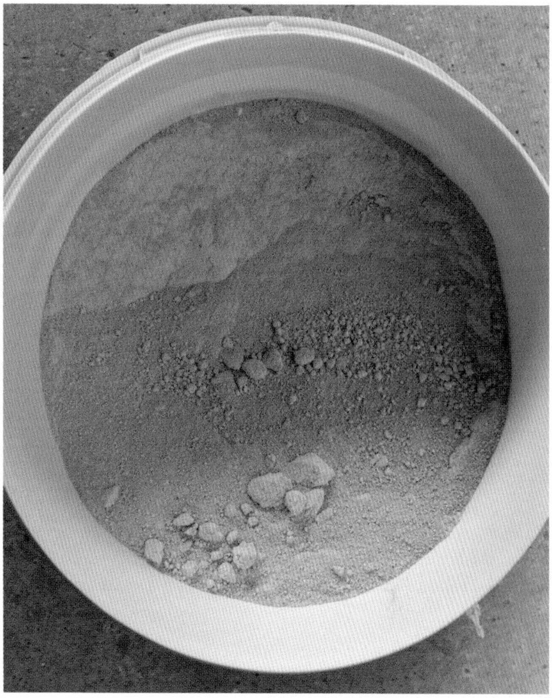

A tub of quicklime shown here in a 2mm to dust form which ensures that a mortar can be produced without larger chunks, causing blowing out of the surface particularly when applied as pointing.

A tub of calcium oxide or quicklime.

Kibbled lime comes in small pieces in a plastic tub, shown here with a plastic liner. Small stones within the material can spit during hot mixing and protective equipment, including eye protection, is essential.

Quicklime

It is important to keep the lids sealed on quicklime tubs when not in use to prevent air from getting at the material. If this happens, the quicklime will absorb oxygen from the atmosphere and 'fall', rendering it useless.

A 2mm to dust quick lime is poured into the centre of a circle of wet aggregates. An exothermic reaction will begin almost immediately.

The wet sand is carefully piled over the lime, and the sand will start to crack and shift as moisture is taken up by the quicklime.

The heap of sand and quicklime is turned over with a shovel. Water is added to the steaming heap of materials slowly until the particles have broken down and/or that the desired consistency of the mortar is reached.

The ability to control the moisture enables the right consistency to be reached for pointing and laying bricks. Once prepared, the mix can be stored in sealed tubs.

Hot lime mixes have several advantages, not least of which, is that they produce historically authentic material with excellent capillarity for the passage of moisture from brickwork. They are more lime-rich than other limes and the moisture content can be controlled by the careful addition of water in slaking. As a result, pointing mortars made from hot lime mixes can be made to be wonderfully stiff and doughy enabling good quality joint finishes to be executed, and good suction and moisture retentiveness for laying bricks.

Linseed oils can be obtained from hardware stores and builders' merchants.

Carbonated Lime Pieces

This crushed material, white or off white in colour, is sold by some lime suppliers in sacks or tubs, the pieces ranging from 3mm to dust in particle size. It can be added as a small proportion of aggregate to a mortar mix and will provide a white fleck element to a mortar.

MIG wire for making frame saw blades.

Oils

Both raw and boiled linseed oils can be used in traditional brickwork. Small quantities of raw linseed oil can be added to lime putty mortar, used in tuck pointing, to make the material a little fattier (*see* Pointing and Jointing). Boiled linseed oil can be mixed with fine burnt sand to form a mastic for sealing narrow gaps around windows (*see* Construction and Repair of Traditional Brickwork).

Crushed carbonated lime from approximately 3mm to dust can form a portion of aggregate in a mix to provide lime fleck in the mortar. This material will not slake on contact with water as it has already carbonated and will not cause pop outs on the joint surface.

MIG Wire

Metal Insert Gas (MIG) wire, used in welding, can be used to make the wire blade for the frame saw. It can be twisted by means of a drill or electric screwdriver with an attachment and the other end looped around a hook or around the end of a scaffold tube.

Pigments

Pigments have been used for applying finishes to historic buildings in England, as well as on the continent, for many centuries. Natural ochre colours work because they contain minerals such as iron oxide and manganese which influence the colour. Pigment is insoluble, but when mixed with a medium such as glue and a fixative such as alum they are suspended and can then provide opacity and body to the brick surface whilst adding a resistant surface without looking like a paint. Using multiple layers of pigment adds to the intensity of the colour whilst single thin coats will allow the hues of the brick to be seen. Pigments can be mixed to darken or add depth to the colours, and samples can be made to ensure that the correct colours for washing and stopping are obtained. Colour washing is a skill generally associated with surface preparation for tuck pointing, but is a useful technique for touching up and bringing colour to brickwork that has been badly stained (including by cement – *see* Construction and Repair of Traditional Brickwork) and to tone down lime pointing by using black washes. It is not a form of lime wash. Pigments can be bought from leading art suppliers and from some conservation material suppliers, and are available in a wide variety of colours which can be exploited to match the similar variety of colours of English brick. Red ochre provides good natural brick shades, and the hue can be altered by the careful addition of lamp black whilst Venetian Red is somewhat brighter. A variety of yellow hues available enables the colour washing of London stock bricks.

Natural earth pigments are imported from the south of France where they are mined and come in a wide range of hues which can be matched to any brick colour including for yellow stock bricks. They are available in 25kg sacks from some suppliers or in small sample tubs as shown.

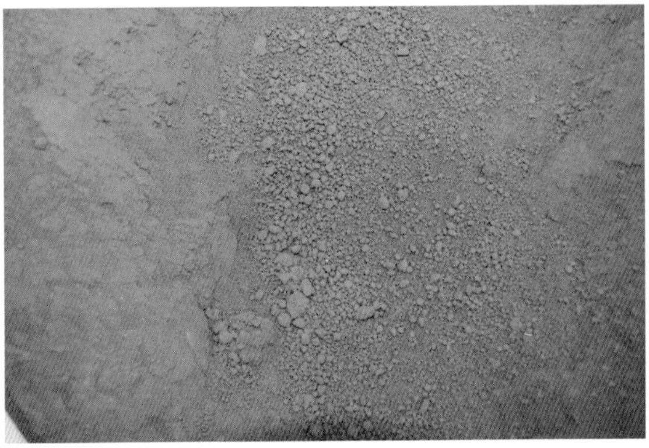

A close-up view of red ochre pigments a colour which can be used in making colour washes and stopping for tuck pointing. It should be stored in dry conditions in airtight tubs.

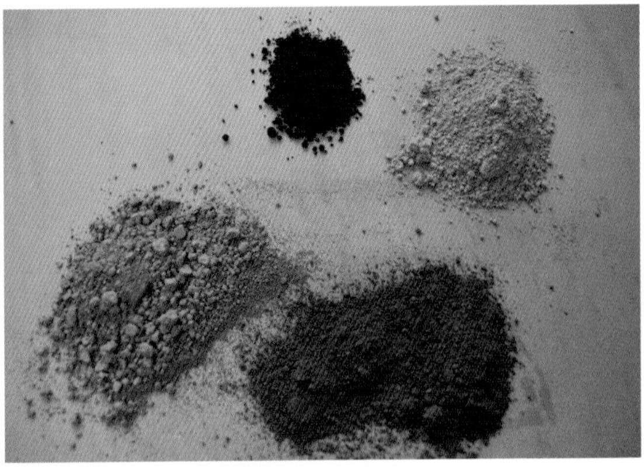

A variety of earth pigments including red ochre, Venetian red, burnt sienna and lamp black. The latter is a versatile pigment used to darken pigment colours or create light soot washes to age brickwork.

Pozzolanic Materials

Pozzolans are materials that can be added to a mortar to give it a quicker initial set, and can be natural such as brick or tile dust or manmade under various trade names in colours such as buff or white. Natural pozzolans can be easily obtained or sourced during site work, such as when cutting or rubbing bricks in gauged brickwork and is a useful commodity when using lime putties for repairs and repointing. Brick dust is available to buy from conservation materials suppliers in 25kg bags. As a general guide, the quantity of pozzolan added is about $^{1}/_{10}$ of the volume of the mortar. Pozzolans do not have to be added to a mortar for it to be effective, and it depends on the context of the building and possibly the conditions you are operating in. There is a small but persistent belief that the 1970s orthodoxy of adding cement to all lime mixes to 'give it a bite' holds true, but today there is a wide range of building limes available for all manner of situations and environmental conditions without the need to add cement which counters the benefits of the lime. That said, it is recommended to take each building and situation on its own merit. Some isolated situations, such as the replacement of roof ridge tiles, might benefit from a small amount of cement in a mix as it is difficult to control the curing of lime in such exposed locations.

Another natural pozzolan is original lime mortar which can be saved when brickwork is raked back for repointing, and makes an excellent pozzolanic additive to mortar once the larger pieces have been crushed down and sieved. it can be used without the addition of other aggregates in very small areas of patch pointing or hole filling mixed with a hot lime or pure lime putty, with the colour and texture being very authentic (*see* Lime Pointing).

Burnt Sand Mastic

Burnt sand mastic is a material formed by mixing boiled linseed oil and a special fine sand. It can be used to seal the gap between timber window frames and brickwork when used in conjunction with oakum tar hemp (*see* Brickwork Repairs). This forms a flexible joint which hardens slowly and will not have the detrimental effects that a cement or silicon might have when moisture accumulates behind it. It can also be effective for pointing flashings as it becomes weatherproof, yet still flexible, and does not require the mothering that lime pointed flashings need (and often don't get).

Chapter Seven

Assessment of Traditional Brickwork

The accurate assessment of traditional brickwork can be used as a means to identify the extent of damage, decay, neglect, and any maintenance issues or natural erosion with a view to carrying out repairs and repointing of the brickwork. In this chapter, a staged approach to the assessment of traditional brickwork will be employed based on an example of a façade and applying the types of knowledge discussed in previous chapters and acquired through training, study and experience of working with traditional brickwork and its construction. Regardless of whether the building is listed or unlisted, thorough brickwork assessment can:

- Identify the causes and symptoms of decay of the brickwork.
- Establish the extent and type of repairs to the brickwork.
- Enable a measured survey of brickwork features and enrichments for drawing and setting out purposes so that they can be repaired.
- Help with forming an understanding and appreciation of the significance of the building and how this can be protected and retained when carrying out the work.
- Help form an understanding of the materials and methods used, and of the mindset of the bricklayers who built it.
- Be used to prepare costings for repairs and/or lime pointing, and to help visualize how a job could be carried out and any logistical and administrative factors that should be considered when working out a price for the work.
- Inform the property owner of related maintenance issues, and those which may need to be diagnosed by the relevant qualified building professional.

To carry out an assessment of traditional brickwork, a five-stage approach can be adopted which might include:

- Understanding the building in the wider context.
- Physical investigation of brickwork including factors affecting its survival.
- Establishing philosophy and method of repair.
- Identifying logistical and administrative considerations.
- Post-assessment works required before work can commence.

Understand the Building in the Wider Context

This part of the assessment process focusses on knowledge that can be attained prior to visiting the building for the first time, and is key to forming the approach to be taken and understanding the building.

Background Research

It is important to point out that all traditional buildings, whether they are listed or not, should be treated with the same care and conscientiousness. It is useful to know when the building was listed. Sometimes, poor alterations or additions took place before the building was listed. Is it Grade II, II* or I and what notable, significant features give it its listing status? Is it of international, national or regional importance? Are there any buildings in the area that are similar, or by the same architect (if known) from which knowledge can be drawn to understand the building? Are there any records which might assist in informing what repairs have been carried out in the past? How was it constructed and in what style? Sometimes clues of original brickwork finishes can be found around the building for example, under lamp fittings or signs or under the eaves.

Architectural Style and Construction

It is important to know the era and architectural style of the building as this will help us to understand its features and how and why they were constructed as well as the brick manufacture technology of that era and how that is evident in the brick and brickwork. It can also inform us of the types and natures of materials and methods that were used in a given era, and what skills would be required in the conservation repair or even in a restoration today. Some basic research in primary and secondary sources will help to shed light on the building style of this era (*see* Bibliography).

Preparing for the Physical Site Assessment

Higher elevations of a property require access to look more closely in order to make informed decisions, so this has to be arranged before the visit takes place. Cherry pickers are one method, whilst ladders can be useful to an extent. Scaffolding is another means of close inspection, particularly for chimneys, but it is rare to have one erected solely for inspection and estimating on a smaller private dwelling. If it is not possible to view all areas, for example if access is not permissible, then this should be explicitly pointed out when the findings of the assessment are prepared for the building owner or manager.

Brickwork assessment should be treated systematically and thoroughly to try to avoid missing something which could then mean the property needs to be revisited or looked at again. One way of approaching a brickwork assessment is by using pre-prepared generic brickwork assessment sheets which can account for all building eras so that the types of features, brickwork bonds or jointing finishes for example can be identified, and indicated by elevation if applicable, on the sheet. Once complete, the survey sheets can be used as the basis for a written report or used to estimate for brickwork repairs of pointing. Photographs are also vital and support the written information on each of the elevations.

Property owners are often knowledgeable about their buildings and can shed light on matters such as damp or water ingress internally, as well as maintenance problems, which will enable these to be pinned down more quickly during the site visit or will raise further questions onto which close examination of the brickwork may shed light. A qualified conservation-accredited building professional may need to be consulted by a property owner if a problem appears deeper rooted than one associated with the brick and mortar themselves.

Physical Investigation of the Brickwork

Time spent on reconnaissance and the gathering of information is never wasted and this is never truer than when gleaning information on traditional brickwork. Initially, it is useful to walk around the building to orientate the building with the compass to determine the positions of each elevation, as different environmental conditions can vary on different brickwork elevations. Next, scan the brickwork whilst standing back from the building to identify obvious areas of decay, cracking and damaged bricks. Finally, examine the elevation closely making notes on what is found including brick and brickwork detail. Once the more obvious areas of concern have been identified, it is then possible to home in on the nature of the bricks themselves on each elevation to unpick some of the clues found in their appearance, influenced by their manufacture and use, as this will be important when trying to source a brick match. Items to identify and take note of could include size, colour, form and texture and nuances such as splits, holes, impressions in the clay and markings of the bricks.

Brickwork Assessment Example

Context

This country house in Shropshire, *c.*1774, is typical of this period with the flat expanse of brickwork punctuated by symmetrically spaced windows and roof hidden by a low parapet wall and a columned portico. It has gauged camber arches above the windows and had been tuck pointed.

Study of this façade example indicates that it is a late eighteenth-century Georgian building and is Grade II listed. This is evident from records, and by the style of build which is the epitome of Georgian construction and, as such, is quite unique in the area. The walls are of red brick, generally of Flemish bond although increased use of headers appear above the windows. The windows are positioned behind rebates which could indicate a date no earlier than 1774, but the bricks appear particularly large for that era, measuring 230mm x 73mm and are possibly Brick Tax bricks, which dates the building from 1784 after the Brick Tax was enacted. The cracking in the elevation above the arches warranted inspection by a conservation-accredited structural engineer who concluded that the cracks could be repaired with stainless steel reinforcement.

Problems identified on the building façade

Front façade	Identified issue	Possible remedial action
A. Parapet	Dislodged masonry cornice	Inspect parapet on both sides, inspect flashings and wall condition. Remove masonry cornice, re-bed and repair replace lead. Repointing of eroded joints, replace/turn around spalled bricks.
B. Parapet	Deep joint erosion	
C. Parapet	Spalling of brickwork	
D. Walls	Sporadic deeply eroded or badly damaged bricks	Remove damaged bricks and replace.
E. Centre LH window	Cracked brickwork	Insert stainless stitching bars through cracking and repoint
F. Lower LH window	Slipped voussoirs	Support arch, remove slipped voussoir and replace. Remove cement pointing from above opening, repoint in lime putty mortar.
G. Beneath lower LH window	Cement pointing	Remove cement pointing and repoint in lime putty mortar.

Front façade	Identified issue	Possible remedial action
H. LH down pipe	Green stained eroded joints.	Inspect down pipes and brickwork behind. Carry out remedial action to brickwork.
I. Plinth	Plastic based paint	Remove paint from plinth and cills.
J. Gauged arches	Cement pointing	Remove cement and repoint.
K. Façade	Tuck pointing fallen out	Remove loose material. Repoint bedding joints where required.
L. Window seals	Cement filled and cracked	Remove cement filling and reseal with breathable, flexible material.
M. Parapet wall (rear)	Torn and displaced flashings and cement repair	Remove inappropriate materials and repair. Lead to be replaced.

Assessing the Requirement to Repair and Repoint the Brickwork

Replacement of Bricks

When considering repairs to this façade, minimal intervention should always be a foremost consideration. Changes to brickwork that are unnecessary, such as brick replacement and repointing where it is not required, may detract from the character of the building, and potentially cause problems. Retention of original historic fabric is paramount when considering brick replacement as once lost, it can never be regained. With this in mind, the era and age of the brickwork and its level of significance should be a factor in establishing the criteria for removal, and this will vary from building to building. Before considering removal, the identification of the symptoms and then the underlying causes of decay should be identified.

Removing the causes of decay may avoid the need to remove some material. In addition, it is also important to establish a set of criteria to consider when making the decision. There may be, for example, some level of natural erosion on the entire brick face which has occurred over centuries, and which has resulted in partial loss of the fire skin, yet the brick is fully intact in which case their replacement is not necessarily warranted. Where deeper loss has occurred and other decay mechanisms are present, such as cement pointing, but which can be removed, this will halt or minimize the decay

Although this brick has some loss of the face and an inclusion has been revealed by natural erosion, the mortar joins are still sound, and the brick condition does not warrant removal.

Brick decay such as this would be justified on the basis that it has eroded deeply and what remains is loose and friable.

process. In this assessment example, sporadic brick decay was identified between first and second floor windows where there had been modern interventions and cracking.

The parapet (A, B, C) shows widespread minor erosion of the brick faces which can have multiple causes. The nature of the brick manufacture may play a part, but more likely is its vulnerability. The parapet wall is exposed, as it is on both sides, and prone to water saturation and ingress due to the dislodged, damaged and open jointed copings. As a result, it is vulnerable to frost attack once saturated, and conditions behind the parapet such as failed lead flashings, cement repairs and a build-up of leaf debris, etc. Repair of the parapet, including copings and leadwork (A), would help to arrest decay whilst other bricks deemed beyond saving should be replaced, and others on both sides of the parapet could be turned around provided enough of the brick is viable. Elsewhere across the elevation, individual bricks have succumbed (D). As there are no signs of cement intervention around these bricks, it can perhaps be attributed to under firing or the presence of large inclusions present in the bricks during manufacture which had subsequently reacted.

Evidence of Pointing Style and Condition

There is ample evidence of historic colour washing and tuck pointing which, though largely lost, is in fine condition in the protected areas such as under the window cills. It is apparent that the historical failure of the tuck pointing was caused by poor application and methodology which had accelerated its demise, although it should be considered that the elevation is south facing, where the wetting and drying process after rainfall is more pronounced, and this factor would contribute to this. Minimal stopping had been used originally, and instead a colour wash had been painted over the bed joints. This action would have made any attempt at forming a housing (to tuck a putty into) difficult, and its absence probably also also contributed toward the loss of the putty ribbon (*see* Tuck Pointing).

The Requirement to Repoint

The first question should be, 'does the brickwork require repointing'? The necessity for repointing is based on the needs of the building and not what the bricklayer can manage or execute successfully, or even what might appear more aesthetically pleasing. Many traditional buildings have lost much or all their topmost surface layer of lime mortar, and with it the joint finish due to natural erosion. Similarly, the arises, or edges of the bricks, may have become worn or rounded off for the same reason. This, in itself, is not a reason to repoint as the joints might still be performing well. As a general rule, if the joint is hollow, vulnerable to retaining water, friable and loose it should be repointed.

It is clear that despite the loss of much of the tuck pointing, the bed joints are generally sound and should not be disturbed although there are hollow and deeply eroded joints across the elevation, particularly where there have been modern interventions and where cracking has occurred. This is notable on the parapet wall (B), on the brickwork above each gauged brick arch (E, F, J). There are

This lime mortar has eroded deeply in this instance; the lime having done its job as a sacrificial mortar by protecting the brick. It is now in need of patch repointing.

patches of cement pointing, notably under each window (G). This should be removed by hand. Conservation pointing would be applied to these areas, ensuring that the pointing was to the narrowest neck of the brick joint (*see* Lime Pointing). Where small areas of tuck ribbon have fallen off, these can be replicated by a bricklayer who is skilled in tuck pointing.

Evidence of a red ochre colour wash on the bricks and remnants of colour on the bed joints. An interesting feature is the brick arrises on perpendicular joints which have all been painstakingly clipped roughly by hand to a bevel, perhaps because it was thought this would allow more room for the desired width of putty ribbon.

Gauged Arches

All gauged camber arches on this elevation have been cement pointed (J) whilst two have cracking which extends into the brickwork above them (E, F). The cracking has been repaired using a hard cement mortar at some point in the twentieth century, but this has reopened providing cracks susceptible to water penetration from windblown rain. In some cases, the cracking has broken or dislodged voussoirs in the arches themselves. It is possible that the header bricks have been snapped, and this may have helped form a weakness in the wall due to lack of solidity and to the cracking in these areas (*see* Context). Advice given by a conservation-accredited structural engineer was that stainless steel reinforcement could be inserted through the cracking on every other course (*see* Brickwork Repairs).

Tuck ribbon has fallen out across much of the façade leaving original bed joints.

An example of a camber arch identified as being damaged. The wall above the arch can be stitched, the arch supported and the damaged voussoirs removed and replaced.

Other Potential Problem Areas Identified on the Façade Brickwork Assessment

Hoppers and Downpipes

Dark green staining behind down pipes (H) can be a sign that these are leaking. Close inspection of downpipes, hoppers and the condition of the brickwork will determine if this is the case and what remedial action is required. These should be repaired before work starts on the brickwork.

Window Seals

Brickwork is sometimes found to be damaged when new windows are fitted. Their subsequent repair and sealing, using cement, often compounds this problem, and brick decay can occur here where moisture is trapped. Where this is found, it has been identified on the assessment (L).

Cement filled window seals and stained brickwork.

Plinth

Whilst this feature is stone, not brickwork, it was identified that the stone plinth at the foot of the elevation had been painted with plastic-based paint (I). It is worth remembering that many of the agents of decay that affect brickwork affect stonework, too (*see* Vulnerability

TRADITIONAL BRICKWORK ASSESSMENT (use one complete copy for each elevation)	
PART 1: BRICKWORK DETAIL	
ELEVATION: East (Front façade)	
Address including Post Code of property	
Current use	**Domestic dwelling**
Original use	**Domestic dwelling**
Date of survey	**05/02/20**
Surveyor	**T. Lee**
Weather conditions on day of survey	**Fine**
Historical era of building	**Georgian**
Date if known (shown on plaque or documented)	**Late eighteenth century post 1774**
List areas unseen during assessment	**Behind parapet wall**
PART 2: CONDITION	
Water ingress	**Yes**
Cement pointing/render	**Cement pointing between windows intended to repair cracking.**
Brick decay	**Sporadic but with clusters of face erosion at parapet level.**

Rainwater goods: Maintenance issues	**Down pipes and hoppers require close inspection and maintenance.**	
PART 3: BRICK (new sheet for each elevation as applicable)		
Form	**Pallet/sand moulded bricks**	
Dimensions (mm)	**230mm x 73mm x 105mm**	
arrises	**Evidence of bevelling by hand**	
Colour(s)	**Red hues, colour washed**	
Frogged	**No**	
Texture	**Smooth with some manufacture pitting, no major inclusions visible**	
Markings		
Form and consistency of manufacture (circle as applicable)	Rounded arris/vitrified/warping/visible inclusion/ splitting/surface popping/**smooth**/sand faced	
Firing method	Wood/**coal**	
Sample (s) taken	**Yes**/no	
PART 4: BRICKWORK		
Brickwork surface condition	Iron fixings, staining	
Bond: Flemish with more headers between windows		
Height of four courses (mm)	**332mm**	
Pointing and jointing of main walling (indicate which)		
Flush	Penny ha'penny/ruled	Weather cut and struck
Tuck **Ample Evidence of tuck pointing**	Bastard tuck	Overhand struck
Cement pointed **Yes above each arch and on gauged arches**	Modern conservation	Lime mortar applied atop bed joint
Height of joint	10mm approximate	
PART 5: USE OF COLOUR		
Evidence of colour washes	**Yes**	
Evidence of pigmented stopping	**No, colour wash over bed joints**	
Coloured patterns	Lozenge/diamonds/initials/other **Nil**	
Coloured headers	Chequer board/linear/random **Nil**	
PART 6: OPENINGS		
Number 8		
Width of window openings (mm)	**1.06m**	

Height of openings (mm)	
Rebated	**Yes 100mm**
Sill	**Stone**
Seal around frame abutting brickwork	**Modern intervention/cement**
Aprons	**No**
PART 7: ARCHES	
Gauged	Number: 7
Axed	Number: **NA**
Rough segmental	Number: **NA**
Soldier	Number: **NA**
Brick on Edge (BOE)	**NA**
PART 8: GAUGED ARCH DETAIL (Survey individually)	
Opening width (mm)	**1006mm**
Depth of face (mm)	**310mm**
Soffit (mm)	**100mm**
Number of voussoir (Odd number required)	**15**
Bond	**Flemish**/half bond/other state
Joint size	**2mm**
Width of voussoir at intrados	**65mm**
Width of voussoir at extrados	**75mm**
Nature of rubber brick	**Pitted**
Colour	Cherry red/orang**e**/**orange red**/malm

of Traditional Brick). This paint should be removed carefully to expose the material beneath, and to ascertain any further remedial action required.

Post Assessment Work

Matching Lime Mortar

Lime mortar will benefit from having been prepared in advance of the construction or repair work to be knocked up later as required. To establish the type of mortar needed, mortar samples taken during assessment can be sent away to be tested under laboratory conditions to ascertain the material content, ratio and lime purity of the original mix. Another method which can be employed onsite, and set out below, is to look at what is in the mortar and decide how it can replicate as closely as possible, and technique can be acquired with practice. In both cases, a decent sized full mortar bed sample is required as well as some knowledge and details of the historical context of the elevation or building. In the case of the latter method, a good range of the regional aggregates is needed from which the sample will be formed. As a general rule, the older the building, the purer the lime is likely to be (less hydraulic). Submerge a piece of mortar in a small bath of citric based acid, and note the rapidity and volatility of the reaction that follows, as this can indicate a purer form of lime, but also note that this can dissolve some aggregate or stone particles entirely.

It is worth noting that the aggregate element of the mix can be made up of a number of different types, to give the appearance and texture required. Thus a 3:1

A ball of lime pointing mortar mixed ahead of the work. Note the consistency should be doughy and mouldable in the hand.

Now stand close to the wall and observe the original mortar. There are definite pink undertones visible. This is because red sand was among those quarried in this particular region. Examination of the mortar will establish texture, aggregate sizes, colours and particles of unslaked lime present. Note the hole formed by a bricklayer's line and pins 200 years ago.

mix of three parts aggregate to one part lime, might have several different aggregates. Knowledge of the type and nature of stone quarried in a given area will give the general colour range of the aggregates used in local buildings. In Shropshire, for example, the aggregates quarried tend to be various hues of red or brown/red. Crush down and sieve a sample piece of the original mortar to ascertain aggregate sizes see what dominant colours of aggregates are present and compare with samples of aggregates purchased locally. Write down the results of all your findings in a notebook or mortar 'recipe book'.

A full bed mortar sample can be taken from the joints of brick which is removed as part of the work.

Visual Mortar Sampling and Matching

Stand back about 3 to 4m from the elevation and look at the colour of the mortar in the wall to ascertain the dominant colour. Here, a buff colour *appears* to be dominant.

Brick Sourcing

Another important task to be carried out during a brickwork assessment, and afterwards, is the sampling and sourcing of bricks. It is important that this isn't left too late as it increases the chances of an inappropriate brick being selected because of time factors. The building should be the guiding factor on the nature of brick required. Initially, a thorough search of the grounds or garden of the property owner's permission might uncover bricks that have sat for many years having been removed following a previous alteration and are perfectly usable if, once

The ingredients to make the mortar include all those required to form the colour, texture, and appearance. Here, in addition to the base colour of washed red sands, yellow aggregate has been included to give the mortar a buff element. A portion of quick lime will provide pin head sized white flecks. A portion of original mortar crushed and sieved will add a little of the original colour and provide a pozzolanic additive.

Samples of lime mortars can be made from the experimental mixes and cured under damp hessian on the elevations for which they are intended. Once cured, they can be broken in two, to examine the texture of the inside compared to that of the original mortar. A successful mortar will not jar to the eye and will blend in well. Note that often, there may be several hues of mortar on one elevation.

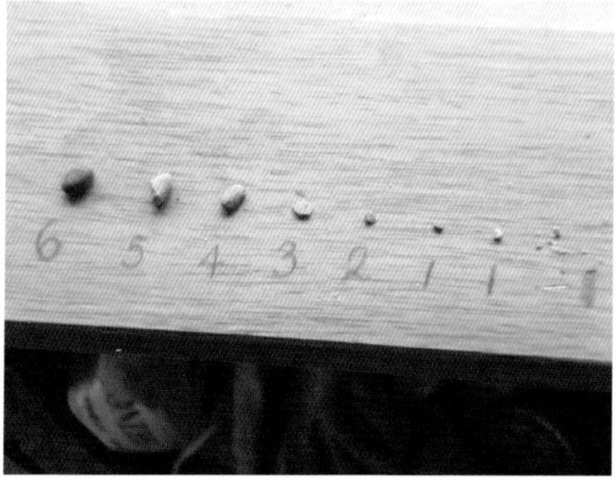

Identifying aggregate size and quantity within a given sized material by crushing and sieving it will establish how much of what type of aggregates are needed in the mix.

Check lime mortar samples against the joints to examine texture and colour.

cleaned, they are shown to be an exact match for a part of the original construction. Quality bricks can be purchased from a handful of traditional brickmakers in England who will match the sample brick using traditional manufacturing techniques, and which are appropriate for the context of the building in terms of dimensions, colour and texture and are also frost resistant with appropriate absorption rates as well as strength for the given year and durable (*see* List of Suppliers). Note that the lead time for obtaining these can be lengthy so this process should start as soon as possible.

Reclamation yards often have large stocks of bricks covering a wide spectrum of historical eras. Sometimes, however, the provenance of reclaimed bricks is uncertain as is their original method of manufacture and purpose, for example whether they were selected for internal or external use. There is also

These 60mm facing bricks have been set aside when brickwork has been dismantled. Recording brickwork by using acetate to trace brick positions and/or photography is an essential component of brickwork conservation.

the possibility that less reputable sellers may have obtained the bricks from an illegal source, albeit unwittingly. Sourcing random reclaimed bricks can be highly problematic as the clay used to make them might differ from that of the region where they are required. It may be too hard or dense, or the arrises may be too well-formed (or not) and contain harmful salts (for example in a chimney and consequently infused with harmful salts). If the brick replacement is too hard and machine made, for example, not only will it jar the eye but it will also shed water more rapidly onto the softer bricks around it, create a hard spot in a wall and cause accelerated decay of the brick and lime mortar joints (*see* Vulnerability of Traditional Brick). For these reasons, obtaining bricks from traditional brick manufacturers is perhaps the best option to ensure quality, as well as the required texture, colour and size.

Sample bricks should be removed from a sheltered position on the elevations where repairs are required, and different brick matches may be required for the different elevations. Both Georgian and Victorian properties, for example, will often have a better-quality brick on the front façade where first impressions of the property were established and on which more money was spent (*see* Context). The brick can be taken from an unobtrusive position in the wall(s) and then a temporary replacement inserted in its place. It should be remembered that for gauged work, if in need of repair, the rubber bricks need to be matched in their own right and this can be done by talking to a supplier of this specialist material. Note that house bricks should never be used for gauged brickwork repairs.

Prioritizing Brickwork Repairs

The results of the brickwork assessment should inform the scope of the work based on the level of its deterioration and determine the methods of repair to be employed and the skills, materials and equipment needed to do it. It should also set out a priority for the repairs based on the degree of decay, the significance of the feature, i.e., the need to save it and the urgency, for example if a feature is unstable and unsafe.

Preparation of Tests and Trials

It can be useful to demonstrate the desired finish by producing a panel of the finished works. A brick exemplar panel can be built using the sourced brick and the lime mortar established from testing. Other materials such as colour washes, stoppings and putty ribbon can be tested and cured under conditions appropriate to the elevation where they will be used. Pointing finishes can also be trialled on the panel, again on the mortar to be used on the work. These tests are a good way for all concerned in the work to examine the suitability of the materials and methods.

Logistical Considerations

In addition to issues directly associated with the brickwork, there are other important considerations to investigate during the site visit or if works are being considered by a homeowner, including:

- availability for dry storage for lime products and other bagged materials
- mains water supply and an outside tap to which a hose can be attached
- availability of mains electricity, or whether a generator be required
- access for deliveries and place to store materials
- access for and room for a skip
- permits for work on pavements for skips and/or scaffolding.

Chapter Eight

Vulnerability of Traditional Brick

Problems Inherent in Manufacture

For bricks to be durable and have the required form for use in construction, the clay with which they are made should contain a number of naturally occurring elements which influence the chemical reaction of the brick clay during firing, and ultimately the finished product. The symptoms of an imbalance of minerals and other materials in the brick clay alluded to previously, however, can both facilitate and be compounded by other external factors including water ingress and modern inappropriate intervention. Poor materials and inconsistent firing can usually be identified by either sporadic eroded bricks, on an otherwise sound brickwork elevation, or possibly large expanses of it.

Traditionally, brickmakers could not alter the mineral balance of the clay but could add elements such as sand, lime, and ash. An imbalance of elements can therefore result in the brick being more prone to the effects of external decay factors. Consequently, whilst traditional brick may be regarded by some as hard-wearing and impervious, and universally usable in each and any brickwork application, in fact they have a nuanced anatomy, as well as physical form, and vary widely in quality. This is a result of their unscientific, inconsistent manufacture by a myriad of small brickmakers which sprang up wherever there was a clay deposit. Materials which make up the body of bricks include sand (silica), alumina, magnesia, sodium, potassium and iron, as well as lime, potash, stones and flint, each of which will contribute to the quality of the brick. For example, small quantities of iron, when it oxidizes during firing, produce hematite (from the Greek for blood) which influences the colour of the finished brick. If iron is present in the form of pyrites, however, this can expand when it comes into contact with moisture and oxygen causing splitting of the brick. Lime is useful as a flux for the cohesion of the clay, but too much can cause complete vitrification, i.e., melting of the clay, resulting in a complete malformation of the brick. Alumina assists the plasticity of the clay before firing but too great quantities can result in misshapen, warped bricks.

Silica (sand) is essential for the toughness of the brick, but in too great a quantity can cause brittleness. Other elements found in clay are pieces of stones and flint, known as inclusions. If small, these are not in themselves influential, simply adding structure to the clay body, and were not removed during the manufacturing process.

The larger ones, however, can react differently under high temperatures and can rupture both during and after firing causing tearing, fissuring and bulging, often resulting in the inclusion protruding

A warped brick found inside a two-brick wall in Admaston, Shropshire.

through the fire skin of the brick. Rapid increases in temperature during firing can result in weak bricks with a blackened core.

Good-quality, well-laid bricks and mortar will naturally decay extremely slowly even with many of the anomalies set out above. Lime is a sacrificial material which will erode before the bricks and in so doing protects the vulnerable arrises of the bricks and provides a warning that repointing is due (*see* Assessment of Traditional Brickwork). This process can, of course, take hundreds of years which is why many traditional brick buildings, particularly if they have not suffered negative human intervention, are as good

Splits caused by a bulging inclusion close to the outside of the clay body which probably occurred during firing.

Inclusion of a particularly large size found in a Georgian era boundary wall. Poorer-quality bricks were often used for works of a more utilitarian nature, or where they couldn't be seen at all.

A handmade coping brick showing a large lime inclusion which resulted in the fracturing of the brick.

A cross section of a seventeenth-century brick from Shropshire showing a blackened core, a result of rapid rise in temperature during firing. Note the white mineral rock inclusion.

This Georgian era brick contains part of a stem of a pipe. Note, the clay body of the brick is deeply fissured from the moulding manufacture process.

as the day they were built. There are numerous agents of decay, some due to inappropriate intervention and, ironically, others due to a lack of it. Whichever the case, agents of decay do not work in isolation, but the factors combine to compound a problem. At the centre of it is usually water and its effect on brick and mortar joints.

Difference in Performance of Solid Brickwork and Cavity Wall Construction

Solid walls

Traditional brickwork was built in multiples of a brick's thickness and has been referred to as one-brick walling, solid walling or sometimes referred to as nine-inch walling due to the length of brick measurement. Strength is achieved by the way in which the bricks are arranged, the strongest being those bonds which have more headers, such as English bond. Solid brickwork bonds are formed by an overlap of one brick over another by a ¼ brick and are established by the particular arrangement of bricks at the quoin. As has been discussed, traditional solid walls can be deceiving as they were sometimes built to appear on the outside as one brick thick, but that headers were snapped and did not extend into the wall their full length as should be the case.

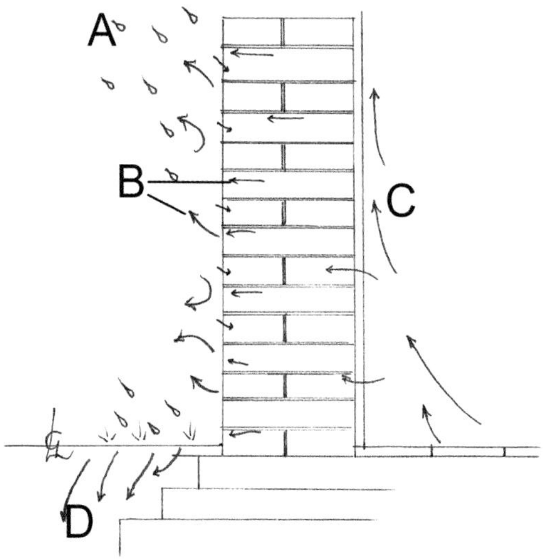

In traditional solid brickwork, rain is absorbed by the brickwork (A) but capillaries through the wall and evaporates from the surface during drying (B). Moisture produced inside the building (C) passes into the walls and outside. Drainable ground outside allows water to dissipate (D).

The construction and performance of traditional brickwork is the antithesis of modern cavity wall construction. Traditional solid brickwork is generally at least one brick thick, and damp proof courses were unknown until the late nineteenth century. During rainfall, moisture enters the outermost part of the wall, and this moisture is drawn in by the lime mortar, allowing it to evaporate away through capillary action. Lime mortar joints enable approximately 80 per cent of evaporation from the wall surface in this way. Lime plaster on the inside of the wall enables vapour permeability, i.e., moisture formed by human habitation is able to pass through the wall, whilst the drafty nature of these buildings together with fires in each room would keep the building dry and aerated.

Cavity walls

Cavity walls were used in an embryonic form as early as the mid-nineteenth century, but the cavity wall emerged as the new method of house construction following the First World War (1914–18). Its emergence was due to the desire to build more quickly using new innovations in construction such as the concrete block, concrete floors and lintels. Perhaps most significant of all was the increase in the use of ordinary Portland cement which could now be produced to set much harder than it previously did. Traditional solid brickwork continued to be built for several decades, but gradually ebbed out as the older bricklayers who were experienced in traditional methods died, and with it, the use of lime in building.

Modern cavity wall construction in new builds is designed to largely prevent water entering the inner leaf of the wall. The bricks and blockwork are constructed using cement mortars, usually of a ratio of 5:1 meaning five parts sand to one part cement, with a plasticizer added to give it workability. The outer brickwork is usually finished with a half-round tooled joint which smooths over and compresses the cement mortar. The outer brick skin and inner block skin of cavity walling are each approximately 100mm in thickness with a form of insulation in the central cavity. The outer skin is built in stretcher bond, a brick overlapping the other by half lengthways, the inner, usually of a block with thermal properties. The two skins are tied together using wall ties with a drip in the centre to allow moisture to drop downwards onto a cavity tray and exit via plastic weepholes. DPCs are inserted on both brick and block skins and are intended to prevent moisture from rising upwards from the ground.

The modern cavity wall is a tried and tested method of construction in new builds but can fail if incorrectly constructed or if bad practices have been used. Problems may occur if the cavity is bridged, i.e., the wall ties are covered, or the cavity filled with mortar during construction allows moisture to cross it to reach the inner leaf, or if the ties are incorrectly inserted, if brick joints allow water penetration, if modern insulation materials are incorrectly installed and become soaked by rain entering the outer skin, particularly in very exposed areas, or if poor-quality bricks are used or if there is insufficient cement in the mortar.

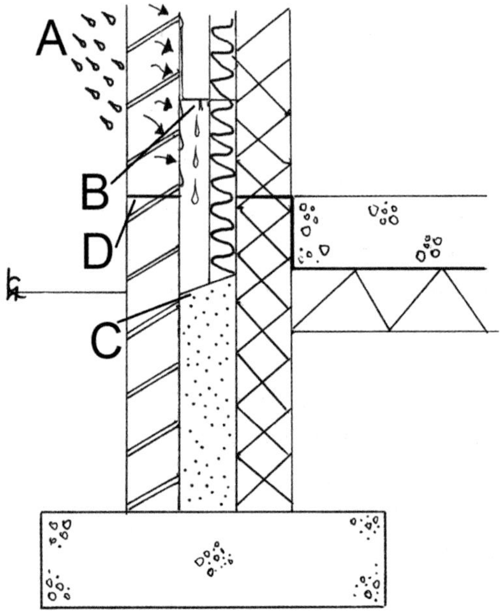

Any water that enters the cavity (A) drips off wall ties (B) and leaves the cavity through plastic weepholes via trays over openings and sloping fine concrete at ground level (C). Damp proof courses are intended to prevent moisture rising from the ground (D).

How Modern Materials Can Affect the Survivability of Traditional Brickwork

Problems with traditional brickwork often occur because of a failure to recognize the effect that modern cement-based mortars, plastic based paints, etc., can have on them and the general belief that what is good for a modern building (to keep out moisture), must also be good for an old one. Regrettably, modern cement mortars are often used as the universal repair medium for buildings of any age or era, as their perceived waterproofing properties as mortars and renders are often wrongly considered as the main line of defence against rain and damp. This misconception can be further compounded by a lack of understanding of the difference between traditional solid wall and modern cavity construction and how they perform, particularly under wet conditions.

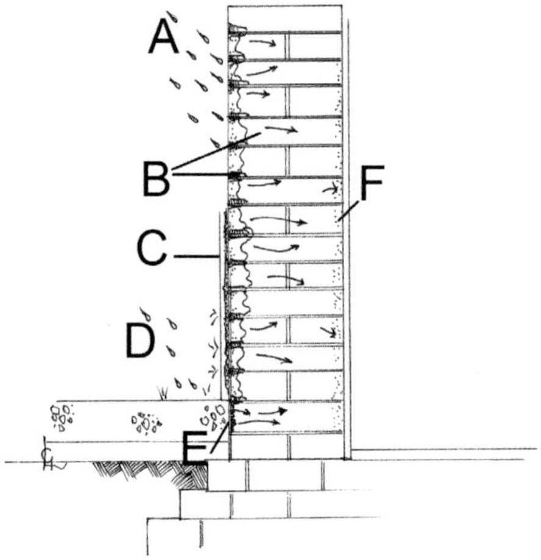

Traditional brickwork and the effects of modern materials.

Traditional brickwork suffers from the effects of moisture when water enters the wall (A) but is trapped on ledges formed by cement pointing and is retained within the walling (B). Cement renders allow rain penetration through hairline cracking and prevents moisture evaporation from the wall (C).

Rainwater splashing from hard adjacent surfaces saturates the lower brickwork, a factor exacerbated by cement renders (D). Concrete abutting soft traditional brickwork creates a permanent damp area potentially causing physical decay and a home for insects (E). Moisture migrates towards the inner wall and is both spread and retained by modern gypsum-based plasters inside (F).

Blocking the joints with hard cement pointing-mortar will seal this moisture escape route, forcing it to pass through the brickwork instead, filling up the countless voids they contain and forming ledges on which moisture can sit inside the brickwork. Moisture sitting inside the bricks freezes, causing damage to the brickwork through spalling or flaking of brick surface. A common problem is the filling of the places where bricks have eroded deeply with cement mortar. This creates a hard spot and potentially destructive repair which usually results in accelerated decay spreading to adjacent lime-built bricks work.

Use of hard cement pointing mortars compounds the problems of water ingress discussed above by trapping moisture inside the walls. Since the lime mortar joints form the main conduit for water evaporation from the wall, and as this can be up to 20 per cent of a wall surface, greater areas are at risk from frost damage and spalling if cement pointed. Hard cement pointing can form horizontal ledges inside the brickwork on which water can accumulate.

During freezing weather, the ice formed can expand, which causes cracking and breaking off the edges of bricks, or an arris to break, resulting in the widening of brickwork joints and the faces of the bricks in the form of spalling and disintegration of the brick. Constant presence of moisture, trapped in this way, will also result in physical wearing of the brick edges. There is little doubt that an understanding of the building and of its materials is a key

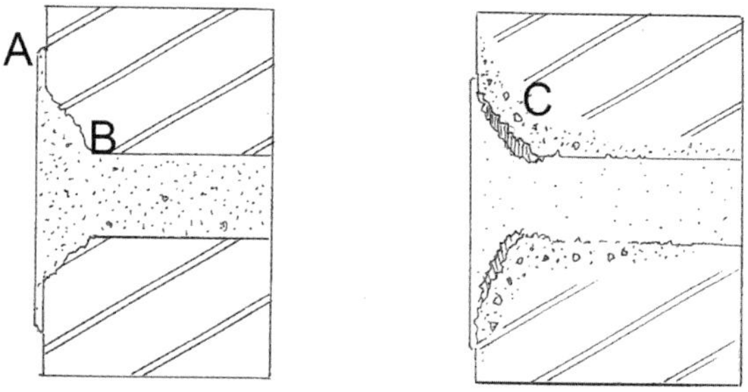

Brickwork can erode over hundreds of years yet remain functional. Poorly advised repointing over the face of the brick (A) and filling up the entire area left by the natural erosion can cause serious problems. Repointing should be to the narrowest neck of the joint (B). Water saturation and subsequent freeze-thaw action can cause the faces of bricks to disintegrate (C).

An example of a ledge of hard cement formed when this brickwork was cement pointed.

Hard and brittle cement mortar surrounds this brick removed from a historic building.

In this brickwork panel from a Grade II Listed cottage in Shropshire, the use of modern cement mortar has been used to plug gaps in the lime-built walling. The original bricks used here were particularly soft probably underfired with many having lost their faces.

Decay of the brick surface due to the presence of hard cement revealing the vulnerable interior and the myriad of inclusion types suggesting a poor-quality manufactured brick. Note the large piece of lime to the left of picture.

defence against inappropriate, ill-informed work but it should also be recognized that a reluctance to finance quality repairs is another key factor.

Cement pointed bricks inserted into period walls as repairs, either singly or in groups, can create a hard surface area which can act like a watershed, directing water quickly onto softer adjacent surfaces such as lime mortar joints and traditional brick. This can sometimes be seen on gable walls that have been cement pointed in an attempt to keep out the elements, but which have caused accelerated decay to the softer lime joints below.

Cementitious Renders

Hard cement renders are applied to traditional brickwork in the belief that it will keep out the elements. Unfortunately, the opposite is often true as once cracks begin to form, and these may be barely visible to the human eye, they can trap moisture from rainfall in against the brickwork which cannot escape but can then capillary up the walls. Sometimes the render pops away from the brickwork just enough to form a void behind which insects can form colonies. Whilst it is, in some cases, possible to remove cement renders, this action, even if done carefully, can be particularly destructive as the render often pulls away at least the fire skin of

An example of a hard, inappropriate modern brick and cement panel inserted into a period wall. No attempt has been made to match the brick or to bond it correctly into the existing work.

A panel of brickwork showing the area of decay surrounded by a cement pointing. The rough texture of the brick faces signifies loss of the fire skin, the protective shell that surrounds the brick.

Cement renders applied over traditional brickwork like this, prevent water evaporation leading to physical decay. The problem can be compounded by water splash from hard adjacent surfaces.

the brick leaving the only option being to reapply a lime render.

Plastic-based Paints

Non-vapour permeable paints seal in the brickwork preventing the evaporation of moisture. Even slight movement of the brickwork will cause hairline cracking, allowing water to enter but not escape. When the bricks become saturated, the paint can often be found to be bubbling in places. Paints can often be removed by professional cleaning systems, but careful testing is still required as the results can vary depending on the type of brick that has been used.

Plastic-based masonry paints can prevent moisture evaporation. Sometimes they bubble and curl as a result of moisture trying to get out of the brickwork. In this example, the mortar joints underneath appear to be in relatively good condition.

An example of naturally eroded brickwork. A patina has been formed by the environment over the centuries, and the lime mortar joints have eroded back from the brick edges. This example is still in good condition and does not require repointing.

Natural Erosion of Traditional Brickwork

Brick decay can be influenced by factors such as the quality of the materials used in the first place, environmental conditions and atmospheric pollution. Brick and lime mortars will gradually erode over the centuries through the effects of wind and rain. Bricks erode slowly, too, but this can take hundreds of years depending on many factors.

Lime mortars will slowly erode but because they are sacrificial this is not a cause of concern until the point is reached when they should be repointed. Many brick-built buildings have mortar joints still effective after hundreds of years and although the surface detail of the joint finish may be lost, it does not mean it should be repointed.

External Forms of Water Ingress

Deeply eroded brickwork joints can allow water ingress from windblown rain or constant exposure to water that is not directed away from the wall. Whilst hollow, crumbling or unsealed mortar joints are one way in which moisture can enter a wall, it is also likely to be problematic if it comes from external sources, particularly if the water is channelled or directed by faulty or broken rainwater goods.

The primary cause of this green staining is a leaking gutter with water splashing from the lead over the doorway on to the brickwork. The hollow joints indicate that this has been going on for some time and is likely to cause damp on the internal wall.

Brickwork is at risk when it becomes saturated after prolonged rainfall, filling the pores, fissures, voids, splits and tears in the brick with water, and subsequently freezing causing catastrophic spalling, or flaking off of the brick faces. Similarly, broken or damaged architectural features, such as cornices or banding courses which tend to be more vulnerable, can channel water quickly and constantly causing rapid decay of the brickwork below or around it.

Maintenance Issues

Forms of water ingress can often be attributable to maintenance issues and neglect. Quite apart from damaged chimneys and roof elements, the sources of the ingress might be cracked or broken guttering and rainwater goods, damaged salt glazed drainage close to walls and below ground level or standing water on concrete adjacent to brickwork.

External forms of water ingress are often attributable to lack of building maintenance, and this is a major factor contributing to the survivability of traditional and historic brickwork as this often involves broken or leaking rainwater goods and blocked drains, etc., and there is little point in executing lime pointing if the guttering is leaking all over the façade. Such issues would have to be fixed prior to work on the same façade but ideally would have been addressed during annual maintenance checks. There may also be issues affecting the brickwork that the building owner has not identified, or is otherwise unaware of, such as leaking rainwater goods, high soil levels, blocked air bricks and other maintenance issues. Over time, even the smallest leak can cause thousands of pounds of damage (*see* Maintenance of Traditional Brickwork).

Biological Agents of Decay

Nature will attempt to reclaim a building as soon as it is built and will exploit any convenient openings that can be found to that end. Where there is a regular or constant source of moisture, green staining can be the result, followed by moss growth and then plant life will quickly thrive and the roots of plants such as ivy, buddleia and others can dislodge joints, bricks and even whole panels of brickwork. Moisture can also undo the properties of the lime mortar making it friable and soil like, and an attractive proposition for both plant and insect life; in effect, returning the joints back to nature.

Embedded Iron

Following the Industrial Revolution in the eighteenth century, the use of iron fixings was seized upon where it provided a practical solution to an old problem such as to tie stone to brickwork. Initially, phosphor bronze was used but was found to be very expensive and it was

Green staining such as this is usually the precursor to moss growth followed by plant growth.

Nature is reclaiming this walling because of a broken rainwater.

Ironmongery and fixings such as brackets, hinges, nails and vine eyes can cause localized staining and splitting of the brick which, in turn, can lead to broader decay issues. Minor spalling of the brick, the emergence of salts, hairline fissuring and staining are indicative of this.

substituted for iron. Later in the nineteenth century, hoop iron of a ¼ inch thick and intended for cartwheels was used as reinforcement around the walls of buildings and as wall ties in hybrid cavity walls. When iron rusts, it can expand to several times its original size, blowing out brick from the surface, cracking and lifting masonry in a process called jacking, and causing rust staining. Although these iron fittings were frequently dipped in bitumen and sand as a means of protection, it is inevitable that they will eventually succumb to rusting and expansion. Movement and opening of brickwork is subsequently left exposed to further water ingress and other agents of decay.

Adjacent Hard Surfaces

Hard surfaces such as roads, pavements, and concrete paths or paving abutting a traditional brick wall can often be the cause of problems of rapid decay to the lower brickwork because of rain splashing from the concrete to the wall and saturating the wall which will then spall during freezing conditions. It is common to see this problem on houses whose frontage is next to a pavement or where concrete paths have been reinstated adjacent to old brickwork.

Insect and Animal Life

Insect populations can thrive where there is a permanent and sufficient presence of moisture and where plant life has gained a foothold. Insects can manipulate soft eroded mortars and other materials and bring soils from outside of the walling into the joints. Woodlice seen indoors in the locality of the walls are a sign that conditions may be damp enough to allow them to thrive.

Birds, such as house sparrows, which like to make their nests under the eaves of old buildings may peck at brickwork if it is soft enough, and will certainly peck at lime mortar joints for the grit or nutrients that they may contain, and for many this would not be seen as a harmful occurrence. Masonry bees will burrow into soft brick or, more usually, mortar joints to make their nests, the volume of which can allow water penetration and in the worst scenario, result in the detachment of brick or masonry.

Constant splashing caused by traffic driven rainwater combined with road salts and traffic pollution can cause serious brick decay which can require considerable effort to put right. Adjacent hard surfaces can also trap and direct next to brickwork. Traditional brickwork in a modern setting such as this is particularly vulnerable.

Insects such as woodlice will thrive where they can get protection and in the moisture found in this brick embedded in a wall and capped in cement mortar.

Masonry bees burrow in to mortar joints and sometimes brick and stone too. A mass of burrows can cause sections of walling to become vulnerable to other agents of decay.

Sandblasting

Sandblasting can be highly destructive, removing the fire skin of the bricks and inducing decay by exposing the brickwork to the elements and associated agents of decay.

Cleaning of Brickwork

Cleaning of brickwork by mechanical means should be avoided unless absolutely necessary, and then only after appropriate testing of the impact has been carried out using only professional conservation-approved systems. Accidental removal of a historic joint finish, the protective barrier that naturally forms on the surface of the brick known as case hardening as well as damage to the actual fire skin of the brick, can occur if adequate testing and impact assessment are not carried out. Cleaning of surface dirt, where required, should as far as possible be confined to natural bristle brush and clean water, and beyond this specialist cleaning should be investigated and tested.

Contaminated Mortars

Traditional mortars often contained, or were made from, materials that were easily and cheaply available.

The effects of powerful sandblasting are clearly shown here by the characteristic pitted and exposed surface and spots of remaining paint. The bricks become much more prone to saturation and vulnerable to the effects of freezing during winter. Note the origina joint has also been pulverized.

Dirt and pollution can build up on brickwork over the centuries. Here, a glimpse of the mortar colour is visible in the centre of the photograph. Despite the surface dirt, the joints are otherwise intact.

White salts evident by the presence of white patches on the surface.

One such ingredient used was fuel ash associated with coal burning and domestic ash. Although highly pozzolanic, such mortars were likely to have been contaminated from the start and could have a detrimental, corrosive effect on the brickwork. Where atmospheric pollutions are carried by rain and fall on building features made of materials such as limestone, they can form a corrosive substance which can be detrimental to the brickwork.

Harmful Salts

The effect of salt crystallization is one of the most common forms of brick decay. In their benign form, salts may appear as a white powder, known as efflorescence, on the face of the brickwork caused sometimes by the crystallization of absorbed ground water and which can be brushed off with a stiff brush, or which will cease in time. Harmful soluble salts can be derived from additives found in cement mortars, and the detergents and additives used to make them, and can exist naturally in the brick clay or perhaps from contaminated aggregates like road salt and sea water or standing water or could be the result of leaching of salts from high soil levels at the base of outside of walls and leaching through the brickwork. The worst form of these harmful salts is cryptoeffloresence, in which salt crystals migrate with moisture from inside the brick to the surface during drying. These crystals subsequently form a crust and break off, taking with them not only the fire skin of the brick but causing serious delamination. Where bricks are soft, and perhaps underfired, the effects of this can be catastrophic leading to widespread sapling of whole panels or elevations.

Chapter Nine

Construction and Repair of Traditional Brickwork

In this chapter, examples are given of some types of brickwork construction and repairs, some of which are works identified in the brickwork assessment of the previous chapter. Brickwork and pointing repairs can range from the smallest maintenance issues, perhaps filling a small section of missing pointing, to entire elevations where specialist assistance is required.

Pre-Work Administration, Preparation and Logistics

Before brickwork repairs can commence, there are a number of administrative and logistical factors that should be considered, and which would have to be in planned well ahead of the work start date. Failure to do so can result in rushed decisions which may be detrimental to the building.

Permissions for Listed Buildings

If permissions (planning consent applications) are required to carry out any work, this should have been sought and obtained by the owner, in writing, prior to the commencement of work. Although repairs might not in themselves require consent if the building is listed, in a complete façade repoint in a conservation area for example, the character of the building may be changed even if the work is considered for the better and therefore, permission would be required. There may also be objections to the proposed work from neighbours. For this reason, such work may still require a communication with local authority conservation officer and a response received by the property owner, again in writing. If in doubt, the local authority planning department should be contacted.

Wildlife

Work should not commence if there are nesting birds and bats in the vicinity, which are protected, and which could be disturbed. Advice from the local authority should be sought regarding them.

Scaffolding and Platforms

Suitable scaffolds and platforms might be required for safe and efficient working. If scaffold is required, this should be arranged in good time with a reputable scaffolder. If possible, the bricklayer would meet the scaffolder onsite to discuss certain elements of its construction and to ensure that it is suitable for the type of work being done. If gauged arches are being constructed or repaired, for example, raised platforms are required at waist height behind the bricklayer on which to place on the brick set ready to construct the arch (to avoid constant bending over to take up a voussoir). For the same work, scaffold lifts should be constructed so that the arch to be repaired is set at about chest height.

Scaffold boards nearest the walls should be moveable so that they can be turned back to avoid the accumulation of lime and dust near the walls or splashing that can stain the wall when washing down. The scaffold may need to be covered depending on the time of year the work is being carried out, including, if necessary, a roof at the top so that no time is lost to bad weather. This will have the important benefit of giving protection to lime mortar, particularly during inclement weather. Plastic sheeting can be laid out beneath scaffolds to make the job of cleaning up easier and to help to keep the property and environment clean. Windows should be covered in lightweight plastic prior to works. An electric hoist or a simple pulley is an advantage for moving materials on to the scaffold. If a scaffold is required, it can be useful to ask the bricklayer to come out to ensure that the scaffold meets the requirements of the work.

Mixing Area, Skips and Storage

A mixing area, if required, should be set up as near as possible to where the work is being carried out, preferably in the shade and on a staging made of pallets with ply sheeting on top to protect the ground. Lime mortar should be stored in the dry, and the bags opened from the end only to minimize waste. Mixing should not be conducted near the walls of a property as this causes splashing of wet lime and airborne lime dust which can stain the brickwork. An agreed location for deliveries and skips should be identified ahead of the work starting.

Water and Power

A water and power supply is essential for successful lime work. It is important that these sources have been identified during the visit to site, and that hose pipes and extension cables can reach the entire elevation from the highest point of the scaffold. On larger projects, it might be possible to have an outside tap installed internally so that a hose can be brought through the window for use on the scaffold.

Pre-Works Maintenance

Any work that impinges on the progress and outcome of the brickwork repairs should be completed in advance by the relevant specialist contractor. This could include damaged and leaking gutters and down pipes (*see* Maintenance of Traditional Brickwork) as there is no point in executing quality tuck pointing, for example, if the rainwater from a leaking gutter is still soaking the brickwork. It could also include the removal of invasive climbers such as ivy, and the cutting back or protection of shrubs, climbers and trellises which prevent access to the brickwork. Trees built in, or close to, walls may be protected and this should be investigated prior to removal. It may also include use of specialist equipment to clean brickwork before work commences.

Constructing New Brickwork in Lime Mortars

Setting Up the Work Area

Spot boards, on which to put the mortar, should be placed along the frontage of the wall, approximately 600mm away from it or, if constructing a corner, a spot board can be set up on each elevation. Spot

Removal or pruning of plants may be essential to provide access for brickwork construction and repairs, as trying to work around plants is often impractical.

boards can be heightened by putting them on concrete blocks, two high, to reduce the bricklayer bending over. The bricks are set out in stacks alongside the spot boards, but not so close that they become spattered with lime (they can be protected by more spot boards on their edges). One way to stack out the bricks is on their sides, so that the bricklayer can make an instant quality judgement when selecting a brick. Alternatively, they are laid out on their beds frog down (if they have frogs), to avoid collecting rain. If bricks salvaged from the building are used, they are first cleaned of mortar residue sufficiently far away from the work area to avoid creating mess before being stacked out. Ensure that mortar mixers and mixing areas are far enough away from the face of the work to avoid splashing and general dirt that collects around them. Spot boards are wetted to receive the mortar which is placed in a heap towards the back of it so that the bricklayer has room to manipulate it with the trowel. No more mortar than can be used efficiently should be placed on the board as lime mortar will soon dry out.

Position and Posture

Bricks should always be laid from the standing position with flexibility at the hips to turn to select bricks and then to lay them in position. The work should never be straddled, i.e., with a foot either side of the wall. The bricks and mortar should be within an arm's reach, as should the bricklayers' tools.

Constructing a Level First Course

When rebuilding a section of walling within a traditional brick wall, say on a façade, the levels of the bricks are taken from the adjacent brick levels by running a line across the brickwork and simply following the existing joint thicknesses. To construct brickwork from an uneven base or footing, lasers are often used to level brick courses whilst another method is to use

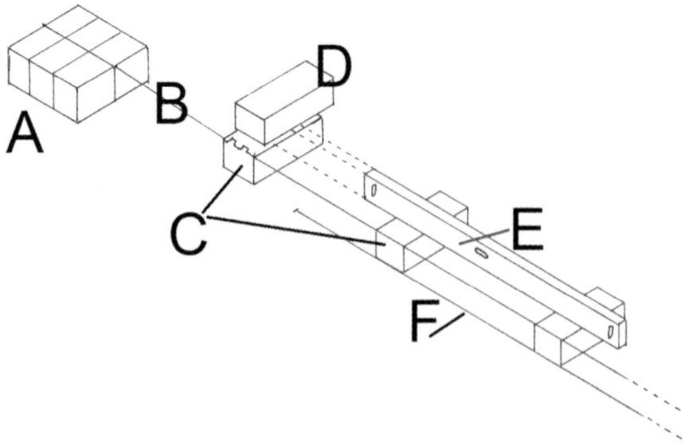

Bricks on edge at both end of the work (A) with string line (B) wrapped around them and pinned down by a tingle plate with a brick on top (D). Bricks spotted out (C) and levelled (E) along the building line (F).

a water level. Another method is to spot out bricks along the building line from the highest to the lowest point of the base by using a spirit level and straight edge. The line is wrapped around several bricks laid on their edge at either end of the work, and the line is trapped on the levelled brick at either end of the work, thus providing a level line for the first course.

Dry Bonding of Bricks (Setting Out)

The length of the wall to be built should be measured to see if the length of the wall works brick, i.e. that whole bricks fill the length measurement with the correct mortar joint (10mm or less) between each. It is good practice to keep perpendicular joints tight from the beginning of the build. The bricks can then be laid out along the length of the wall in their dry positions to determine where the cuts will be placed. The ends of the wall can be marked on a thin layer of mortar using the blade of a trowel.

Broken Bond

Having measured the gap for the proposed wall to find that it does not work to full brick lengths, then brick cuts will have to be used to fill it in a manner

Example of a broken bond over an opening where it appears less obvious. Three headers have been inserted here in order to maintain ¼ bond.

which is repetitive from the bottom to the top of the wall, unless the broken bond can be hidden under a window or door. The broken bond should form a pattern which is pleasing to the eye, and must appear deliberate with cuts being uniform in size and the pattern regular and not random. A broken bond should generally be placed in the centre of the wall or, alternatively, hidden under openings whose positions form part of the initial setting out. In brickwork, no cut smaller than a header in width should be seen in a wall apart from at the quoin where it forms the overlap of the bricks or bonding, such as in the form of a queen closer. In the formative years of brickwork development, such conventions were not always rigidly adhered to as the rules that govern bonding were developed gradually. In replacing historic traditional brickwork, as opposed to building new, the original conventions as found should be adopted to rebuild even though this may appear to go against the grain of modern brickwork teaching.

Core Brickwork Skills

In the context of constructing traditional brickwork, typical applications include rebuilding or repairing ½ brick or 1 brick walling. The former, in brick noggin used in rebuilding areas of face work of an elevation often where the headers have been snapped (*see* Context of Traditional Brickwork) repairing garden wall bonds, or facing badly eroded brickwork. The latter, used in the repair of parapets, boundary walls, the repair of solid walling generally and new work in handmade brick and lime mortar.

The core skills of the bricklayer are the same in modern cement work and traditional lime work. For both, the key to laying a good brick is judging and

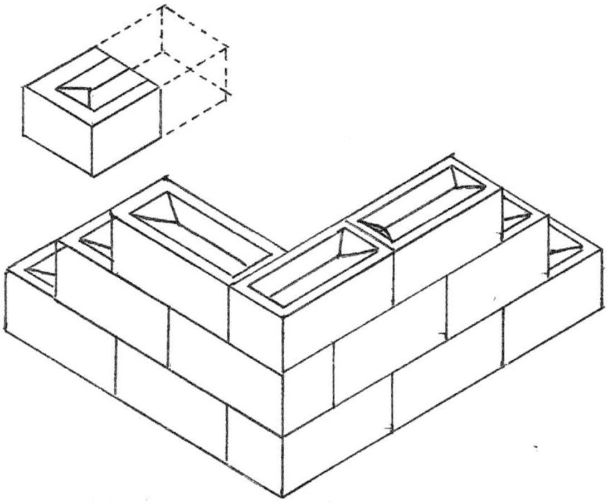

½ brick (100mm) quoin in stretcher bond gives ½ lap or bond.

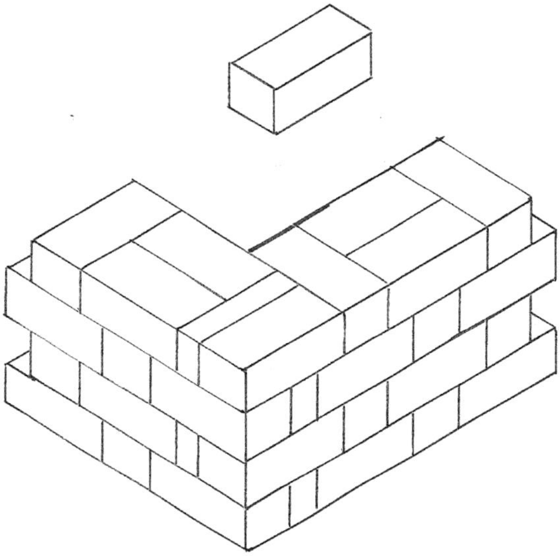

One-brick walling is so called because it is as thick as the longest brick used in it. This Flemish bond gives ¼ bond its weakness lies in the internal straight joints formed as a result of the bond.

laying the correct depth of mortar bed, spreading it well and dexterity in handling the brick with a good eye and attention to detail. Other skills of the bricklayer include the gauging of the work to ensure the courses are of the same height, levelling and plumbing the work to ensure it is upright and aligning (ranging) and squaring it.

Gauging the Brickwork

Accurate gauge will ensure equal bed joint sizes and determines the height of courses for the work. This measurement of a course is the height of a brick plus a joint, which should match that of the existing building. The gauge should be checked in one fixed position on the wall, i.e., on a wooden peg inserted against the wall, the top of which should be level with the top of the bottom course of bricks. The bottom course is not gauged because the joint thickness underneath of it is likely to vary according to the level of the base, considering that it is being laid on existing work that may itself be out of level or on an uneven footing. When integrating brickwork back in to existing traditional work, the gauge should match that of the existing.

Levelling the Brickwork

The level is to ensure that the brick is laid level, and that the faces of the bricks are as perpendicular as possible. When levelling an uneven, badly-formed brick, it should be levelled as best as possible longitudinally.

Plumbing the Brickwork

Plumbing is a term which is derived from the use of the traditional lead plumb bob, and plumb level from the Latin word for lead *plumbum.* To check plumbing,

Brickwork is gauged, here by means of a gauge or storey rod, to ensure the courses (brick and joint) are of equal height.

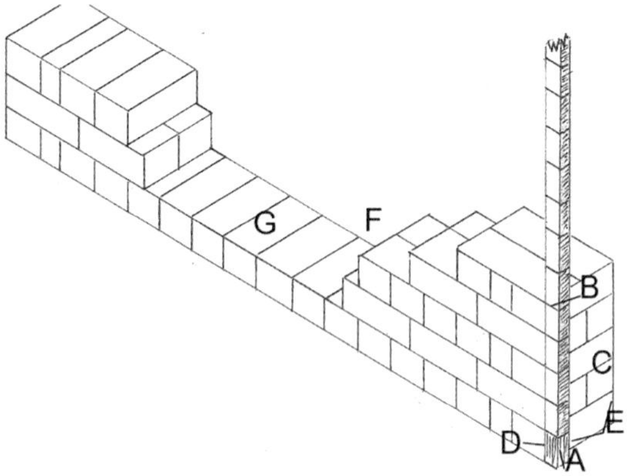

Gauging brickwork with a gauge rod (A), marked to course height (B), and at stopped end (C). Plumbing points at (D) and (E). Racking back (F), and header course (G).

The quoin brick is first positioned by eye to ensure that brick arrises are aligned, and then levelled through its length.

The brick is levelled across the brick. This will ensure the faces of the brick are as perpendicular as possible.

Ensure bubble is central to the two black lines on the spirit level bubble.

The work is plumbed using a spirit level to ensure it is perpendicular with the bubble in the centre of the two lines. The bricks should touch the level as much as possible, but this is sometimes difficult to achieve with some malformed handmade bricks.

place a foot against the base of the level held against the wall and adjust accordingly the brick being laid.

Ranging and Squaring

Ranging is the checking of face alignment of the brickwork to ensure the face of the work is flush with the spirit level throughout. Particularly misshapen brick faces may not all be able to be left flush in this manner. Squaring with a steel square at the quoin will ensure that new work is at a 90^0 angle.

Wall Lengths

On long runs of wall up to 12m in length, a tingle plate can be used to prevent the line from sagging in the centre. The tingle plate is placed on a bedded tingle brick and held in position with a brick on top of it, at which point the bricks can be laid to line. Tingle plates can be made from thin aluminium plate or plastic. The line should be taught, and daylight should be just visible between the line and the brick which will be straightforward, provided the ends of the wall have been built plumb and ranged. If no daylight can be seen, the brickwork will be built 'too hard to the line', and this will cause it to bow considerably, potentially without the error being spotted until quite a lot of new brickwork would have to be taken out to rectify it. Similarly, if the work is built

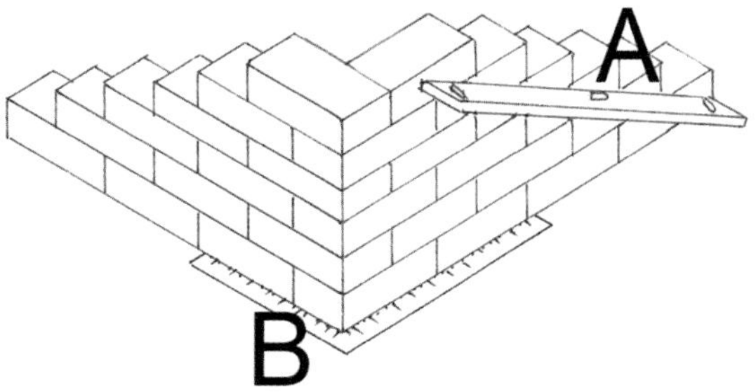

Ranging a ½ brick quoin (A) and squaring (B) on a ½ brick quoin using a steel square. The former to ensure the brickwork is flat, and the latter to ensure the corner is a 90° angle.

with too big a gap between wall and line, the result would be a concave wall.

Joint Thickness

Some bricklayers prefer to execute tight (sub 10mm) perpendicular joints (also known as perps, dots or cross joints) starting from the bottom of the work. This will look better, avoiding unsightly wide joints higher up the wall, but will negate potential problems of bonding later on, particularly if using a traditional brick with variations in length. Tight 'perps' are achieved by paying attention to the joint width when setting out the brickwork. When rebuilding traditional brickwork with particularly thick bed joints, it can be found to be mortar hungry and this factor should be considered when estimating the mortar materials needed.

Rearing the Corners of the Wall

Once the bottom course has been levelled and laid and the broken bond worked out (if there is one), there are several options to construct the wall. One option is to use steel profiles onto which lines are attached. These are positioned on the corners of the

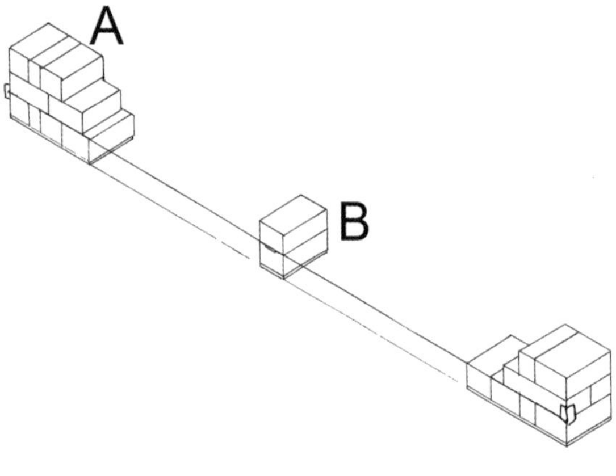

Racked back brickwork at either end (A) with line held by a tingle in the centre (B). Generally speaking, it is prudent to construct the bottom course of walling completely before racking back the ends.

When rearing the corners, perpendicular joints should be kept vertically aligned to ensure that bricks will fit when the centre is filled in.

building to be constructed, which are marked with the gauge, and this removes the need to build up the corners first. Another option is to use lasers set at the required heights whilst another, the method discussed here, is to rear the corners before filling in the remainder of the wall.

Toothing and Racking

This is a technique used in brickwork to enable a greater height to be reached on corners before the filling in of the walling, later. Straight lines of toothing should be avoided because they can potentially form a weakness if they are not bonded in properly when the centre of the wall is filled in. Combining toothing with racking back prevents an excessive use of both methods, yet still achieves a good height on a corner. When racking back, the bond should be maintained by ensuring that the overlap of the bricks and the perpendicular joints is consistent and vertically aligned.

If it isn't, and the bond is allowed to wander, it will be difficult if not impossible to fill in the centre to line. Once the ends of a wall are racked back or corners built, the centre of the wall can be filled in using corner blocks and line, or line and pins fixed to each end of the wall. These are often used because they can be moved quickly and the tension on the line can be quickly readjusted if necessary.

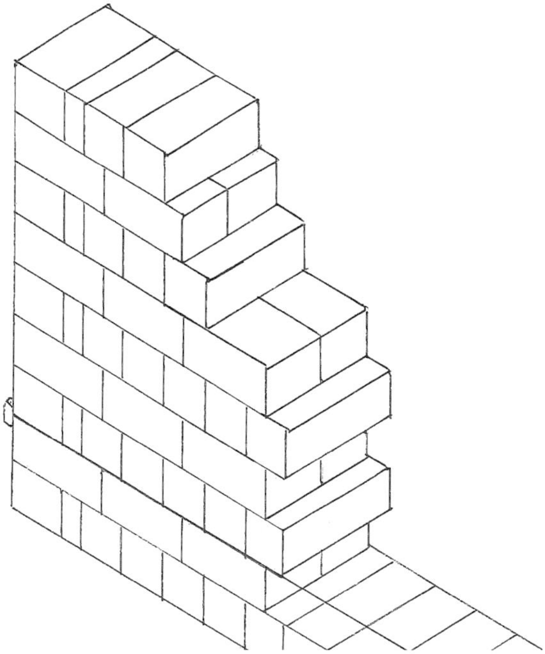

Toothing and racking back combined here on English bond walling.

When laying bricks to line, bond should be maintained with the bricks below.

Running in the Brickwork Using Lime Mortar

A key skill of bricklaying is judging the thickness of the mortar bed and this skill comes with practice. When picking up the mortar, hold the trowel loosely, not in a clenched fist, and make it an extension of the arm so it is flexible. Do not allow the mortar to smother the handle and the hand when picking it up but pick up just enough to fill the trowel. Fatty, lime-rich mortar can be manipulated into a shape akin to a large quenelle to make it easier to place it on the wall. One method is to lay enough mortar for one brick at a time so that the mortar won't lose moisture sitting on the wall. Lime mortar should be spread no more than the length of a spirit level before laying the bricks, for exactly the same reason. This is less of an issue when using lime putty mortars because they are fattier and more moisture retentive (*see* Materials) than hydraulic mortars, which can tend to become less workable more quickly. Making lime mortars

Spreading and judging the correct depth of mortar bed is a key skill of the bricklayer. Lime mortar is generally coarser than cement mortar because it contains graded aggregates and can therefore be less yielding than cement mortar.

Laying bricks to line, pushing down the brick with the hand until the top arris lies next to the line built, with a trowel blade of daylight between.

too wet in order to make them more spreadable can result in rapid moisture loss, and hairline cracking will potentially occur. All lime mortars will respond well to a damp atmosphere and fine mist spraying.

When placing the bricks, it is done with hand pressure and minimal tapping; line up by eye to ensure that face of the bricks is vertical and in alignment with adjacent bricks. There are two methods of physically laying the bricks. Some prefer 'pushing', which is when they are laid in front of the bricklayer when walking forward, or 'pulling', walking backwards laying to line as they go. There are several techniques for laying bricks but, apart from laying to line correctly, the key is to ensure a full perpendicular joint and cleanliness and neatness of the work.

Traditional Brickwork Repairs

The repairs discussed here are a selection of those that might typically be found when conducting work on traditional brickwork in a variety of situations.

An Approach to Conservation Repair

When carrying out brickwork conservation repair, one method is to adopt a systematic approach. In this scenario, regardless of the size of the job be it a small maintenance repair or an entire elevation, only one job is tackled over a given elevation at a time, unless there is a particularly good reason to do otherwise. There is little point in trying to execute quality pointing or brickwork repairs until the preparation phases are complete. This methodology will help to ensure that both ongoing and completed work, including prepared lime mortars, are not corrupted with dust and debris created during the earlier phases of work. This phased systematic approach also makes for a

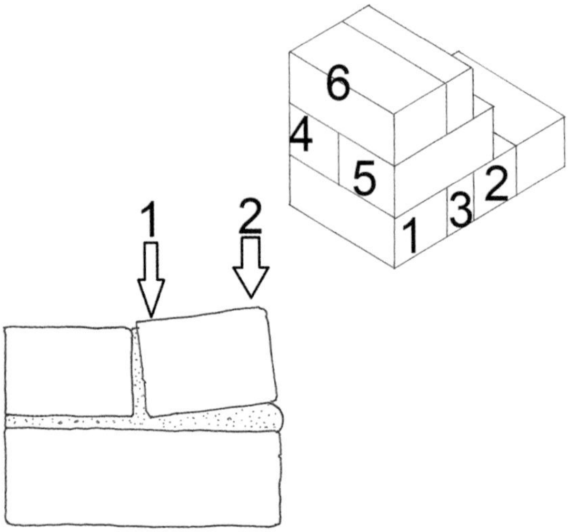

In constructing brickwork (top right), the order of bricks laid can be as shown. When placing a brick next to another lengthwise (bottom), push down with the fingers on the inner edge (1) and then on the outer edge (2) for the brick to sit level (2).

To guarantee full joints, ensure that bricks are fully buttered so that the joints are solid with mortar.

Surface preparation can be one of the most time-consuming phases of work. Here, iron indicated by the dark stains, poor repairs and cement mortar are all present.

Phase	Main Task	Tasks Details	Associated and Ongoing Tasks
1	Protection of property	• Sheet up windows • Turn back scaffold boards	
2	Recording	• Record by photographs • Acetates • Notes	
3	Wall surface preparation	• Removal of vegetation • Removal of random iron fixings • Removal of cement pointing including from any arches • Raking out of joints for pointing to sufficient depth • Removal of sporadic and clusters of decayed or cement bedded bricks • Clean out voids • Cleaning brickwork and washing down if appropriate	Prepare gauged arches in workshop. Prepare and mix sufficient quantity of lime mortars at least 24 hours in advance.
4	Brick removal and replacement	• Drill out modern bricks and cement plugs, clean out voids • Measure, cut, and offer replacement bricks	Number and store bricks noting course number and position.
5	Remove damaged arches designated for removal and prepare openings	• Remove brickwork above arch if required • Prepare and set out openings for new arches	Prepare pigmented plastic repair mixes.

more efficient working practice by focusing resources on one key job at a time, and this facilitates thorough quality control of each phase of work.

Protection of the Property

Protection of the property from dust and debris is an important standalone phase of the work. Good-quality work should be presented well, and this includes not only leaving the surrounding area in pristine condition but also protecting the aspects of the property that might be prone to damage and dust collection. Windows, for example, can be covered with plastic sheeting. Temporary plastic down pipes can be fitted if the rainwater goods are removed so that rainwater removal from the roof can be controlled during the work.

Recording of Work

Before any intervention, and before the dismantling of any brickwork, copious pictures can be taken of the area, structure or elevation so that the work can be rebuilt exactly in the way it was originally. Photographs are a useful record of the process of the work so should be taken throughout. Additional notes and drawings can also be made to supplement the photography. This can be useful particularly after a period of time has elapsed before the work starts. Plastic acetate can be fixed to the brickwork and used to trace the positions of existing bricks, marking those that are identified for removal. It is also important to record as much detail about the positioning of enrichments to remove speculation during the repair.

Initially the nail can be loosened by carefully drilling either side of it, then grasping it tightly with pincers and working it loose.

Surface Preparation

Removal of Iron and Other Fixings

Anything fixed or inserted into the wall, and in particular the mortar joints, can impede or prevent pointing and repairs. Often, traditional buildings have centuries of iron fixings such as nails and vine eyes, old downpipe brackets and redundant metal fixings used by power and telephone companies over many decades. The removal of these should be considered and dealt with carefully because, whilst some may be unsightly, they can cause damage to bricks and joints when forcibly removed. Whilst there is also an element of thought that some fixings are historically important and should be left where they are, iron when rusting can cause serious problems to brickwork including the spalling and staining of it. Iron fixings can usually be removed using pincers or pliers, but in some cases may have to be drilled out using an appropriately-sized masonry bit.

Large nails and fixings can cause localized decay as a result of expansion when they rust.

Removing Cement Mortar

Cement pointing in walling can be removed provided it has been deemed necessary, and in so doing so will not cause damage to the brickwork. Removal of cement mortars can be time-consuming and constitutes a large part of the preparation phase of the work. It is common to find different qualities of cement application depending on how much effort the original contractor put in to applying it decades before.

Cement Mortar Laid Thinly Over Lime Joints

Sometimes, the original lime mortar can be found to have not been raked back at all, but the cement mortar simply tooled over the lime joint surface. This poor attention to detail can be of great assistance to those seeking to remove the cement because it is sometimes possible, with very careful use of hand tools, to remove the cement by hand, exposing the lime joint beneath. Although it is likely that the original joint finish beneath is lost, the lime joint may not require repointing and can potentially be left as it is.

Using a mason's mallet and ball headed chisel to lightly tap away surface applied cement revealing the lime joints beneath.

Removing Loosened Cement Mortar

Sometimes the cement pointing may have shrunk back from the brickwork, separated from the brick and become loose. This can be recognized by the cement mortar having a hollow sound when tapped with the end of a chisel and/or visibly protruding from the joint. These factors can enable the mortar to be removed relatively easily, resulting in minimal damage to the brick arrises. Strips of cement should not be levered out from one end as this can cause damage to arrises.

Alternatively, using a 2 ½ lb club hammer and tungsten-tipped chisel, create a small opening in the cement and, working into the open joint, lightly tap out slices of the surface cement without digging the chisel point deeply into the lime mortar.

Hard Cement Pointing and Void Filling

Using good-quality tungsten-tipped chisels or mason's quirks, cement mortar can usually be removed effectively by hand. Yet even with careful use of quality hand tools, attempting to remove hard cements can result in damage to the brickwork. Indeed, in some cases, the findings of the assessment of the brickwork may deem it unwise to attempt to do so, particularly if the brickwork is not suffering from the effects of the cement mortar because of the risk of damage to the brickwork. Plugs of cement, inserted to fill voids where there was once a brick, often require considerable work to remove creating unnecessary vibration and impact on the walling.

An example of cement mortar which is cracking, perhaps due to the effects of moisture. Potentially, this can make the work of removing it easier.

Drilling out plugs of cement and inappropriate, modern bricks can be an effective way of weakening it prior to its removal, lessening the impact on the wall surface.

Following drilling, a firmly held steel punch can be used to create an opening in cement joints, and cement filled voids, by creating fissures in it.

Use of Small Grinders to Remove Cement Mortars

If the removal of hard cement is deemed necessary, the use of power tools may be an option to consider. There will always be an occasion in conservation where necessity prevails and this course of action will be resorted to on a case-by-case basis and should always be weighed against the impact of the work on the brickwork. Unobtrusive tests should be carried out by hand and by machine to assess the impact of this on the brickwork, to the satisfaction of all parties concerned. Ensure that appropriate protective equipment is worn during the operation, including eye and ear protection and dust mask. Holding the machine firmly, direct the thin blade in the centre of the cement joint and cut deep enough to only weaken the cement. A skilled operative using a small grinder with a thin diamond-tipped cutting blade can cut a horizontal line centrally through the cement joint so that hand tools can then be used to collapse it. Work should be carried out in short bursts with time in between to allow dust to settle and to assess the impact the machine is having and to allow the operative to rest. Once cement has been weakened in this way, the cement can be chopped out using hand tools.

Raking Back Lime Mortar Joints

Once the cement has been removed, the joints can be raked back approximately 25mm deep or more, depending on the condition of the back of joint, as sometimes joints needed to be consolidated further. The joints are raked out, ensuring that they are consistent in depth and that the backs of the joint are as square as possible so that there is a firm bond between newly applied and original lime mortar. This can be done using a reciprocating saw (*see* Tools and Equipment) which will make short work of raking out lime mortar (they cannot be used to remove cement as it will damage the machine) or by hand. Hand methods of lime removal using drags, or quirks, are an option depending on the size of the project.

Removing Dust and Debris

Dust and debris from the joint can be removed from the joints, preferably by hoovering it up and in doing so, the original lime mortar dust and aggregates can be saved and reused as a pozzolanic additive in subsequent mortar mixes, its use making a very authentic mortar colour (*see* Materials). Blowing out the dust is an alternative method, but this means that the

Using a brick pick as a 'drag' to rake back lime joints. This is a useful technique where machinery should not, or cannot, be employed.

mortar dust cannot be saved and is likely to be blown all over the scaffolding or elsewhere on the property. If the dust is not removed, subsequent wetting of the brickwork will create a lime effluent that will run down the face of the brickwork causing staining which will then have to be removed, thus creating another unnecessary job. As stated previously, all jobs on the elevation should be carried out systematically in phases, and in no case should stages of the work be undertaken at once on the same elevation, i.e., cement removal, raking back, and pointing as this makes quality control more difficult. Thorough quality control after each phase will ensure that there are no inconvenient discoveries once the work of pointing begins.

Using a blower can be an effective way of removing dust and debris from walling once raked out. It is an effective way of preventing staining by lime effluents when the joints are washed out.

Mortar removal

Once cement mortar has been removed from the structure or elevation, this can be completely cleared away from sheeting so that any lime mortar which is subsequently dropped can be easily collected for reuse.

Discovering Ineffective Lime Joints During Surface Preparation

Sometimes, having removed the cement pointing, the condition of the original lime bed joints underneath is worse than expected, and bad enough to warrant further removal of bricks or even disassembly of sections of brickwork for relaying, something which may not have been apparent when the brickwork survey was carried out. In this scenario, the original lime mortar has practically turned to soil over hundreds of years because of the ingress of moisture into the wall (often combined with insect action), perhaps through failed copings, for example, and its inability to evaporate away due to the cement pointing on the exterior, and bricks can often be removed by hand with no effort whatsoever. There is no point in trying to execute lime pointing if this is the case. Instead, the brickwork should be removed until sound and stable work is reached, and the bricks cleaned and re-laid before pointing is carried out.

Washing Out Joints

Once modern brick repairs have been removed, and the brickwork joints raked back deep enough, the

Historic lime mortar can turn to a friable mixture of soil and lime after decades of neglect and inappropriate repair of a building or structure. In this example, the mortar contained very little binder and the bricks could be removed very easily by hand.

walling can be thoroughly washed out, preferably the night before the pointing work is due to commence so the brickwork is cold to the touch the following morning. The washing out of the joints should occur when the bricks to be replaced have been removed to avoid the risk of washing out recently applied lime mortar joints. Washing out has several benefits: it will help the pointing mortar adhere to the insides of the raked-out joints; it helps to prevent the rapid drying out when the mortar is inserted in to the joint; and it will ensure the mortar will not be corrupted by debris which may prevent a sound joint being made.

Once washed out in this way, the brickwork will subsequently only require spraying prior to pointing and then mist spraying during pointing. The best means of washing out the joints and for the subsequent wetting and fine spraying of the work is to have a hose on the scaffold with an adjustable head. A small spray bottle is adequate for the brickwork directly in front of the bricklayer, but not for anything of scale.

Cleaning Brickwork by Hand

Once the brickwork joints have been washed out, this is a good opportunity to clean the brickwork, should it require it. This should be carried out using a natural bristle brush and water to clean off surface dirt or green staining. Beyond this method, cleaning should be approached very carefully, and professional advice should be sought as even some methods can, if used incorrectly, be too powerful on certain substrates and as such testing and trials are always recommended.

Brick Replacement

Replacing bricks as a part of a programme of repairs or maintenance is a common element of traditional brickwork repair. Brick replacement can be the next stage of the systematic approach to the work, and could involve the removal of inappropriate bricks bedded in cement which were identified during the assessment of the brickwork (*see* Assessment of Traditional Brickwork). The removal of bricks should be justified, for example, it might have serious, deep facial erosion or loss of structure (*see* Assessment of Traditional Brickwork).

It is often the case that the bricks used to 'repair' a wall in previous decades have been inappropriate, perhaps too hard, dense, or of incorrect colour and size. If they have been inserted using a full bed of cement mortar top, bottom and sides, they can be difficult to remove solely by using hand tools, and the impact of the hammer and chisel may cause vibrations to the surrounding brickwork causing hairline cracking to mortar joints. If the bricks are inappropriate, there is no need to try and salvage them whole, in

Soil and green staining can often be removed effectively by hand using clean water and a stiff brush.

Holes have been drilled along the length of this modern brick to weaken it and aid its removal using hand tools.

The deeply fissured, friable nature of the clay body of this brick suggests that this brick should be removed and is unlikely to be viable for reuse.

This 1680s era facing brick matches the existing brickwork. It has been pre-soaked to reduce the loss of moisture from the mortar when it is inserted, and to help with the initial curing of the mortar.

which case they can be drilled to weaken them before being carefully removed using hammer and chisel.

Original bricks which have been assessed as requiring replacement due to spalling or damage can be removed and turned around so that the innermost undamaged face is exposed, provided that they are still viable. Turning bricks around should never be considered the only solution because it is inevitable that some will be unviable or will simply break up when removed, and for this reason it is wise to consider obtaining extra matching bricks as replacements to match the existing work in colour texture and size. Moreover, the bricklayer would have selected the best side of the brick when laying and the interior might be of a lesser quality, though it often falls well below the bar set for brick removal.

Once the brick to be removed has been identified, it can be removed by hand or by certain reciprocating saws which can allow it to be dislodged without damaged. The void is then thoroughly cleaned out, ensuring that there is no remaining mortar which would impede the fitting of the replacement brick. Headers are more difficult to remove because even the longest blades of a reciprocating saw cannot reach far enough back to free the bricks from the wall unless the headers have been snapped (*see* Anatomy of a Seventeenth-century House). Because of this, badly eroded header bricks can be chopped back far enough

The void is buttered with mortar on the bed and in a wedge shape to the sides to ensure mortar is forced behind the brick when inserted.

The brick is buttered on top with a wedge of mortar and inserted angled slightly downwards before it is aligned with the bricks on either side of it. It can then be checked using a spirit level to ensure it sits flush with surrounding brickwork.

The brick is tapped firmly into position using a rubber mallet which, unlike a club hammer will not damage or mark the face of the brick. The wedge of mortar inserted into the void should ensure a tight, compacted fit.

Check that the brick is sitting flush with the surrounding wall by using a spirit level or straight edge.

Point up around the replaced brick using a matching mortar and a suitably sized pointing iron to minimize marking of the brick. Until the pointing of the façade is undertaken, the joints of the replacement brick can be set back 20–25mm.

to allow for a header slip to be inserted. During the initial assessment of the brickwork, count all eroded bricks – both headers and stretchers – which are deemed fit for removal and allow for enough replacements. The replacement brick should be a match to the existing ones. If the removed brick can be reused, carefully remove it from the void and place it safely to one side, ensuring its position in the wall has been recorded.

Reuse of Brick

All brick that has been removed from the building to make a repair, should be carefully conserved ready for reuse (*see* Conservation Principles). When brickwork has to be dismantled, perhaps to remove a bad cement repair or to rebuild a wall, it should be done extremely carefully so that further damage isn't inflicted on the

Handling bricks

Deft and careful handling, clean work and correct tools will reduce the chance of staining of the brick faces with soiled gloves.

brickwork, and so that as much original brick can be conserved as possible.

Any piece of original brick that has been removed should be regarded as potential cut for inserting back into the wall and should be measured for size. The cutting of full original bricks to produce smaller cuts should be avoided whilst there are smaller pieces to utilize for the same purpose.

Dismantling Existing Brickwork for Repairs

Brickwork should be photographed before removal. It should be carefully dismantled, removing only what is absolutely necessary, and without damage to the bricks which are then laid out, numbered and in courses. Toothing is a means by which brickwork can be tied back into the existing walling. The decayed and damaged bricks should be carefully cut out and removed. The projecting bricks should then be made free of debris and old mortar so that inserted bricks are not prevented from being seated properly. A reciprocating saw is a very useful tool for creating toothing and for minimizing intervention in sound brickwork as it can cut through lime and loosen the brick without applying force to remove them (*see* Tools and Equipment).

Heaping too much mortar on the brick before insertion will cause it to pile against the surrounding brickwork and may result in staining of it.

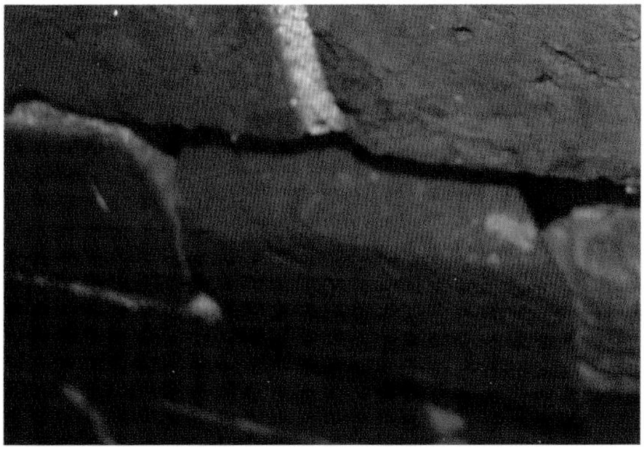

From a piece of original salvaged brick, make a cut to fit the shape of the void ensuring that there is a good bed of mortar for it to be bedded into, and test to fit.

Remove damaged brick back to sound material and create a surface on to which a new joint can be made. Wash out debris with clean water.

Pack enough lime mortar into the void to ensure a tight, firm fit around and behind the brick piece to be inserted.

Form a tight joint between the two pieces of brick with pigmented mortar and use a little colour wash to blend in the joint between the two. Joint up to match the surrounding mortar finish.

Toothed brickwork ready for constructing a new panel. It is important that the toothings are clean and free of debris.

These bricks have been removed and laid out in their positions and courses on the scaffold boards.

Preparing Existing Walls for Laying Bricks

Traditional brickwork repairs often entail laying or inserting bricks on existing surfaces. These surfaces should be free of dust and debris and well-dampened, prior to laying of bricks, to reduce absorption of moisture from the lime mortar and to help it to adhere to the brick surface. Damping surfaces in this way should be done regularly, particularly in warm weather. Availability of water onsite is crucial for the successful construction of traditional brick and lime mortar and its subsequent curing. Failure to keep the surfaces damp, to dip bricks and then to cover and protect work, particularly in hot weather, can lead to lack of bond between bricks and mortar and the rapid drying out joints, a symptom of which is for the joints to turn white, whatever colour the mortar was intended to be (*see* Problems When Using Lime Mortar).

Laying Misshapen Bricks

Handmade bricks can often be misshapen or in some cases, bowed longitudinally and this can affect the way they are laid. If the bricks are laid incorrectly, the result can be hatching and grinning, meaning the faces of the brickwork sit at angles to one another across the face of the work which looks unsightly and causes the brickwork to not be flush when measuring with a spirit level. Handmade bricks should not be laid 'cocked up' as this can impair the correct

Remove only loose and badly seated bricks and remove old surface mortar and debris using a bolster and a 2 ½ lb club hammer.

Brickwork surfaces should be dampened down before bricks are laid to enable better adhesion of the mortar bed.

laying of the next course. Laying the bricks with the bow shape downwards is the way to prevent this. When laid correctly, the bricklayer will endeavour to adjust the brick on the mortar bed, level it and ensure that one part of the face of the brick, however misshapen, is touching the spirit level when plumbed. Some bricks have very uneven arises and, as such, the line forms a guide to which some of the brick is laid to which leaves a trowel blade's width of daylight between brick and line.

Dressing Bricks

Traditional bricks may require some preparation before they can be laid to ensure a correct fit. It is important to avoid leaving scutch marks on brick faces. Bricks should be suitably cleaned of old mortar debris, etc., before they are laid. This work can be undertaken before work on a structure commences to improve efficiency.

Dipping Bricks

Dipping bricks when constructing or repairing traditional brickwork serves two purposes. It will prevent the rapid absorption of moisture from the lime

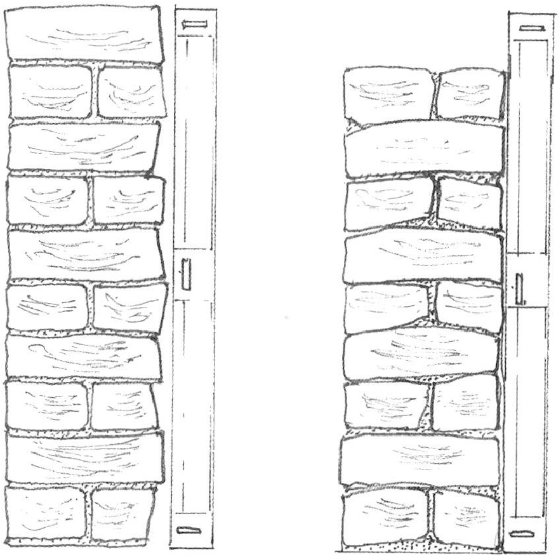

Hatching and grinning is the result of poorly seated bricks and makes the work look unsightly and unprofessional (left). Adjusting the bricks so that when laid, the faces are as flush as possible with the spirit level is the correct way to lay (right).

mortar and, if the bricks have been pre-soaked, can also provide a reservoir of moisture for the lime during the initial curing of the mortar around the brick. In cooler, damp conditions this is a quick plunge, but in hot conditions bricks benefit from having been soaked in advance followed by a quick plunge just before they are laid. When the brick is submerged, the bubbles that are formed occur when the water forces out the air from myriad tiny voids in the brick.

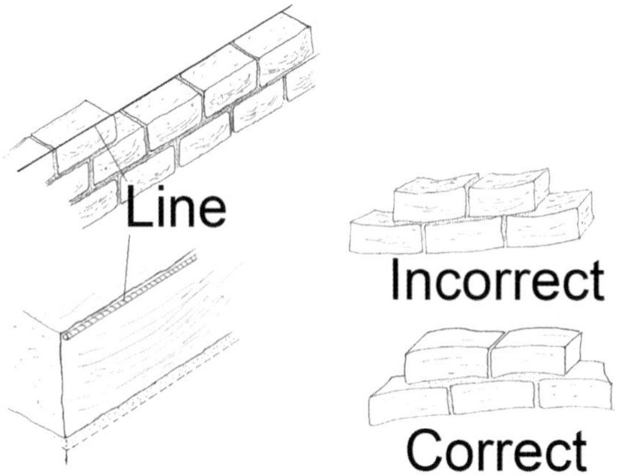

'Cocked up' bricks (top) will make laying of subsequent courses difficult. Laying the bricks bow downwards (bottom) will help prevent this. When laying to line, the top brick arris runs along the brick line. The lower brick arris should be aligned with the arris of the course below. This can be achieved by considering an imaginary line on the lower brick arris (dashed line).

Completely submerging the brick in water for a few seconds will prevent too much moisture being instantly sucked out of the mortar bed. In hot weather, bricks can be thoroughly soaked in baths until all bubbles have left, the air having been displaced by water.

Dressing bricks is necessary to ensure a correct neat fit in to the wall. Here a comb blade on the scutch hammer is used to accurately trim the brick bat. The brick is held against the fleshy part of the thigh with fingers kept well out of the way of the hammer blade.

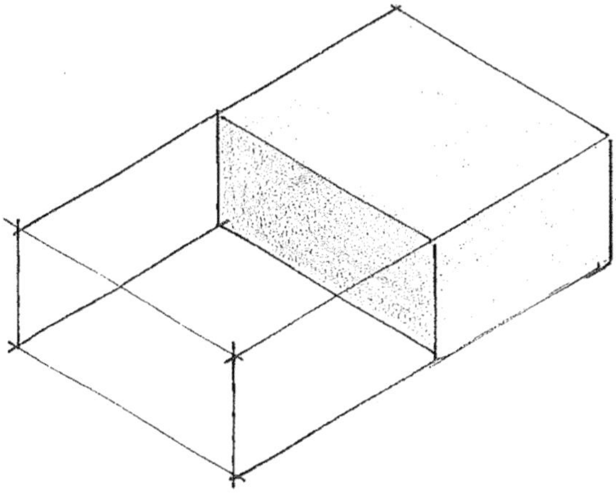

Half a brick or half bat.

Cutting Bricks before and During Construction

Whatever types of cuts of brick are required for the wall, they can be cut either by machine or by hand before the work starts so that the flow of bricklaying is not interrupted during the build. Whilst the machine-cutting method is perhaps a more efficient way of doing this, hand skills using hammer and bolster are an essential part of the bricklayer's craft.

Mortar

Note that if carrying out brick replacements and minor repairs across an elevation, a container of mortar can be a more practical method than the spot board.

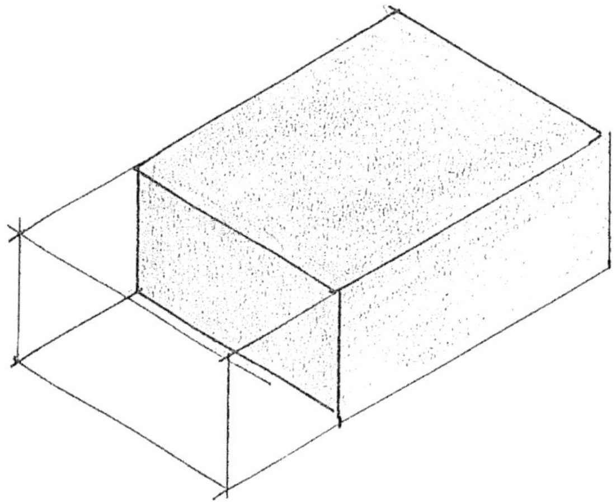

A ¾ bat.

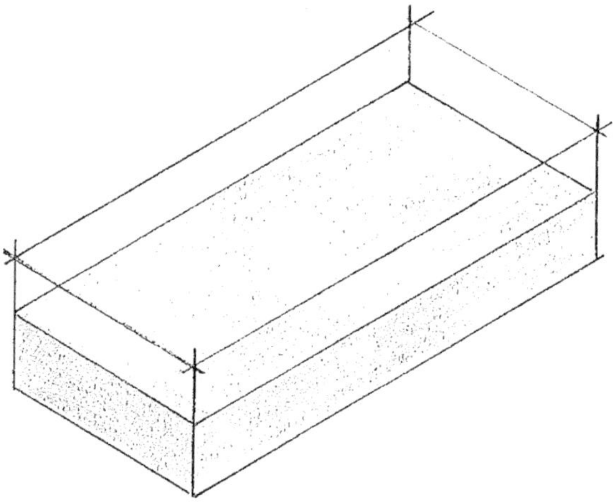

A split brick.

Use of Steel Reinforcement

Cracks in walls can be stitched or sutured using high-grade stainless helical fixing rods (*see* Materials). The bars can be bedded every two courses across the crack, approximately 50mm in depth, prior to pointing and then pointed over with lime mortar. In the example below, there has been some movement in a boundary wall which has opened up and ruptured the vertical joints in one specific area forming a potential weakness. Moisture has penetrated inside the wall via failed joints of the copings.

When preparing to insert steel reinforcement, joints have been raked out to a depth of approximately 50mm depth then thoroughly washed out with a hose until the water runs clear.

Offer up the rods to the apertures to check they are suitable for the steel to fit and tap them in to the mortar behind.

Point over the apertures to blend in with the remaining pointing, compressing hard to ensure that the bar is fully embedded and that there are no voids within the joint.

First, select the location where the bars will be inserted. Cut out the horizontal mortar joint just over the length of the rod across the vertical crack, ensuring sufficient depth. Remove any cracked or broken bricks which may lay across the vertical crack using the method described in brick replacement, above. Grouting of the brickwork using liquid lime mortar or consolidation of deeply eroded joints may be required before steel is inserted.

Small Brickwork Repairs

Small groups of brickwork can be targeted for repair using well matched replacements and/or turned around bricks.

Insert matching brick headers using a line and pins to achieve a level course.

A group of damaged and badly decayed bricks in a cement pointed elevation.

Bed the final stretcher course to line. Rake back the joints ready for pointing.

The badly damaged bricks have been removed by hand or by using a reciprocating saw. The voids, as well as the joints, are thoroughly raked and cleaned out.

The spirit level is another method to check alignment of bricks in the repair if line isn't used. Ensure the ends of the level are positioned on existing surrounding brick or stonework.

Once the bricks have been replaced, the area is ready for pointing. The area should be fine-mist sprayed regularly.

Beat the lime putty conservation pointing with a churn brush once it is leather hard. Brushing too early can result in lime bloom. (*See* Problems when using Lime.)

Plastic (Pigmented) Repair

Plastic repair is another term for a mortar, pigmented or otherwise, used to form a repair to brick or stone. In traditional brickwork repairs, the technique is useful where the removal of a brick is considered unnecessary or unwise (consider the principle of minimum intervention) but there is a small piece, perhaps a corner or a deep recess in the face of the brick, that may have a detrimental effect on the brickwork and also from an aesthetic point of view. It should never be used to coat all the eroded bricks as a deliberate finish. When preparing the pigmented mortar, make samples to match the brick and test them unobtrusively on the intended elevation, perhaps on a spare brick. It is worth remembering that on walls above head height, small red ochre pigment repairs would be invisible and even lower down on the elevation, one would have to search hard to find the repair. Cover and protect the test samples to cure them sufficiently and then check the colour is appropriate. The constituents of pigmented mortar for a plastic repair could include building sand, fine sand, NHL 2 lime, pigment (colour to suit brickwork), a little brick dust and rabbit skin glue in solution (*see* Tuck Pointing).

This technique works best when the repair can be supported by two or more sides of the brick. The colour of the pigment should be matched to the brick to be repaired, and this may require several tests but, in fact, the red and orange pigment hue will be

A missing corner can be an instance where a pigmented plastic repair could be used.

From this mixture, small amounts can be taken and mixed with the rabbit skin glue solution to form a doughy, putty-like material useful for a variety of applications.

Applying the pigmented mortar with a small tool. Spray the area with a fine mist as work proceeds and then cover with a pad of dampened hessian.

Texture the pigmented lime mortar using a piece of lath, or similar. Protect the completed repair with layers of hessian.

practically invisible when viewed from the ground (*see* Minor Face Repairs in Gauged Brickwork).

Repairing Window Rebates and Seals

The replacement of windows in traditional brick buildings can present an opportunity to carry out attractive and practical repairs using the traditional materials and skills. High-quality expensive timber or UPVC windows are often fitted and then the gap between the window and the brickwork sealed with hard cement mortar and or silicon mastic from a tube which in time, which can trap moisture against the timber and the brick once they begin to split and crack causing physical decay. Repairs around original timber windows and openings can often be found to have been carried out badly using cement mortars as an afterthought or as is more often the case, silicon. There are traditional methods to seal around windows which are breathable and could be considered to use instead, and which will conserve the timber for years to come. Two methods will be discussed here.

Brick buildings built after 1774 were required to have a brick rebate to protect the window frame (*see* Historical Context). Poor cement repairs and staining of the brick rebates are quite common where a window has been replaced in the past, sometimes resulting in 25mm or more of unsightly and damaging

An example of an unsightly and potentially damaging cement seal between frame and brickwork, potentially trapping moisture against both timber and brick and possibly resulting in the physical decay of both.

cement. An opportunity to reverse poor repairs and a lack of craftsmanship can be taken when a window is removed for replacement and the entire window opening is revealed.

Another method of resealing around window frames is to make a seal using oakum tar hemp (*see* Materials) used in conjunction with either lime pointing or a burned sand mastic (*see* Materials). Both methods can form a flexible and breathable joint that will not trap moisture against timber or brick. Timber sash windows can have deep recesses as deep as the original box. Sometimes this was seen as an opportunity to use newspapers and even stockings to fill them! Today, once old debris has been removed, they can be filled with lime mortar before creating the seal.

The inside of the rebate, and in particular the edge to which the window frame will abut, can be cleaned off to remove cement and any badly protruding brick which would prevent a good fit of the window frame. The brick rebate can be touched up with red ochre colour wash to enhance the red of the brick and camouflage mild cement staining (which cannot be removed).

Caulking Window Surrounds

The hemp is wound into a rope or braid of a suitable thickness for the gap by placing it over a scaffold tube and then twisting or braiding it by hand. It can then be offered up and gently pushed in to retain it in position.

The hemp rope is then hammered in using a special caulking iron and club hammer. Ensure that the hemp rope is not too thick, so it causes damage to timber and makes insertion difficult, yet tight enough to form a good seal between brick and timber.

Lime mortar has been applied over the top of the hemp to a depth of approximately 10–15mm to form a good seal. Note the dark area on the timber is where cement had been placed.

Burnt sand and double boiled linseed oil is another material which can be turned into a thick paste which can be applied over the hemp to a depth of about 5mm to form a durable flexible seal between brick and an oak window frame that blends well with the oak trims used here.

Chapter Ten

Gauged Brickwork Arch Construction

The gauged arch has been chosen here because it is a typical feature of property dating from the seventeenth and eighteenth centuries, and can be seen in England's cities, towns and villages all over the country. As has been discussed previously, this feature is often subject to the ravages of modern methods and ignorance, demonstrated by the grinding out and widening of the extremely narrow joints, followed by the use of cement mortars which prevents moisture evaporation and can accelerate decay in the soft bricks from which these features are constructed. Damage such as this is usually carried out by people unskilled in gauged work, or those who do not understand the implications (*see* Context and Vulnerabilities).

Two types of gauged arch will be discussed here. The flat arch, which has no rise of camber, and the camber arch, which has one – albeit barely noticeable – and was designed to remove the optical illusion of sagging of the flat arch. This class of work is called 'gauged', but this simply means 'measure' and this informs us that all elements of this work are subject to the utmost accuracy and attention to detail, often using the finest quality of brick available. Today, there is a strong tendency, largely for economic reasons, for pre-formed arches to be specified. These are arches that are accurately surveyed and then cut in a workshop and mounted on a steel lintel ready for insertion into the building, providing an excellent cost-effective and ready-made feature. Alternatively, gauged bricks can be supplied ready cut to the exact measurements of the voussoirs for an arch ready for laying by the bricklayer, again producing arches of sublime quality – provided they are installed by a skilled bricklayer. Whilst both have their merits, and can look superb when installed, some believe that it is in the interests of the craft for a bricklayer to be able to draw, make, set out and construct a gauged arch from scratch. Often, gauged arches have simply been badly treated and require careful repair to bring back their character.

An example of an arch in a precarious state of repair. In this example, there would only be three courses of brick to remove above the arch to enable access to construct it.

There are several components to the successful learning, understanding and constructing of gauged work. The first component, perhaps, is to develop a body of knowledge of the subject and a broad understanding of the historical context of the skill. The second is to be trained by someone already skilled in this work whilst last, but by no means least, is to gain experience and practice. There are some excellent primary and secondary sources that discuss all aspects of traditional gauged work. Here, some modern methods, materials and techniques will be described because they have been found, in the authors' experience, to be practical and effective onsite particularly in a very busy work schedule, but which do not detract from the finished work or the skills needed to produce it.

Working Platform

The scaffold, or work platform, must be erected to suit the bricklayer doing this work and it is worth meeting with the scaffolder to ensure that this will be the case. The arch to be constructed should sit at approximately chest height to the bricklayer. A raised platform within the scaffold at the rear of the lift is needed to lay out the arch to keep it out of harm's way and enable the bricklayer to select bricks and return them without having to constantly bend down. A well-secured plastic covering for the platform will protect the work from the elements and enable work to continue in inclement weather.

Removing a Damaged Arch

Generally, if more than half the arch is badly eroded and must be repaired, then the whole arch should be removed and for this adequate support of the brickwork above will be required. A portion of the brickwork above the arch should be removed first to be able to access the arch properly from above. Recording of work is an essential part of the process to make sure that all ways are identified to aid the setting out of the work. Photograph the area, and make notes before any work is carried out so original work can be rebuilt correctly. Make careful note of any aspects of the brickwork and opening that will aid the construction of the new arch.

The damaged arch should be carefully and safely restrained and supported to prevent collapse, because once one voussoir is removed the others can drop out more easily. Not only can this be dangerous, but it could also damage the window or door beneath and result in a sound, reusable voussoir being damaged. Those voussoirs that can be reused should be

Removal of the brickwork above an arch is an opportunity to remove inappropriate repairs and halt decay. Here, successive cement repairs, cracking and sagging of the brickwork are visible.

Carefully remove the brickwork and number it for course and position. Tooth back the brickwork on either side of the opening so that new brickwork can later be constructed to a line. Ensure that the area behind the arch is clean and free of loose material, filling any holes either during or prior to arch construction.

numbered and their position in the arch identified, cleaned and stored carefully.

Preparing the Drawing Paper and Arch Drawing

The first step in constructing a new gauged arch is to thoroughly survey the existing arch and the opening (*see* Assessment of Traditional Brickwork). Next is to draw the arch in a 1:1 scale. Drawing gauged arches takes a lot of practice and involves a great deal of patience. Errors, where they are made, will multiply as the work goes on. For the drawing, depending on the size of the opening for which the arch is to be prepared, a large sheet of ply placed on a table or even on a smooth garage floor will suffice. The drawing should have a legend on which the key pieces of information about the arch are written, including measurements of the opening, the depth of face of the arch, joint size, voussoir size, distance of the striking or vanishing point and the soffit width. Arch sizes vary depending on the opening, but there must be room enough on the floor or drawing board to create any striking or vanishing point position and the full width of the arch.

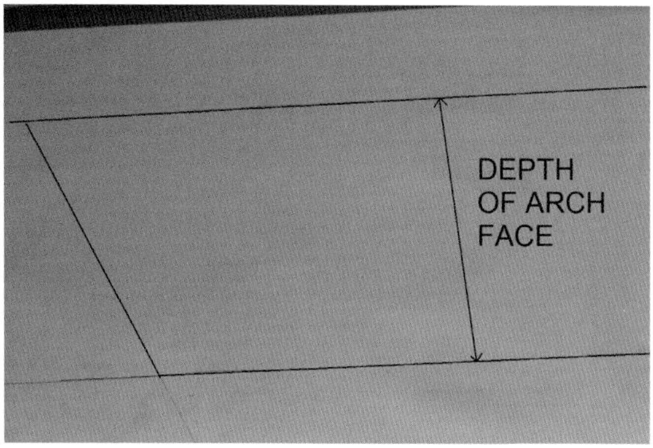

Leaving a gap of about 150mm at the top of the paper, draw two parallel horizontal lines, with the distance between them being the measurement of the depth of face of the arch surveyed on the building opening.

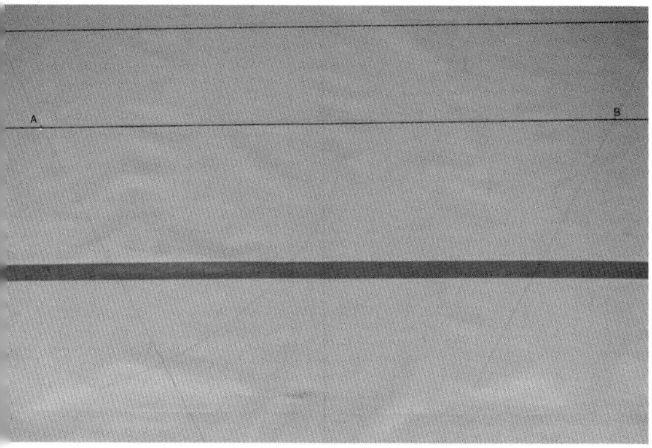

On the lower of the two lines, the setting out line or intrados, mark out A and B at either end of the span of the opening.

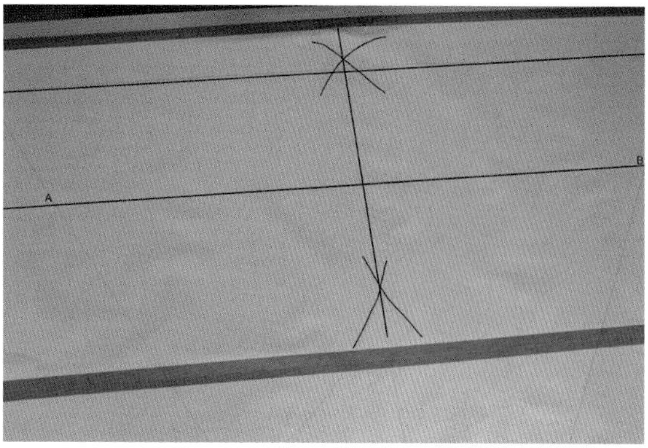

Set up a perpendicular line by forming intersecting arcs at the top and bottom of the paper by placing the trammel point first on A, adjusting the trammel to just over halfway in the opening. From A, draw an arc in the gap at the top of the paper and one below. Reverse this process, this time from point B. Draw the centre line by drawing an accurate line through both sets of arcs where they intersect. This line marks the centre of the opening.

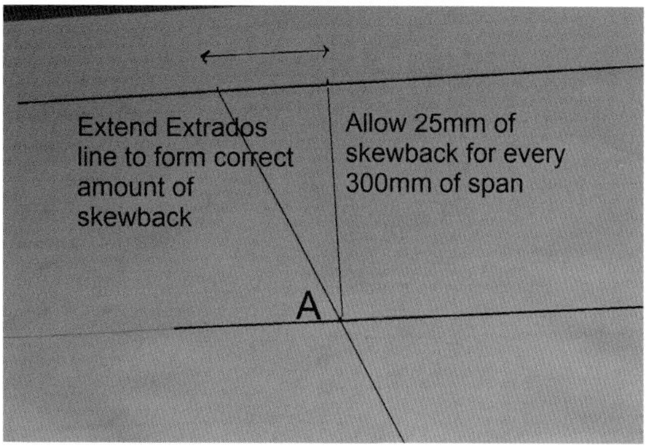

To form the angle of the skewback, allow 25mm for every 300mm of the opening measurement. In an opening of 1.2m, 1200mm/300mm = 4 x 25mm = 100mm. Elongate the extrados line of the drawing by 100mm and mark the positions on the paper.

Layout the paper on the chosen drawing surface and stick it down using decorator's masking tape so that it won't curl at the edges. Draw a margin around the paper, and in the bottom left or right-hand corner (or wherever convenient) draw a box or legend which will contain the construction information of the arch (*see* above). This information should be detailed enough for a skilled bricklayer to pick up and understand the dimensions of the construction.

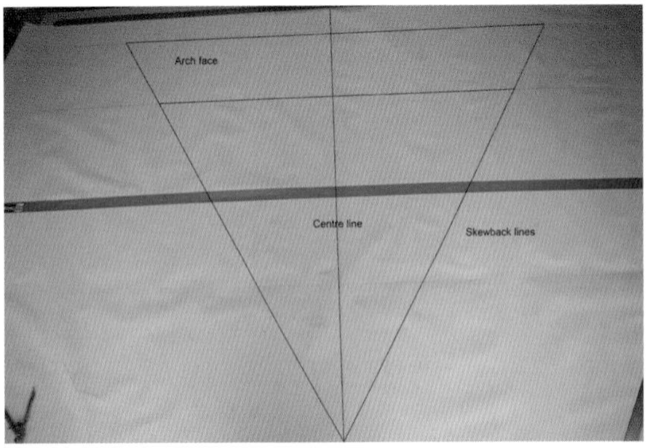

Draw a line through each skewback position marked on the extrados, through points A and B on the intrados and down to bisect the centre line. The shape produced is a 1:1 scale outline of the arch that will be built in the opening.

Marking the Positions of the Voussoir's Lines

The next task is to work out the position of the voussoirs and to mark them, and the joints, on the drawing. One method is to divide the opening into the number of voussoirs required (there must be an odd number with the key brick in the centre) and prick out the position of the key brick which sits equally astride the centre line. Prick out the measurements of the voussoirs between the key brick and skewback. Once the positions are confirmed, mark them in carefully with a retractable pencil.

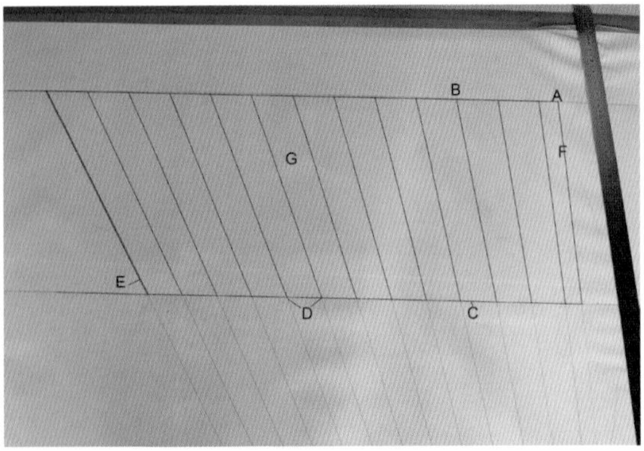

Positions on drawing include centre line (A), extrados line (B), intrados line (C), positions of voussoirs marked on intrados line (D), joints parallel to voussoirs lines (E), key brick (F), even number of voussoirs (G) on either side of the key brick.

Draw the lines from the striking point, through the marks on the intrados and up to the extrados. This will produce the familiar shape of the brick voussoirs.

Using a 2m rule is the best way to ensure neat accurate and continuous lines from striking point through the arch face.

Marking Out the Joints

Prick out the joint width using dividers from the drawing set and then lightly pencil mark them in on the drawing. Draw in the joints by drawing lines parallel to the voussoir's lines, first to the key brick and then to the remaining voussoirs. It is important to remember not to attempt to take the joint lines from the striking point as this will produce wedge shaped joints! Note that the joints at the skewbacks at each side of the opening must be included in the width of the opening.

Bonding Arrangement

The bonding arrangement of the arch is drawn in so that templets can be made to the correct size. Evidence of the bonding will come from existing work on a property and with reference to historical context. For example, in Flemish bond, a header and closer were created using one voussoir, the closer being formed by the addition of a false joint.

Forming a Camber

There are various methods of forming a camber, but one method is by springing a steel rule under three tacks inserted into the arch drawing, one just above the centre point of the setting out line on the intrados and one each at A and B on this line. The rise of the camber can be worked out at 3mm to every 300mm of arch span. With the ruler placed in the appropriate position, a camber line is drawn with a pencil tc

Forming of a camber using a steel ruler sprung over small nails (bottom of photo) on the portion of the arch drawing that has been taped to the portable arch bench.

produce the distinctive rise. This step is not required for a flat arch.

Making Templets

Once the life-size drawing is complete, the next stage is to prepare the templets that fit the voussoir shapes of the drawing. One modern method is to use clear plastic acetates which are available from some craft outlets. These are positioned on top of the drawing and stuck down to prevent them from moving, using drawing pins or decorator's tape. The shape of the voussoir is then traced onto the acetate using a fine, black permanent pen and then cut out using a sharp Stanley knife and a steel ruler on a cutting mat. The templets are then numbered to the drawing and kept in a safe place until they are ready to be used to mark the bricks ready for cutting.

Squaring Rubber Bricks

When selecting rubber bricks, ensure that they are appropriate for the era of arch being constructed (*see* Materials). Note that the finished size of the voussoirs at the extrados should never be bigger than the bricks used in the surrounding wall construction. The bricks are prepared for cutting by squaring off one bed face and one stretcher face. Using pre-squared gauged pieces (*see* Materials) will cut out this initial squaring, but all bricks should be checked for square as a matter of good practice. Squaring ensures a 90° angle between bed and face, and enables one voussoir edge ready-prepared for the templet to be held against it. When the bricks are rubbed on the stone, they are rubbed in a clockwise, circular motion using the fingertips to apply pressure where the brick needs to be rubbed and then to check using the back of an engineer square. Hold the brick up into the light and check that no daylight can be seen between blade and brick.

Once the bed of the brick has been squared, next square on stretcher face, again checking that no daylight can be seen using the square. Once the brick is squared in this manner, it should be put out of the

Check that there is no daylight under the square by placing the blade upside down on the brick then holding the brick up to the light drawing the blade towards the holder.

Hold the stock of the square tight against the squared bed when checking face of the brick for square. Hold the brick up to the light to ensure no daylight can be seen underneath the blade.

way or stored carefully as the edges are very easy to damage. Like all aspects of brick conservation work, it is best to do everything systematically so that all of one type of job is finished on all the voussoirs before moving on to the next phase.

Cutting the Excess of the Rubbers

Once the bricks have been squared, the excess material from the brick can be removed. It is economical to purchase rubbers with the size of the voussoirs in mind to avoid too much waste. The templets are brought in, and each held against a squared edge of the face of a brick. An outline of the voussoir shape is drawn around the templet and the brick is numbered for its position in the arch. A scribe line can also be scored around the pencil line to act as a guide of cutting of excess brick.

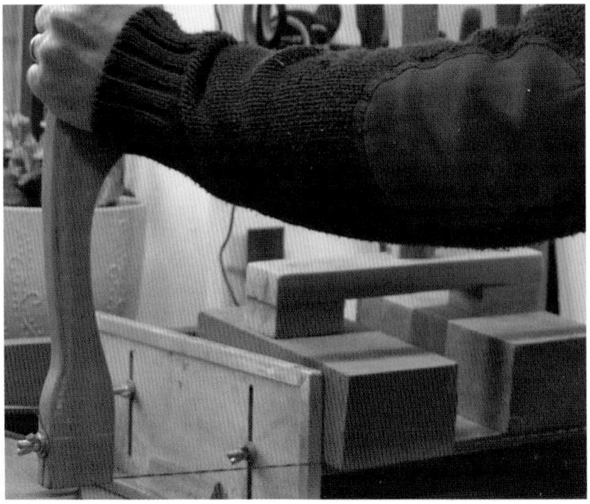

Using a bow saw to make a cut underneath the brick will prevent the offcut from snapping off leaving a ragged edge. Note the bridge and strut keeping the two bricks firmly in position.

The marked bricks can then be placed in the cutting box with an adjustable base so that the cut line is showing above the side of the box and cut with the bow saw. If the bricks have lots of inclusions, such as flint (*see* Materials), a masonry saw can be used to cut off the excess brick just over the cut line. This is an extremely dusty process, particularly if the saw is a dry-cut saw, and should be done outside with ample protection of the ground using plastic sheeting and with particular attention to wearing correct Personal Protective Equipment (PPE) including a suitable dust mask. When cutting, it should be taken as close to the scored line as possible so that there is less to have to rub on the stone. Once cut, the voussoirs can be placed again in number order and stored carefully ready for the next phase of rubbing to fit templets and arch drawing.

Rubbing the Voussoir to Size

The rubbing of the bricks is a painstaking process requiring practice and experience. Respiratory protection is required to carry out this work, and regular clearing of dust using a hoover is recommended. The arch voussoirs must be thoroughly squared, and attention to detail will be immediately apparent firstly when the acetate, which accurately represents the voussoir size on the drawing, is placed on it to check the size, secondly when it is placed on the arch drawing and thirdly when the arch is installed! When rubbing, it is recommended to rub the soffit bevels on the intrados leaving a generous amount of rub left in the top end in case of accidental damage and for adjustment. The soffit bevels of the camber arch, unlike those of the flat arch, are all different. This is because the camber is not formed as part of a circle but is arrived at from the height of the rise in relation to the width of span (*see* above). It is important that the soffit bevels sit neatly on the lintel or turning piece. For a camber arch, they must follow neatly over the camber and any discrepancy will be immediately obvious. A final rub can still be carried out when constructing the arch onsite.

Once rubbed down to the pencil line and not beyond, set the voussoirs down in their correct position on the arch drawing ensuring that their position is carefully marked on the bricks.

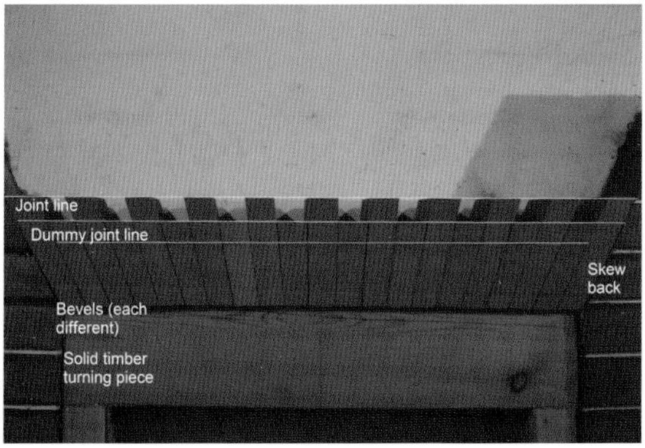

An illustration showing the lower half of a gauged camber arch set out dry, emphasizing the desire for level horizontal joints and neat soffit bevels. In reality, gauged arches are not constructed in this manner but are built to full face height in pairs of voussoirs, equally from either side of the opening. Note the small rise of the camber.

When rubbing the bricks, great care should be taken not to over rub as, once this happens, the brick will not be suitable for its position in the arch wasting effort and material. Rub the voussoir down to close to the pencil line using the templet to check the shape whilst regularly checking for square so that all sides of the piece are at right angles.

Arranging the Arch on the Drawing

The radiating lines of the drawing are no longer needed, but the arch itself is still very important. This part of the drawing can be taped to a timber arch bench which is laid out on trestles. Special 1mm thick DPC can be inserted between the bricks to act as the spacing of the joints. Once all spacers are inserted, the arch can be secured by fixing battens to the bench beneath the intrados and at the extrados to prevent movement of the voussoirs. At this point, transfer the voussoirs positions at intrados and extrados to a piece of lath for the former, and a wooden staff for the latter. These will be used to transfer information when preparing the opening and setting out the arch. Finally, the arch set can be carefully packed up in boxes, wrapping each voussoir in bubble wrap or similar for carriage to site.

Preparing the Opening

The flat and camber arches follow a very similar method except that a flat stainless steel lintel would be used for the flat arch, and a timber turning piece of the correct rise in the centre used for the camber arch.

When constructing a flat arch, the lintel is inserted first ensuring a minimum of 150mm of bearing each side of the opening and making sure that the lintel is set back a little from the face brickwork. For the camber arch, the timber turning piece should be firmly secured in position using a framework of timber supports and folding wedges so that it cannot move during arch construction. It should be positioned just back from the face of the wall so that it does not interfere with bricklayer's lines. Once securely positioned, transfer information taken from the drawing via the lath and staff and apply to the lintel or turning piece.

A lintel can be used on which to position the arch long enough to allow a minimum of 150mm either side of the opening. and it should be levelled both ways and bedded about 5mm back from the front of the window position. This allows for a timber trim to be secured under the soffit to hide the front of the lintel at a later date.

Once the lintel has been firmly positioned on lime mortar and has set, the skewback cuts can be prepared. To do this, the position of the striking point should be established. The measurement is taken from the drawing and carefully measured from the upper edge of the lintel (bottom edge of arch) via a plumb line and tape measure. A batten can be fixed just inside the window opening, the striking point position marked upon it and a small nail inserted.

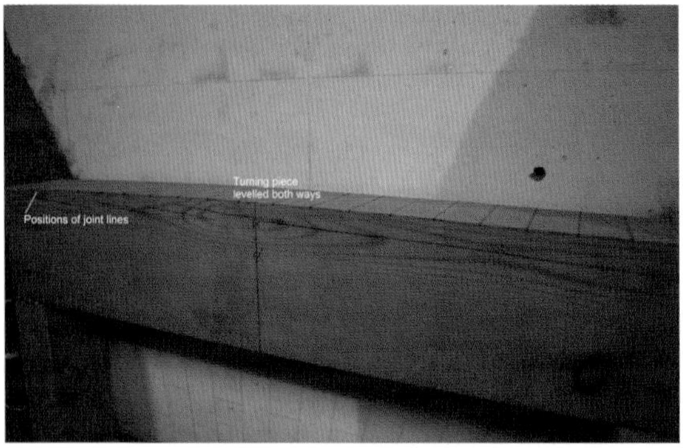

Marking up turning piece for a gauged camber arch. The turning piece must be level both ways. The bricks are laid just to the pencil lines (A and B). The consequences of not doing so will immediately become apparent.

Attach a length of seamstress twine or fishing line to the nail at the striking point and extend the line to ensure it reaches beyond the extrados of the arch. This will be used to check the voussoir positions when they are laid.

Marking up a lintel during setting out. The markings can be transferred directly from the arch drawing to the intrados via a piece of plasterer's lath. Using an adjustable square to extend the marks on the lintel will help to ensure that the voussoir is laid square to the opening.

Preparing the Skewbacks

The bricks can be dry-bedded in the positions where they would actually be laid, or placed, on spacers equivalent to joint thickness. This is so that the cut line will be in the correct place when the brick is bedded. Establish the line of cut on the skewbacks by means of the line taken from the striking point, through the mark of the end the voussoir arris made on the lintel or tuning piece, and up to the marked staff placed on top of the arch. Carefully mark the bricks along this line with a pencil and then re-draw the line on the bricks using a steel ruler or sliding bevel.

Construction

The arch can then be constructed working from the skewbacks to the centre, from each side and laying the voussoirs left-hand side and right-hand side alternately. The voussoirs can be pre-soaked but as they are being selected, plunge them into clean water for

Taking the line form the striking point through the correct mark on the lintel or turning piece at the intrados will establish the correct angle of cut for the skewbacks. Here an adjustable square is being used to check the position of the line on the lintel mark.

Method of marking bricks for cutting to angle with the brick seated on weep vents commonly used in cavity wall construction. Note that a line is set up across the opening to ensure that the skewback bricks are laid level.

Checking the bedded skewbacks for correct angle. The importance of the accuracy of the position of the striking point in this operation cannot be overstated. Note that the mortar joints of the newly laid skewbacks are tight as are the originals.

just under a minute. Either dip or float the bricks in the lime mortar, or butter them using the flat-fronted trowel (*see* Tools and Equipment). Position the voussoir according to the mark on the lintel or arch centre, checking using the striking point line and extrados staff marks, and bed with a light tap with a rubber mallet. Minor rubbing of the voussoir may be needed on occasion and a rubbing stone is taken onsite for this purpose.

When laying the voussoirs, two or more lines set up across the arch position to keep the arch aligned as it is constructed otherwise there may be a tendency for the faces of the voussoirs not to be square to the adjacent brickwork. The bricks can be dipped in lime (traditional method) or buttered using a continental-style trowel, according to the preference of the bricklayer.

Once the arch has been constructed, the voussoirs may sit slightly above the extrados line. These can be rubbed down to the line neatly, so that the brick course above can be laid to line with the bricks either side of the opening. The bricks above the arch can then be re-laid in their correct positions. No further work can take place on the arch until the joints have set sufficiently, perhaps up to a week.

An arch set on scaffold platform ready for construction. Note the platform set up to the rear of the lift with the numbered voussoirs with the extrados towards the bricklayer.

Plunging the voussoir in water for about a minute is necessary to ensure adhesion of the lime mortar and to prevent rapid drying.

The key brick is the final brick to be laid in the arch and should be a tight fit. The rear of the arch is filled with mortar as work proceeds so there is no void behind it. Note, the three lines have been used here to ensure face alignment.

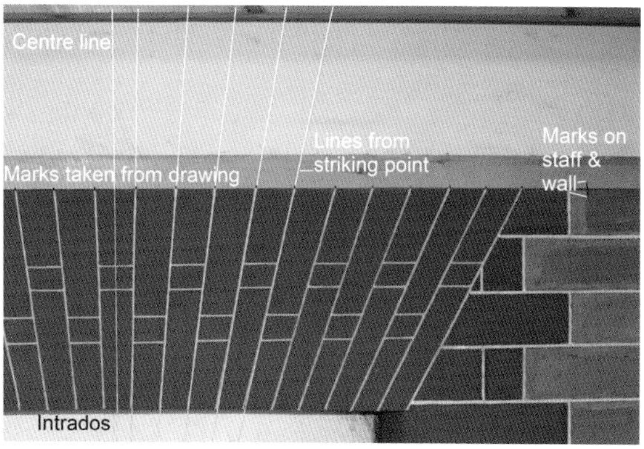

Accuracy during construction is ensured by the alignment of marks at the intrados and extrados using the cord from the striking point.

Checking Accuracy of Position of Voussoirs

Accuracy during construction can be tested by using the marked staff to check voussoir positions on the extrados and use of the line from the striking point (several lines are shown to emphasize this but only one is used). The wall and staff are marked with pencil lines so that when the latter is laid on top of the arch, the lines coincide to ensure staff is placed at exactly the same point each time the positions of the voussoirs are checked at the extrados. By these means, any inaccuracy will very quickly be identified.

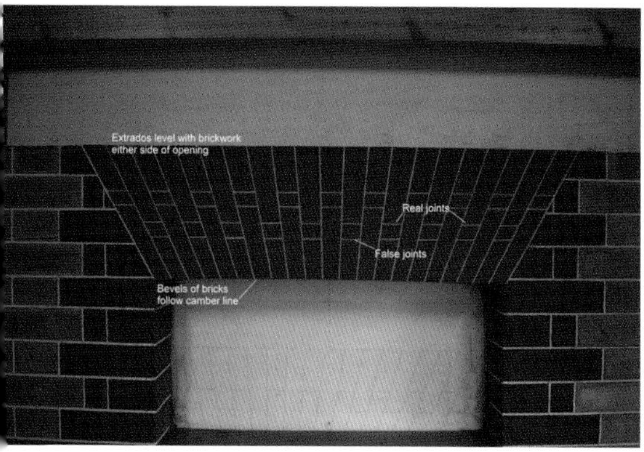

A camber arch with the supporting turning piece removed. Note the curvature of the camber, with each bevel being different.

Example of a gauged camber arch in Flemish bond, showing cement pointing and general neglect. Note the angled brick extensions or Dutch joints towards the top of the arch.

Finishing the Arch

When the arch has properly set (after about a week), the face of the arch can be rubbed down flat with a pumice stone to remove any minor aberrations. The arch extrados line can also be rubbed down so that it is in the exact line of the adjacent brick work. Brush off all dust and then wash off the arch. Finally, using the tip of a small tool to remove the dust staining will reveal the white joint lines. A degree of pointing up is often necessary and specialist tuck irons would be used for this task. Sometimes, gauged arches were tuck pointed to match the surrounding façade work (*see* The Use of Traditional Brick to the End of the Eighteenth Century).

Repairing a Gauged Arch

Apart from inappropriate intervention and modern materials, gauged arches crack or slip for structural reasons, often natural settlement. Often, they are repointed with cement, the joints having been first widened by inappropriate use of grinders. In repairing these arches, one should be mindful of the soft nature of original rubbers and that further unnecessary damage could easily be inflicted. Voussoirs in gauged arches were often extended in length because the bricks needed to give the desired depth of face, and the angled joints were blinded out using pigment and or brick dust.

Remove vine eyes, nails etc. from the arch and carefully remove cement to a depth of approximately 25mm using fine tungsten-tipped chisel by hand and hacksaw blades. Note how the joints have been widened when the arch was prepared for cement pointing.

After cleaning the arch with clean water and natural bristle brush, fill small holes and minor damaged areas using the pigmented mortar techniques previously discussed. Blind out the joints that were originally used to lengthen the voussoirs and to re-establish Flemish bond.

Fine mist spraying throughout the work is important to provide adhesion for pointing mortar and to prevent drying out.

Using a straight edge, make horizontal housing incisions 1–1.5mm deep on the stopped-out joints.

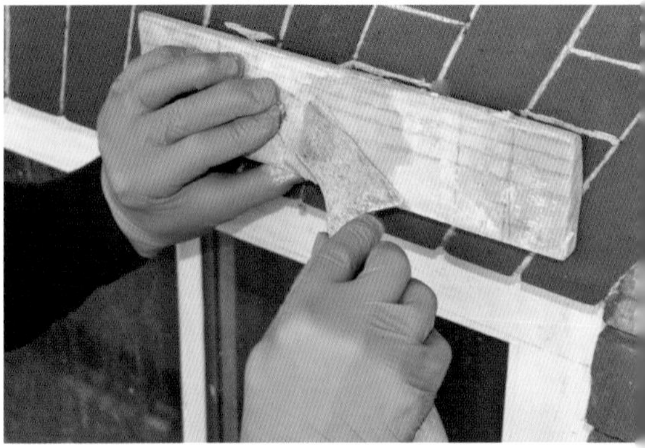

Repoint the arch using an appropriately sized tuck iron and a lime putty mix. A very fine or silica sand is required here.

Chapter Eleven

Lime Pointing

Pointing is a term given to finishing the bed joints in a specific way following the construction of the brickwork. Jointing, in contrast, is carried out as the work proceeds. Pointing finishes were deliberately applied to improve the finish of a façade, often applied as a thin veneer over the bed joints before it had fully hardened. Today, all finish styles could be regarded as pointing because, when applied, it is usually as remedial work and because, in conservation (or restoration), a full depth of structural pointing is applied, usually 25mm or more. Lime pointing performs the practical function of preventing water ingress due to the way it is compressed, as well as being aesthetically pleasing. Executing authentic historic pointing requires a combination of practical skill, sound knowledge of materials and knowledge of the historic context of the methods originally used.

Traditionally, most types of buildings would have originally had some form of jointing or pointing finish except for utilitarian buildings such as farm buildings, canal bridges etc., which tended to have flat joints. One notable exception are horse stables of high-status houses which were often highly decorative. Even the humblest of country cottages in the Georgian era can be found with a ruled or penny ha'penny joint. In this chapter, some key finishes from within this period of study of this book are explained.

Preparation for Pointing

Prior to the commencement of any works where scaffold is required, the boards nearest the building are turned back so that any water or debris can fall straight through to ground level and not down the face of the brickwork. Buildings can sometimes be seen with a horizontal smudge running across the building at scaffold lift height. This is staining caused by lime splashing against the walls where the boards where not turned back during the working day. Work is generally carried out from the top to bottom of an elevation so brickwork, windows and other features could be sheeted up and protected from lime, dirt and debris.

Plastic sheeting can be used to catch the cement and brick debris on the lifts and so facilitate the task of cleaning up between phases as well as conserving valuable original mortar which can be used again (*see* Materials). Before pointing work commences, coverings such as hessian sheeting, which are used to protect the mortar from drying out, are prepared and made ready at hand (*see* Materials). Hessian should be thoroughly wetted and draped over the nearest

A simple awning like this will reduce the rate of moisture loss through drying when used in conjunction with fine mist spraying of the brickwork and pointing.

scaffold bars ready for covering but should not be applied to the walls soaking wet as they could cause mortar to run down the face of the work. The hessian will soon lose most of the excess moisture and will be ready to fix in position covering work that has been completed as the work progresses, keeping the work cool and out of the glare of the sun.

Should any shade need to be created, particularly on south facing elevations, or wind breaks erected then this should be done before the pointing begins. Pointing can be adversely affected by the sun and can quickly bleach. The covering or 'wrapping' of a scaffold during colder and wetter months is a consideration and highly recommended for working in autumn and winter. It will help to keep out frost, minimize the effects of desiccating winds and enables work to continue in wet and cold weather. Even with the scaffold covered, the use of hessian and garden fleece will provide extra protection for the lime. One disadvantage of having the scaffold covered is that the brickwork will not benefit from rain showers which assist in curing the lime by keeping the hessian damp, but this is a minor consideration. In cold weather, covered scaffolds can be heated to keep temperatures at the levels suitable for lime use.

Preparation of Mortar for Pointing

Experience dictates that lime mortars benefit from having been mixed up in advance of a minimum of twenty-four hours. The materials ferment together and take on a fatty, more workable quality making them easier to apply. Grittier aggregates, when used with hydraulic lime mortars, can tend to be more difficult to pick up on a jointer, but this is not the case when using lime rich and air lime hot mix mortars mixes. If the mortar mix is too wet, there will be more chance of cracking due to rapid moisture loss and staining of the brickwork when it is applied, and so would have to be 'gauged up' to take out the wetness. It can also be dried out sufficiently by spreading the mortar onto a clean scaffold plank which will absorb the excess moisture. A hot lime pointing mix can be made to a ratio of one part lime to three parts sand. With the expansion of the quicklime on slaking, this will result in a mortar rich in binder.

The prepared mortar should be the consistency of modelling clay – doughy and malleable. Once made, they can be stored in sealed tubs where the mortar cannot be contaminated. The composition of the mix should be noted so that colour and texture do not vary in subsequent mixes. Experience will inform the bricklayer what area can comfortably be undertaken in a day, but the area covered by 25kg quantity of mortar will depend on the depth of the raking out. Quality not quantity is one approach to be taken, as there is little point racing through an elevation in lime pointing if the brickwork is left filthy with staining or incorrectly applied mortar. When opening the tub of stored putty mortar on the day of use, some

Pointing mortar should be doughy and retain its shape when squeezed into a ball.

Preparing material such as this pointing mortar ahead of the work is an efficient practice which also makes for a better mortar.

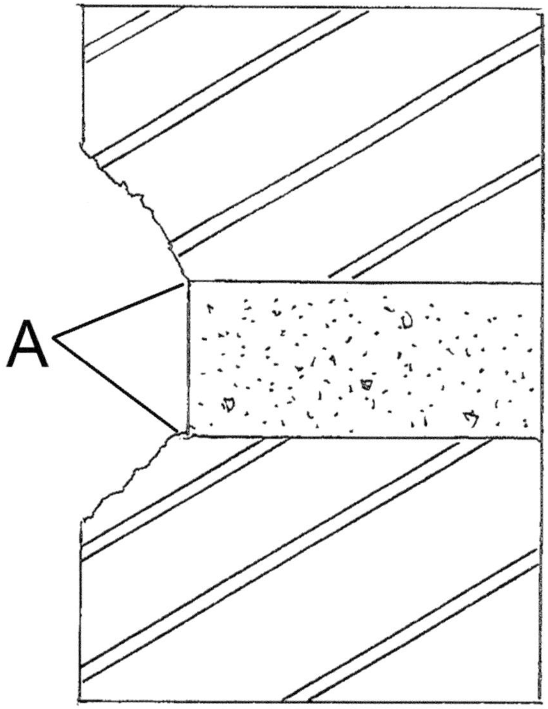

Historic brickwork that has eroded joints should be pointed to the narrowest neck of the joint (A), as shown here. This will ensure that the joints do not appear overly wide whilst protecting the neck and retaining the character of a building.

Lifting off the pointing mortar with a jointer from a plastic hawk. The mortar should be flattened out on the hawk.

Pointing using a flat plastic hawk, made from modern felt protector attached to a wooden handle for convenience (*see* Tools).

water may have accumulated on top but this will be absorbed when the mortar is knocked up. No attempt should be made to add more water in the mistaken belief that it is too dry.

Conservation Pointing

Modern conservation pointing is a method that can be employed to patch point where there is no evidence remaining of another traditional joint finish having been used, or where patch pointing of small areas are involved. Bricklayers may use slightly different techniques to apply and finish mortar joints when carrying out conservation pointing. But different techniques in application do not necessarily matter, provided the finish is the same and it is protected and cured properly. Key to the success of the work is that the substrate is raked back sufficiently, say 25mm depending on the condition of the mortar (it may have to be deeper). The mortar is compressed into the joint by using a jointer which fits the joint (*see* Tools and Equipment). Although the conservation joint could be regarded as 'flush', in reality the joint should be finished slightly back from the arrises of the brickwork by 1–2mm. This is because of wear to the arrises over hundreds of years which widen the mouth of the joint and, if filled completely, give the appearance of an excessively wide joint which is both stark and ungainly to the eye, increasing the ratio of mortar to brick in the brickwork generally.

One method is to pick up the mortar from the board or hawk by the appropriate jointing tool and inserting it into the joint as cleanly and neatly as possible. To do this, the jointer must fit in to the joint horizontally so that it can be compressed. For some, the trickiest part of this process is to be able to lift the mortar from the hawk cleanly.

Another method is to place the hawk up to the arris of the brick and push the flattened mortar directly into the joint until it is full and then to strike it off flush with the brick. The risk in this method is staining caused by the edge of the hawk against the brickwork, so the edge should be wiped clean regularly. If the mortar has not been sufficiently flattened on the board, this too will cause staining.

Using a small tool to pick out any overhanging lime mortar.

Using a small hawk to push flattened lime putty into the joint.

Once the mortar has been inserted, texture or 'usher' the surface to iron out hairline cracks and imperfections using a piece of lath or similar. This method will prepare the joints for the brush tamping phase. This process offers the opportunity to remove minor lime marks that may have been left on the brickwork.

Where joints are very tight, tape such as the blue decorators' tape can be used and affixed either on the brick side of the joint or over the joint with a slot cut in it to it to push in mortar. Either way, this method is extremely time-consuming though it will keep the brick arrises lime free. For narrow joints of 2–5mm, tuck irons can be used for this work (*see* Tuck pointing).

Small lime marks can be removed as the work proceeds by using a small piece of 'rubber' brick which lightly pumices off the mark, or by using the rough side of a household kitchen sponge pad to flick off specks of lime. On no account should a wet brush be used to try and remove a lime stain as it will exacerbate the situation and will result in lime 'bloom' on the brickwork. When the joint has sufficiently set, that is to say it is 'leather hard' and can be compressed with a fingernail possibly even the day after pointing has taken place, it can be given a unified, weathered finish by banging with a churn brush. This method exposes aggregates within the lime and opens the pores of the joint, facilitating evaporation of moisture and presents a unified even finish. If this is carried out too early, the brush will pick up the wet lime and it will be applied to the surface of the brickwork causing staining and will result in an unnatural stippled effect on the joint. Horizontal brushing of the joints will result in tram lines created in it which will not be pleasing to the eye.

Using the churn brush to tamp a conservation mortar joint. The mortar is beaten using the brush with a flexible wrist movement. Brushes used for this purpose should be kept dry and separate from those used to clean utensils, etc.

Note that putty mortars will remain flexible and moisture retentive for longer than hydraulic ones and would need to be left longer before they could be beaten in this way. This method of a brushed finish is for a modern conservation joint only.

Throughout the pointing process, a fine mist should be applied to keep the surfaces damp and once a reasonable are of pointing has been applied, it should be covered by the now damp hessian which can be applied by nailing it up over the completed area but preferably hanging over it to create a micro-climate underneath. The hessian should be applied in enough damp layers to keep the moisture in the inner most layer until the following morning when re-wetting of the hessian can take place.

A panel of completed conservation pointing. Note the even and weathered joint finish, dressed back between 1 and 2mm from the brick arris. Note the brick cleanliness of this example.

Provided that the mortar is well matched, and the correct preparation and methodology used, the conservation joint enables the subtle blending in of new with existing lime pointing and is therefore ideal for patch repairs. Moreover, its use will avoid stark contrasts in colours and techniques which would otherwise be the case if attempts were made to copy or parody original joint finishes. Some have suggested that this form of pointing is 'easy', giving rise to a theory that anyone can do it. Whilst it does have fewer elements than other traditional pointing finishes, and perhaps less precision is required, it is still very easy to make a complete mess of it due to poor use of tools, lack of experience and understanding of the materials used. The most common errors are careless use of tools resulting in dirty brickwork and lime bloom – a result of tamping the lime too early.

Pointing mortars, however well matched, are new materials and will still potentially be brighter than the original mortar. Although in time they will begin to develop patina, various techniques at tinting the joints can be carried out. Whilst some are opposed to this false ageing of the joints, others are averse to the newness of the lime mortar. Sample panels are a good way of demonstrating the finish colour and style of joint, and trials for the use of stewed tea or black pigmented water can be carried out on them. Whichever option is chosen, if indeed it is considered necessary at all, careful testing on an unobtrusive place should be considered. Note that using washes in this way does not compensate for joints which have been allowed to bleach white through lack of protection, and have failed as a consequence.

Double Struck Joint

This type of joint was used in the Medieval, Tudor and Jacobean periods. It was a way of dividing the generally wide joints of these periods into two to create shadow and interest to the eye.

The joint is first filled more or less flush but with no texturing or smoothing of the joint.

Using a dotter, pointing trowel or suitable jointing iron run the blade at an angle under the topmost arris of the brick, at a blade's thickness, to form the upper angle and repeat this action on the lower half of the joint.

Execute the perpendicular joints by treating each side of the joint in the same way.

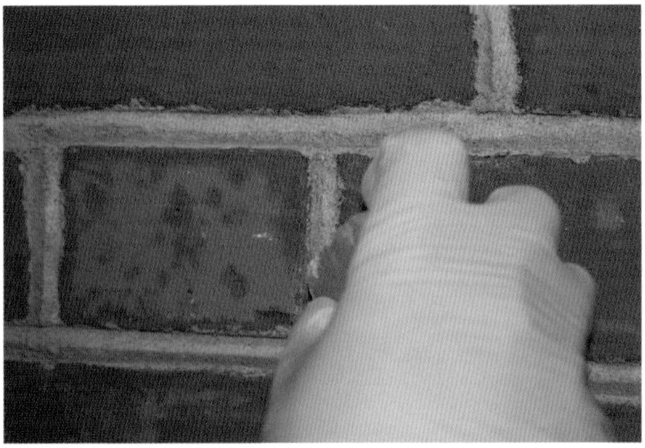

Use a piece of rubber brick, a sponge or brush to remove small lime particles. Wait twenty-four hours to brush with soft brush at 45°.

As with conservation pointing, the joint is filled flush before being tooled to produce the double struck finish. A straight edge is not required here, but instead the brick arrises provide the guide for the jointing iron.

Penny Struck or Ruled Jointing

Georgian bricklayers often used a method of joint which created a geometrical pattern on the joint and which drew the observers' eye away from the ragged edges of the bricks used. This method, the ruled joint or penny struck joint as it came to be known, was widely used in the seventeenth and eighteenth centuries and even early in the nineteenth century, before weather struck and cut finishes proliferated when bricks became much more uniform in size and shape. The method of surface preparation is as described above. A putty lime mortar is perhaps the best mortar to use for this joint because it is fattier, retains moisture for longer and a crisp, neat compression line can be achieved in the mortar.

Sometimes, this joint can be seen as having been executed by using a brick trowel run across the top of a spirit level to create the line. Not only is this method historically inaccurate, but it will

The bed joints are filled and compressed first, like in the previous finishes, ensuring the bricks are kept free of staining as far as possible.

The flattened bed joints are ruled first, making sure that the tuck iron is at 90° to the straight edge. With a firm grip, compress the iron whilst drawing it to the right, using the front $^2/_3$ of it.

The mortar is then applied into the dampened perpendicular joints by compression, taking care not to disrupt the ruled joint above.

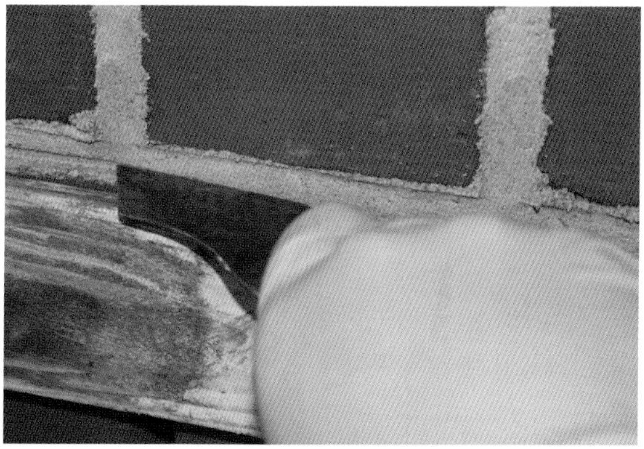

Using a straight edge to rule the horizontal joints.

'he joints are flattened approximately 1mm back from the arrises. f the joint is taken to the edge of the arris, it can appear overly vide and can dominate the brick.

result in an incision rather than a compression of the joint and one in which it is difficult to accurately gauge the depth therefore producing a wavy line. A spirit level is not used to produce this joint as it is in tuck pointing because the ruling will not stand out sharply like a tuck pointing ribbon. Instead, the straight edge, or feather edge, is used and held centrally to both bed and perpendicular joints. The width of the compression should really reflect the width of the joint. Rulings of up to 5mm wide have been observed but on joints of approximately 10mm, a 1–2mm tuck iron is more common.

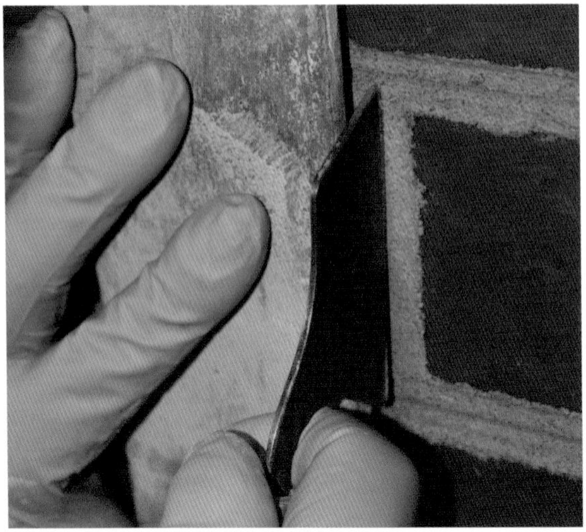

Rule the perpendicular joints by holding the straight edge vertically and central to the joint over a number of courses.

Brush the joint lightly with a soft brush the following day, ensuring that the ruled lines are not blurred or smudged. The ruling compression should be crisp and precise.

Make the compression to meet the two horizontal rulings, taking care not to cross the lines.

Pick out mortar where it shouldn't be using a small tool.

A panel of brickwork with joints raked back to a depth of 25mm, cleaned of debris, washed out and ready for colour washing. This illustrates the level of surface preparation required for all pointing styles.

Tuck Pointing

Tuck pointing is notoriously difficult to repair or blend in to existing brickwork because of the difficulty in matching the colours and patina of the original stopping and putty ribbon, so careful testing and trials would be required. When patched in on an elevation, it will form a sharp contrast with areas left untreated. If, however, an opportunity arises to complete a full elevation as an evidence-based restoration, the effects can be stunning. Another approach is to repair specific stages of the work by colour matching and refilling the stopping and even incising the housing into it, but not applying the ribbon.

Tuck pointing is a skill which takes a great deal of practice before it can be performed on a property. In past centuries, it is likely that specialist teams of pointers followed the bricklayers and applied the pointing. Nowadays, there are perhaps one or two firms that specialize solely in tuck pointing, but those traditional bricklayers trained and practised in this skill can produce excellent work, too. Following a systematic approach, tuck pointing can be executed in a phased approach as set out below:

- preparing the scaffold, shade and protection
- preparing the surfaces
- setting out
- making the rabbit skin glue solution
- making and applying colour wash
- making stopping
- making the lime putty to form the ribbon
- execution
- protection aftercare and covering.

Preparation of Surfaces

Preparation of the wall surfaces for tuck pointing is the same as with other pointing methods discussed and should be approached in the same way with the joints ultimately being sufficiently raked out to a depth of approximately 25mm, clean, free from debris and sufficiently dampened so that the stopping adheres correctly. Preparation for working in inclement weather is important, so protection from sun and rain should be set up before work starts. During warm weather, shade or awnings will help prevent it from drying out too quickly but mist spraying should be employed through the work.

Rabbit Skin Glue Solution

Rabbit skin glue solution is formed by mixing boiling water with the glue granules to form a consistency not unlike a thin wallpaper paste in consistency (*see* Materials). Boiling water is applied to the granules in a bucket which should then be thoroughly mixed to prevent globules of rabbit skin sticking to the bottom of the bucket. Once prepared, it can be stored in a sealable container such as a five-gallon container, shown here. A capful of household disinfectant can be added to negate the unpleasant smell of the solution.

Colour Wash

Colour wash is a remarkable application which acts like a coating on the wall but is neither a paint nor a form of limewash. It is highly effective in creating a unifying base colour to brickwork prior to the insertion of stopping into the brickwork joints. It is made from the combination of boiling water, rabbit skin glue, alum used as a fixative and pigment (*see* Materials). Different shades of red or yellow can be used to achieve the desired colour, the latter for London stock bricks in the south of the country. For yellow washes, iron sulphate is added to the mix as this will give lustre to the bricks. Testing of the colours on the elevation to be colour washed should be carried out prior to committing to the colour.

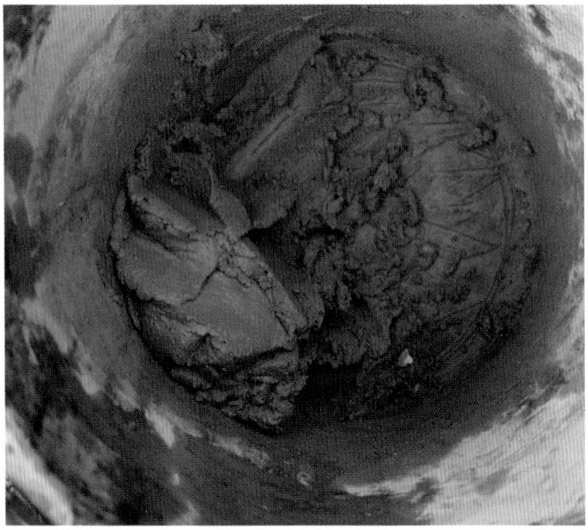

A portion of stopping mix ready to use. The colour of the finished material can be made to suit, but it can be found that quite a lot of ochre must be added to give the required depth of colour, which is why trials and tests are important. Adding a measured amount of colour wash into the stopping mix can provide extra depth of colour.

Stopping

The stopping is a coloured mortar which should be matched as closely as possible to the bricks with which it is being used and tested on the elevation to be stopped up. It is made from a mixture of building sand, silver sand and NHL 3.5 or NHL 2 lime, depending on the building era, and mixed with natural pigments. Natural pigments can be obtained from a good conservation materials stockist, from some specialist art shops or directly from the quarries where they are produced, for example in the south of France. Unlike modern chemical colours which fade, natural earth pigments combine completely with the lime particles and form a homogenous material. To ensure that the materials are fully combined, dry sand, pigments and lime are sieved together up to three times. When mixed, the stopping should have a doughy consistency, the moisture obtained not from fresh water but by means of the addition of solution of glue size. This will help to form a set, provide some weather resistance and provide a durable finish ensuring that the colour wash will adhere to the wall.

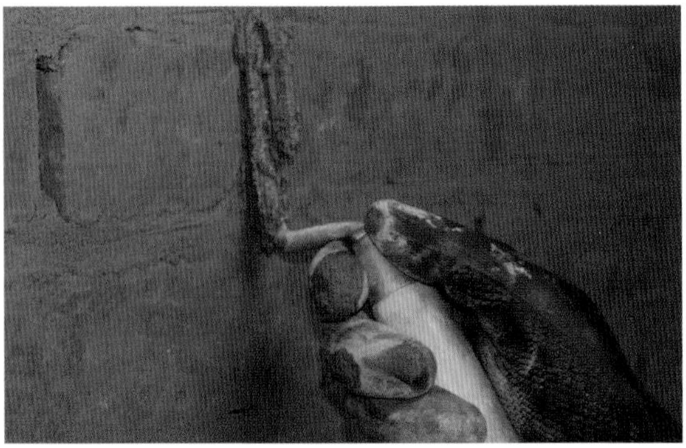

Insert the stopping into the joints using a jointer and then flush off with the brick. When inserting the stopping, the arrises do not need to be kept clean as in normal conservation pointing.

Putty Ribbon

The putty ribbon is made from a mixture of the fine silica (110 sand) and NHL 2 lime. Kiln-dried sand is not suitable to form the putty mixture because the aggregate particles are too big (*see* Materials) and will be dragged out when the ribbon is cut using a Frenchman, creating an untidy, ragged line (*see* Techniques below). A small amount of boiled linseed oil can be added to the putty as needed to make it feel fattier and more workable. The consistency of the putty should be doughy, yet not too dry as it will be difficult to mould it to the back of the straight edge and will not smooth out well over the housing. The putty is flattened out on the back of the straight edge to make it easier to pinch off in application. 'Tuck pointing putty' can be bought from some suppliers, but it can have a tendency to be too wet and sticky making it hard to apply and risking the leaching of the lime into the stopping.

Use of Tools

The length of tuck iron (*see* Tools and Equipment) to be used for the bed joints depends on the preference, experience and/or skill of the user and any evidence of existing work. Using the longer tuck irons, usually with 125mm blades, covers areas more quickly whilst the shorter irons, usually 75mm blades, are better suited for the perpendicular joints – but some prefer to use the latter for both bed and perpendicular joints.

Tuck Pointing Stages

Tuck pointing must be set out from the top of the elevation ensuring that all joints, both horizontally and vertically, are equidistant starting with the top of the elevation. Vertical joints should be lined through top to bottom using a plumb bob. To ensure consistency in setting out, traditionally tuck pointing was sometimes applied directly over bricks which were not scored to receive the ribbon and was therefore prone to falling off due to lack of adhesion.

A piece of plasterer's lath, or a piece of roofing batten, can be used to flatten out the stopping and iron out hairline cracks.

The stopping is lightly brushed with a soft broom head or similar. This will remove loose particles and work the stopping into the brickwork.

Apply another coat of colour wash to the wall surface to add lustre to the colour and to help blend in the stopping.

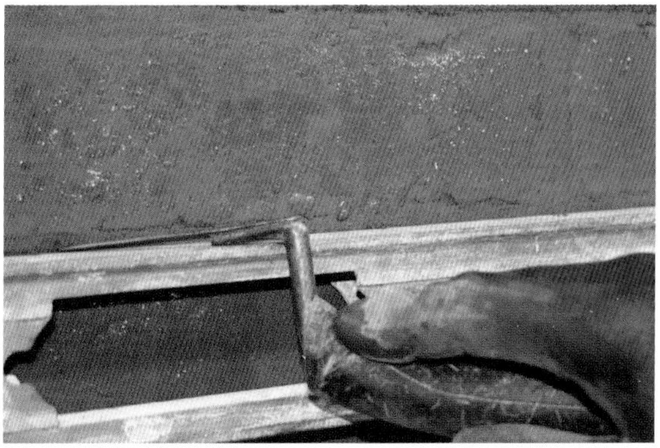

Form the horizontal housing by running a knife or appropriate tool over a spirit level held firmly, centrally in the joint, creating the housing.

Unlike the process of conservation pointing, in which the mortar is set back from the brick arrises, here it is used to fill all recesses and rough edges along the arrises in order to effectively create an appearance of a continuous slab of red (or yellow) masonry. The stopping should be left until it has gone off a little. If it is too wet, the stopping will bleed into the ribbon. Too dry and the ribbon will not adhere when applied and is likely to drop off.

The housing is the name for the incision into which the putty will be tucked. It can be incised through the centre of the joints using a small knife or the tip of a flat jointer, starting first with the bed joints and then the perpendicular joints. The housing is incised between 1–2mm deep whilst the stopping still green enough to do so.

Incising the housing on the perpendicular joints. The long spirit level will enable several joints to be housed at one time. Ensure that the incision meets the horizontal one but does not go beyond it.

Once the housing has been completed over a given area, it is very lightly brushed at a 45° angle with a soft brush. This will remove loose particles and lightly rough up the edges of the housing to enable a better bond with the ribbon when it is applied.

The straight edge is offered up to the housing and held in position. The tuck iron should sit central to the housing line when it is offered up to the joint. The putty is spread thinly to be able to pick up just enough to apply on to the housing.

It is important that the housing is made by incision and not compression; this is so that the edges of the housing are a little rough to provide a key for the putty ribbon. Note that if the stopping is too gritty, the blade will drag out particles of aggregates spoiling the housing and making it more difficult to apply the putty.

Applying the Putty Ribbon

Using the tuck iron, pinch off enough putty from the back of the straight edge so that when it is applied to the housing, the minimum amount of material is pushed to the sides to be trimmed off and tram lines are formed which will form the cutting lines for the width of ribbon required.

Once the putty has been applied and smoothed over to produce a flat ribbon with a ragged top and bottom edge, it is ready for trimming along the visible 'tram lines'.

Applying horizontal putty ribbon using a 75mm tuck iron. Apply three blades' worth, working from right to left. Then run over all three applications once with the tuck iron to unify them before one more pass over the entire length of ribbon.

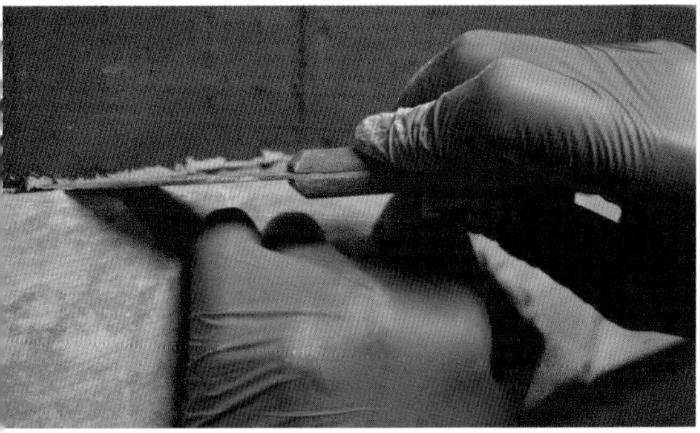

The straight edge is once again placed in position, ensuring that it is possible to trim the bed joint along its top and bottom edge. When trimming the horizontal joint and bottom edge of the ribbon first, the nib of the Frenchman should face downwards and vice versa for the top edge.

When a sufficient number of horizontal joints have been applied and trimmed, the perp ribbons can be applied. A number of perps can be applied and trimmed without moving the straight edge from its position. When applying the ribbon, apply twice starting with the bottom half of the perp followed by the top, and then run the joint through from top to bottom ensuring that the perp joins the horizontal ribbon.

Frenchman

Sharpen Frenchmen on a wet stone regularly to ensure clean cut ribbon.

The perp joints can now be trimmed. Position the straight edge so that the LH side and RH side can be trimmed without moving the straight edge away from the wall. The nib of the Frenchman should be facing to the left for the former, and to the right for the latter.

Touching up with a fine make-up brush and some colour wash will cover very minor lime staining around the ribbon. Note, spraying with a fine mist at regular intervals is crucial.

Crisp and precise division of colours is important for visual impact. The colour wash has unified the bricks, yet on closed examination the surface nature of the brick can still be seen.

Forming Colour Contrasts In Eighteenth-Century Brickwork

As has been seen in previous chapters, contrast was much favoured in the eighteenth century. Achieving authentic and durable colours on brickwork requires knowledge of materials and their application. The colours used are generally a deeper version of the colour of the existing brick, formed by making stopping and washes of different colours. They look particularly striking when used in conjunction with tuck pointing, although such contrasts are often found with penny struck or ruled jointing, too.

Protection of Fresh Lime Repairs and Pointing

Lime work should be carried out in consideration of the elements that might affect it. As has previously been discussed, awnings and shade should be set up before work starts in summer and/or covered scaffolds that provide this protection. Lime work should be protected during the project by spraying and covering up stretches of completed work. Putty limes do not require the same levels of hydration as hydraulic limes because they carbonate from the atmosphere. They will still bleach, however, if left exposed to direct wind and sunshine too early. After work, brickwork should be covered according to the time of year considering factors such as temperatures, the effects of wind, frost and heavy rain. Failure to do so can lead to damage of the work, staining and bleaching of joints. Various materials can be used for protection, but the primary aims are to retain moisture around the brickwork under or within the coverings, and to protect it from the effects of the wind.

Protection of lime mortars can take different forms. Here a chimney has been first wrapped in wet hessian, then a layer of garden fleece and finally a plastic sheet to protect the work from desiccating winds.

Chapter Twelve

Maintenance of Traditional Brickwork

Maintenance Checks

Regular maintenance of a traditional building can avoid the build-up of costs for much larger repair work that can arise if a small problem is left unattended to. One priority for maintenance checks is the prevention of moisture penetration into the building, so the check could include all those fixtures and fittings designed to shed water away from the roof, walls and footings and direct it away in to drains and gullies.

Maintenance checks can be carried out by the homeowner who might carry out some minor repairs but where these become more complex, or where there are apparently daunting issues such as large damp patches appearing on the inside, conservation accredited building professionals or specialists can be brought in. They can identify and diagnose the problem particularly on larger more complex buildings. Specialist craftsmen and women are often able to identify problems relating to their own craft discipline, for example, an experienced carpenter is likely to be able to pick out problem areas relating to the woodwork whilst a qualified conservation bricklayer will be able to identify problems directly relating to, and affecting, the brickwork.

Maintenance checks should take place at least twice a year, once in spring, and again when all leaves have fallen in late autumn so that blocked gutters, etc. can be addressed without having to redo the process. Paying more attention to the brickwork on a much more regular basis can only be a good thing and is likely to increase the awareness of the things that look out of place.

A maintenance check should be thorough and systematic, working from the chimneys down to the base of the walls and leaving nothing out. There is little point in leaving an area of the building unchecked when it has a direct bearing on the survivability of the brickwork (or any material). Working alone on a maintenance check where heights and confined spaces are involved has many potential hazards and should be avoided, and professional help should be sought. In all cases, it is important to inform others that a maintenance check is underway.

Equipment for Carrying out Maintenance Checks

Access equipment such as ladders, platforms or cherry pickers may be required to access all areas. The people doing the maintenance check should have good PPE such as masks and even protective disposable suits if, for example, access to the roof space is required. Masks are important here because if pigeons

A leaking gutter is the cause of this erosion above a doorway. Note, the eroded joints and build-up of moss associated with the presence of moisture. This problem requires action before it becomes more than a maintenance issue.

have been nesting their droppings can be extremely harmful, as can the fibres from modern insulation (if it is present). Good lighting is essential, so torches and if necessary 110-volt lighting systems. Recording what is found by means of photographs, handwritten notes or pre-prepared maintenance sheets is useful to avoid missing areas of concern which is easy to do in larger and more complex buildings. A camera or a phone to take pictures could be regarded as essential to record what has been discovered, and digital recording devices can also very useful. Whilst drones can be a very useful tool, they are not fool proof.

Flashing can become split and work loose over decades. In this case, the brickwork into which it is inserted also needs remedial attention.

What to Look For

Seeking the examples of decay mechanisms and their symptoms, found in the chapter about the vulnerabilities of traditional brickwork, is the object of the check but there could be other seemingly innocuous things that are also discovered whilst carrying out the check. One approach is to use the assessment approach seen in a previous chapter and work around the building (*see* Assessment of Traditional Brickwork). In this manner, the building can be divided into numbered elevations which will make it easier to find the items when it comes to the owner or outside help rectifying them. It is useful to start the maintenance check at the chimneys and work downwards looking at:

- chimneys and roof coverings
- rainwater removal
- walls
- drains, gullies and vents
- ground level (at the foot of the walls) particularly where there are adjacent hard surfaces
- inside roof spaces.

Walls

Walls should be checked for areas of mortar erosion, loose mortar, cracked bricks, spalling and staining. Vegetation growth including climbers should be controlled to ensure they do not gain access to brickwork or underneath soffit boards.

Chimneys

It was normal to have a fire in each room of a traditional brick house which served to keep the house warm and to allow air to circulate. Today they are often be regarded as out of sight, out of mind and have the potential to become conduits of damp into the heart of the building. Because chimneys are very

A chimney top in a poor state of repair. Dangerously loose bricks, cracked and dislodged flaunching and hollow joints, make this a repair priority.

exposed, they will take the full force of the elements and as a result can suffer from accelerated erosion of joints, split and loose flashings and in some cases loose or displaced brickwork. This is sometimes compounded by the chimney being active and having done its job as intended, in some cases over centuries.

Traditional chimneys have often been repaired with modern materials at least once in their lifetime, and these repairs often exacerbate the situation. It is quite common to find the cement flaunching cracked and the pots unstable. It is difficult to ascertain the true condition of a chimney in a maintenance check without looking at it closely, and for that access equipment would be required.

Rainwater Removal

Examine gutters, hoppers and downpipes carefully to check the water is flowing freely, particularly during the pouring rain when it is possible to see where they are leaking or boiling over and the effect on the brickwork. Check flashings to ensure they are sound and fit for purpose.

Flashings

Flashings are often too high on the property to observe sufficiently without access equipment, but they can

Green staining could be an indication that this pipe is leaking, and that moisture is being retained on the wall. Plant growth will begin if this problem is left untreated.

Turf-clogged gutters can force water to spill over onto brickwork, soaking it and causing physical decay over time as well as the potential for damp inside.

Adjacent hard surfaces cause rain to splash against the softer brickwork and leads to plant growth in the hollow joints.

be a source of problems and should be checked (*see* previous section titled Chimneys). They may have been untouched for decades and may have become torn and dislodged by the wind. They may not have been installed correctly after a modern repair and been inserted using inappropriate materials. Commonly, not enough lead is inserted into the brickwork to make it sufficiently robust, with the lead wedges having fallen out. Sometimes associated problems with the brick and mortar around the flashing turn a maintenance check in to a sizeable repair and this should not be underestimated.

Pea gravel can be used to fill a trench dug along the base of walls in conjunction with a weed membrane on the soil. In some cases, a perforated pipe can also be an effective way of removing water. Here, broken brick has been used as a bottom layer of drainable material.

Drains, Gullies and Vents

Examine drains where plant growth appears or where there are broken or dislodged bricks or fittings. Late nineteenth- or early twentieth-century glazed gullies and pipes are prone to cracking and, if this is discovered, there is a chance of an accumulation of water against the footing brickwork below the gully.

Ground Level

At ground level, check that soil levels and paths next to walls are lower than the floor level inside the house by at least two courses. If this is not the case, it might become a further action project. Examine the base of the walls and identify patterns of decay causes by rain splashing or pooling water including spalling, eroded joints, etc. Air vents were often inserted in buildings long after the original date of construction but were placed there for a purpose, usually ventilation under wooden floors. Check they are sound and not covered by soil or vegetation.

The maintenance check might uncover green staining and moss growth especially if the area has been hidden by plant pots, etc. Concrete laid up to soft brickwork can be problematic when it is abutting traditional brickwork, and particularly if it is above the internal floor level as it prevents the removal of

Badly applied cement-based mortars contrast with the original time-worn mortar above.

water and provided a breeding ground for woodlice, etc. The symptoms will almost certainly be apparent if there is a problem. Action would include the removal of a strip of the concrete and filling with a drainable material such as a pea gravel.

Modern Repairs and Interventions

The insertion of service pipes such as water, gas and waste into a building can be unsightly, particularly where they have not been made good and cement mortars have been used. This type of problem might require specialist outside help to rectify if such repairs allow water ingress.

Further Action

Once the maintenance check is complete, a list can be drawn up of those that are manageable by the property owner and those which have been found and constitute bigger jobs where contractual or craft assistance is required. The combined findings can be coordinated into a project of repairs prioritized based on their level of severity. Where accumulated brickwork defects have been identified, this might be the point at which brick specialist advice is sought.

Good Practice in Maintenance Repair

Prior to a program of repairs, problems found with rainwater goods should be addressed first as there is no point carrying out pointing repairs, for example, if gutters are still allowing water on to the wall. Tackling empty joints and holes in brickwork can easily become a bigger job, so work should be confined to the problem area not on good, sound mortar. Even minor works instigated following a maintenance check should be approached like any brickwork conservation project in which all aspects including materials matching, retention of original materials, and minimal intervention are considered however minor the work is.

Lime bloom, caused by careless brushing of fresh joints into the brick, is unsightly and creates more work in trying to remove it. Note sagging gutter with vegetation in it.

Problems Associated with the Use of Lime Mortars

For the unacquainted and unskilled, using lime mortars with traditional brick has a number of potential pitfalls which can result in unsightly or unsound work. When working with lime it is not possible simply to pick it up and 'have a go' without training and education in its use and to imagine that good-quality work can be produced. Many buildings today are being defaced because the property owner has been convinced by an operative or company that they can 'use lime'. On the other hand, problems can also occur if a pointing or brickwork specification for the work produced by a building professional is lacking in sufficient detail or has insufficient quality control.

Working with lime requires sound knowledge of the materials and their limitations, and knowledge of historic buildings and how they were finished so a clear understanding of how a historic joint or conservation pointing should look. Moreover, building limes cannot be used like cement mortars which, because of their comparatively quick set, can be applied and left with minimal further action.

Troubleshooting

Symptom/example	Cause of problem	Remedial action
White, bleached joints which turn to powder if outer skin of joint is punctured with a nail	Joints have flash dried due to failure to prepare the surface sufficiently i.e., not raking out deep enough; failure to protect the work from the sun/wind during and after works, and failure to keep adequately damp during works	Remove pointing, prepare surfaces, re-point with awnings and shades then re-apply
White smears and stains from carbonated lime on brickwork from hands and tools	Poor hand skills	Use of some conservation-accredited solutions to remove staining
Brickwork joints appear wider than original	Mortar joints have been overfilled and have coated the arrises with wet lime	Remove pointing, clean brickwork, and repoint
Cracking and crazing of joints	Mortar too wet on application	Remove pointing, prepare surfaces and re-point
Joints do not conform to a known historic method	Lack of knowledge and understanding of historical context, resulting in brick joints which are an amalgam of different ideas	Undertake training in historic methods. Remove pointing, prepare surfaces and re-point
White hazy staining appears on the brickwork, known as 'lime bloom'	Beating or tamping a joint with a wet churn brush and/or too soon after mortar application	Malt vinegar for light hazing removal; bespoke solution for deeper staining
Dimples in lime mortar when tamped with churn brush	Lime still too wet for brushing	Smooth over and/or re-apply mortar then brush when lime is leather hard
Obvious colour contrast between the new and original mortar	Failure to match materials sufficiently	Remove pointing, prepare surfaces and re-point
Flaking and scabbing of lime joints	Failure during winter months to work in a temperature-controlled environment and insufficient protection	Remove pointing, prepare surfaces and re-point
Varying colours of mortar within one façade/structure	Poor gauging/batching of materials for making mortar; different operatives with varying levels of skills	Remove pointing and re-apply using good site practice
Lime effluent staining brickwork particularly but not exclusively from putty limes	Lime mortar exposed to too much direct water or rainfall causing running lime effluent	Malt vinegar for light lime hazing or proprietary cleaners for lime stain removal

Failure to apply mortar to the narrowest neck of the joint

Even traditional brickwork that is in very good condition is likely to have suffered some degree of natural erosion of both the brick arises and faces as well as the lime mortar joint. The implication of this is that if the joints are overfilled, they will appear disproportionally wide on the brickwork as a whole and make it look unsightly and amateurish. Jointing should always be to the narrowest neck of the joint or 1mm back from the brick arises, depending on the condition of the brick.

Applying mortar too wet

Overly wet mortar will also lead to more shrinkage and cracking which is not only unsightly, but can result in poor-quality and weak joints. It can also coat the arrises of the brick, giving the impression of a wider and unsightly mortar joint.

Staining bricks with lime mortar

Each time a tool, a gloved hand or a wet churn brush with lime on it touches the brickwork face, it will make a mark and stain as the lime quickly carbonates. This may not be immediately visible, but within a day or two the wall will be thoroughly marked and/or covered with what is known as lime bloom, a misty white staining that detracts from the character of the brickwork. Poor hand skills, a lack of training and/or rushing the work are often the main causes of this.

Lime mortar has been needlessly applied to fine gauged brick joints in what could be described as unwitting vandalism. To rectify this would require complete removal of the pointing, rubbing down of the arch and tuck pointing the joints of the voussoirs.

Stark against the red brickwork, these white joints suggest rapid drying and bleaching of the lime mortar joints.

Insufficient mixing of lime

Problems can occur if mortars are not mixed sufficiently so all the particles are distributed properly throughout the mix. Lumps of insufficiently mixed materials and lime particles can bleed down the face of brickwork and calcify, causing unsightly hard deposits which are difficult to remove by hand. Unmixed lumps of material can also form voids within a mix which, in turn, can create weaknesses in the mortar.

Inadequate protection from the elements

In either cold or warm weather, building limes are vulnerable and can fail if not adequately protected. Using one sheet of hessian for example will not adequately protect lime work from the sun and wind. With this in mind, as much materials on hand should be used to protect the lime so that there is less chance of rapid drying or wind and sun damage.

Remedial measures

If a mortar mix is too wet, it would have to be 'gauged up' by mixing in more dry components and mixing until it was the desired consistency. Alternatively, some mixes – if only a little wet – can be spread out on a board to lose some moisture. Lime staining can be removed using proprietary brick cleaner, but acids are not necessarily good for brickwork particularly if they are not diluted before use and then neutralized with water. One policy is to work with finesse, pumicing off small lime marks using a piece of rubber brick or flicking off lime particles with the rough side of a washing up sponge. Using small spots of colour wash on stubborn marks can also be effective. Often, very poor work cannot be improved and therefore complete removal of the defective work to start again is the only solution.

<table>
<tr><th>Date</th><th>Key event</th><th colspan="2">Historic Era</th><th>Examples of some notable buildings</th></tr>
<tr><td>c.1050</td><td>Anglo Saxons reuse Roman brick in churches</td><td rowspan="13">MEDIEVAL

TUDOR</td><td rowspan="13">RENAISSANCE</td><td>Holy Trinity Church c.1020</td></tr>
<tr><td>Post 1066</td><td>Normans use reclaimed Roman brick</td><td rowspan="4">St Botolph's Priory, Colchester 1100</td></tr>
<tr><td>1100s</td><td>Flemish immigrant craftsmen aide and influence brick manufacturing skills in Eastern England</td></tr>
<tr><td>1190</td><td>Bricks made locally for use in Abbotts Lodging, Coggeshall Abbey</td></tr>
<tr><td>1240</td><td>Hanseatic League created including Eastern counties towns such as Hull and Kings Lynn</td></tr>
<tr><td>1278</td><td>Bricks imported for use in Tower of London</td><td rowspan="2">Little Wenham Hall, Suffolk c.1270/1280</td></tr>
<tr><td>1303</td><td>Municipal brickworks founded at Hanseatic Port of Hull</td></tr>
<tr><td>1477</td><td>Edward IV statute for tile making governing their manufacture</td><td>Tattershall Castle 1433</td></tr>
<tr><td>1450s</td><td>Start of great era of English brickwork in mansions and residential castles. Bench moulding replaces moulding on the ground</td><td>Waynflete Tower 1475–80

The Deanery, Hadleigh, Suffolk, 1495</td></tr>
<tr><td>1500s</td><td>Brick chimneys and brick noggin appear. The word 'brick' now used</td><td>Hampton Court Palace 1515
Layer Marney Tower, Essex 1520</td></tr>
<tr><td>1548</td><td>Statute protects brickmakers from doing their work unmolested</td><td>Leez Priory, Essex 1536–1537</td></tr>
<tr><td>1568</td><td>London Tilers and Brickmakers merge and receive coat of arms</td><td></td></tr>
<tr><td>1570s</td><td>Brick size regulations put on statute books</td><td>Burton Constable, Yorkshire, late 16th Century</td></tr>
</table>

Date	Key event	Historic Era		Examples of some notable buildings	
1605	Edict by James I that building fronts and windows be built in stone or brick	JACOBEAN	RENAISSANCE	Kew Palace *c.*1631. Moulded brickwork, carved brickwork and colour washing	
1631	Flemish bond becomes the new bond of choice, replacing English bond				
*c.*1600s	Sand moulding gradually replaces slop moulding and greatly improves brick form, though clamps continue to be used			STUART	Bramshill House, Hampshire 1605–1612
*c.*1650s	Updraught kiln adopted which improves efficiency in brickmaking				
1666	Great Fire of London				
1667	Edict by Charles II banning the building of new timber framed buildings and for building in stone or brick only	RESTORATION			Groombridge Place, Kent, *c.*1670–1674
1660s	Sir Christopher Wren (1632–1723) drafts building Regulations and designs buildings influencing the development and use of brick. A second great era of brickwork craftsmanship underway				Tyttenhanger Park, Hertfordshire, 1660
*c.*1680–1690	Introduction of the horse powered pugmill enables greater mass of pliable clay to be produced increasing production				East Range, Hampton Court Palace 1689–1694
1670–1680s	Rise of facadism as once timber buildings are now wrapped in fashionable brick				
*c.*1690	Frog introduced in brick manufacture improving the form of brick and saving clay	William and Mary		Hampton Court palace, Middlesex, south front 1689–1702	

Continued

Date	Key event	Historic Era		Examples of some notable buildings
*c.*1700s	Controllable kilns replace clamps providing more efficient manufacture	GEORGIAN	PALLADIAN NEOCLASSICAL	Chicheley Hall, Buckinghamshire 1719–1723
1725	Edicts banning the abuse of bricks in manufacture relating to the use of 'Spanish' for internal fuel Georgian deceits in brickwork such as tuck pointing appear and take root. Gauged brickwork highly sought after but very expensive			Church Row, Hampstead *c.*1720s Sherman House, Dedham, 1735
*c.*1750	Canal building enables spread of brick into non-traditional brick areas			Bradbourne House, East Malling, Kent, 1774
*c.*1776	Statute by George III sets out brick sizes as 216mm × 102mm × 64mm			Bedford Square, London 1775–1780
1784	Brick Tax introduced to pay for American War of Independence			
1800s	Mechanization begins in earnest In opening decades of 19th Century. Deeper excavation for clay and expansion of brick industry			

apron A panel of projecting brickwork, often gauged, under a window. Common in the eighteenth century.

arris The edge of the brick. In modern factory-produced bricks this is often sharp, but often not in the case of traditionally manufactured brick.

batt A piece of brick cut to a specific size to achieve bonding, i.e., ½ batt, and ¾ batt.

bed joint The horizontal mortar bed on which bricks are laid.

binder A bonding agent that combines with aggregates and water to form a mortar, i.e. lime.

bleeding (of lime) The running of droplets of lime effluent down the face of brickwork.

bonding The arrangement of bricks in a particular way to achieve strength as a primary aim but also pattern.

bonding timbers A section of timber used in internal walls during the seventeenth to nineteenth centuries to eke out the number of bricks used, to provide horizontal reinforcement and to help maintain levels.

bowsaw A traditional tool used to cut rubber bricks in conjunction with a cutting box.

brickearth The uppermost Pleistocene clay deposits used to make bricks up until the nineteenth century.

brick noggin The use of bricks to fill in panels using different patterns where once there was wattle and daub with a view to fire prevention, fashion and reduction of drafts.

brick on edge (BOE) Bricks laid on their face side, latterly to provide a coping but traditionally to provide a footing for walls and or to strengthen a wall (*see* also rowlock bond).

brick replacement The removal of badly eroded bricks and their replacement with a new or salvaged brick.

brick slip Sections or slice cut from of brick of around 50–60mm of either the stretcher or header face and used to cover a badly eroded brick in order to avoid its complete removal.

brick tax One of numerous taxes levied on building materials and in force from 1784 initially to help pay for the American War of Independence, but only revoked in 1850.

camber The slight curvaton applied to the intrados of a gauged camber arch to remove the impression of sagging.

carborundum stone A piece of fine stone for rubbing gauged work enrichments.

chuff A badly formed brick, usually underfired and riven with cracks.

clamp A traditional method of firing bricks from the Medieval period to the early nineteenth century.

closer A ¼ cut of brick enabling quarter bond in one brick walling.

closer gauge A wooden device used to mark-up bricks for cutting to a consistent size.

colour wash A traditional means of providing colour to walls using pigment and glue size.

conservation The philosophical approach of work to protect a building now and for the future.

corbel The projection of a number of courses often found under eaves or under projecting brickwork features.

course A single row of bricks.

cutting box An adjustable wooden or metal box used for the reduction of rubber bricks to the correct size prior to rubbing.

dentil course Projecting header bricks in a course of stretchers to form a patten Dog toothing. A decorative brick projection, usually at eaves, in which bricks are laid at an angle of 45°.

diaper bond Use of coloured bricks to form diagonal patterns in brickwork. Named after the weave of a traditional baby's nappy.

dot A perpendicular brickwork joint.

dressings Coloured areas around openings sometimes colour washed, sometimes in a higher-quality material.

Dutch bond An alternate name for English cross bond.

efflorescence white powdery deposits on brickwork associate with salts in clay.

English bond Alternate courses of headers and stretchers and the strongest of bonds due to number of headers.

English garden wall bond Three to five courses of stretchers to one course of headers. Often used to the sides or rear of a building.

erosion The loss of material through natural or man induced means.

face work The most attractive brickwork on the façade of a building.

fireskin The hard outer skin of the brick created during firing.

flared headers The smallest (header) faces of the brick darkened or vitrified by their position in the kiln or clamp and associated with wood firing. Used for forming coloured patterns in Medieval, Tudor and Jacobean brickwork.

Flemish bond A brick bond consisting of alternate headers and stretchers on the same course.

Flemish garden wall bond Three stretchers to each header on each course.

frog The indentation in a brick formed by a kicker fixed to the pallet.

front A type of brick of good quality used in face work.

garden wall bonds Brickwork bond consisting of three to five courses of stretchers to one course of headers or one course of Flemish bond.

gauge rod A timber staff marked with joint increments to ensure equality of course height in a wall.

gauged work The use of rubber bricks to produce extremely accurate and artistic brickwork enrichments.

Gault bricks Bricks made from a clay with very high chalk content found in Eastern England.

great bricks Oversized bricks used in the Medieval era.

green bricks Bricks prior to firing.

grizzles Poor-quality bricks.

grub saw A small, toothed saw used for marking gauged bricks before cutting or for removing mortar from very fine joints.

hack barrow A type of barrow used to take bricks to be dried.

half bat Half a brick.

header Smallest face of the brick.

header bond Walling constructed with the smallest faces exposed.

hot lime mix A method of making mortar by mixing quicklime with aggregates.

hydraulic lime A type of lime containing clay and other mineral particles which provide a chemical set when mixed with water.

inclusions Pebbles, flint or organic material which has not been removed from the clay before firing.

jamb The sides of a window or door opening.

jacking The upheaval of brick and masonry caused by corroding iron within the structure.

jointing The finishing of mortar joints as the work proceeds.

kiln A permanent method of firing bricks.

kiss marks Markings on bricks created by the method of stacking unfired bricks or tiles another.

legend A box on a drawing containing information pertaining to it, i.e. the dimensions of a gauged arch.

lime bloom The discoloration of brickwork by carbonating lime usually associated with incorrect work practice.

lime mortar A mortar made from calcium carbonate (lime) of varying levels of purity, aggregates and water.

lintel A piece of concrete, steel or traditionally wood, used to support a wall on the inside of an opening.

London stock brick A brick with an indent or frog fired with an internal fuel and of a familiar yellow colour found in London and the Southeast.

mathematical tile A tile used to imitate brick which was hung on the outside of buildings.

mature Used to describe the time that lime putty has had to slake down all lime particles.

monk bond A bond consisting of two stretchers to each header on every course.

mould A wooden frame, later steel lined in which clay is placed to form the brick.

moulded bricks Bricks which have been made in special moulds to form the shape required.

oakum tar hemp Hemp infused with natural sap and which can be used as a breathable flexible jointing materials between brick/stone and timber.

ochre A naturally occurring clay earth pigment used in brickwork for making colour washes.

penny struck joint A name for a flat joint with a compression of between 1–3mm created using a penny and ha'penny fixed in a piece of wood but later a purpose made tool.

perpendicular joints The upright joint in brickwork referred to as a perp.

pigment A natural earth material traditionally used to ruddle (mark) sheep and used historically to colour brickwork to unify the varying hues of brick.

place brick A brick made directly on the ground but whose name became synonymous with bricks not suitable for face work.

plastic repair A small repair made to brickwork using pigment, aggregates and binder.

plinth A section of walling at the foot of a building which often projects. Traditionally used under timber-framed houses to protect the timber.

plumbing A term used to check the vertical accuracy of brickwork, today using a spirit level.

pointing The application different profiles or mortar finishes on top of the bed joints after construction work has been completed.

pozzolan A natural or man-made additive to mortars which provide a quicker set.

pug mill A cylindrical device which appeared in the seventeenth century, drawn by horses in which clay is placed and which is intended to remove inclusions and forming the clay into a more workable mass.

putty A form of lime of the purer type and used to make mortars for pointing and laying.

quarter bond The overlap of on brick over another, usually 56mm.

queen closer A cut of brick lengthways placed beside the quoin header to provide the bond of a solid wall.

quoin The corner of a brick structure and often applied to projecting stone or brickwork.

rabbit skin glue A natural glue used to make sizes for colour wash and brickwork repairs.

racking back The method of building up the corners or ends of a wall before filling in.

raking out The removal of mortar from brickwork in readiness for pointing.

ranging The face alignment of a section of brickwork (usually a racked corner) using a spirit level or straight edge.

rearing A name given to the construction of brickwork corners.

rebate A brickwork section designed to hide or cover part of a timber window frame.

reciprocating saw A type of electric saw which provides a directed cutting tip rather than the rotary action of a disc, used with caution for the removal of bricks from a lime-built wall.

relieving arch An arch built within a wall and used to 'relieve' or take the weight for the decorative arch over the window opening.

restoration Restoring a building to a given point in history based on physical and documentary evidence.

rowlock bond Another name for brick laid on their edge.

rubber brick A brick of very fine consistency used for making gauged enrichments.

rubbing stone A round piece of York stone approximately 475 × 75mm used to rub rubber bricks to exact size.

ruddle A traditional colour used in marking sheep for identification and used to coat buildings (*see* also colour wash).

ruled joint A linear compression on a joint created latterly by use of a specialist tools and straight edge but originally by the use of a penny over the straight edge held between thumb and forefinger, hence penny rolled, or penny struck.

rustication A method of using recessed joints or offsets on quoins to create shadow.

semmel An underfired brick, usually pinkish in colour.

silica sand Sands which are very fine, and which can be used to producing fine pointing finishes.

skewback The sloping bricks either side of an arch.

soldier course Brick laid on their ends.

spalling The delamination or crumbling of brick surface often caused by sulphate attack or freeze thaw action.

spanish An internal fuel of domestic ash and refuse used in brickmaking which cut the costs of fuels for firing. Used in the manufacture of stock bricks.

springer The bricks either side of an arch.

squaring The process of creating ashlar block from a rubber brick ensuring that each face is at 90°.

stock A piece of flat wood over which the brick mould is placed and on which the green brick is taken out for drying.

straight joint Two vertical or perpendicular joints appearing directly above one another in brickwork and seen as bad practice in face work though it appears internally in Flemish bond. Common in Medieval brickwork but a cardinal sin in modern work.

streight arch The traditional name for gauged arches constructed directly over window and door frames.

stretcher The longer side of brick visible when laid.

stretcher bond A pattern of bonding consisting of bricks in ½ lap longitudinally and synonymous with cavity wall construction in modern housing. Traditionally, sometimes used in brick noggin.

strike The bow shaped implement used to remove excess clay form the mould during production.

striking point The central point from which the angles of radiating voussoir lines are derived in a gauged arch.

string course A horizontal course of bricks used at eaves or to define the division of a building into floors.

struck joint A type of joint finished in a cut or impressed linear fashion, i.e. double struck, penny struck.

templet An exact shape cut from wood, cardboard or acetate used for cutting and rubbing brick voussoirs.

tingle A piece of thin metal or plastic used to keep a line true on longer brickwork runs.

trammel A device used on a timber lath to produce geometry for arch drawing.

tuck iron A specialist tools used to apply putty ribbon and usually comes with either a 75mm or 120mm blade with might have one of several different profiles.

tuck pointing An artistic style of pointing which emerged in the 1730s which initially was intended to disguise the rough edges of bricks and make the brickwork look like expensive gauged work but later became the standard finish for premier facades.

tumbling in Bricks laid at right angles to a slope as often found on a gable walls or buttresses.

vitrification The melting or slumping of brick clay that occurs at high temperatures.

vitrified headers Headers placed near the fire channels of the kiln and which burn dark blue to grey colour.

voussoir A wedge-shaped piece of brick or stone used to form an arch. In brickwork it applies to the shaped bricks in gauged or axed arches.

Bibliography

Brunskill, R.W. *Brick and Clay Building in Britain* (Yale University Press, 2009)

Brunskill, R.W. and Clifton-Taylor, A. *English Brickwork* (Ward Lock Limited, 1977)

Campbell, J.W.P. and Pryce, W. *Brick, A World History* (Thames and Hudson Ltd, 2004)

Cave, F.L. The *Smaller English House* (Port Hale, 1981)

English Heritage *Practical Building Conservation: Mortars Renders & Plasters* (Ashgate Publishing Company, 2011)

Hodge, J.C. (1972) *Brickwork for Apprentices* (3rd Ed) (Edward Arnold, 1972)

Holmes, S. and Wingate, M. *Building with Lime: A Practical Introduction* (Intermediate Technology Publications Ltd., 2008)

Lynch, G. *Brickwork History, Technology and Practice Volume 1* (Donhead, 2008)

Lynch, G. *Brickwork History, Technology and Practice Volume 2* (Donhead, 2008)

Lynch, G. *Gauged Brickwork, A Technical Handbook* Second Edition (Donhead, 2006)

Sear, F. *Roman Architecture* (Batsford, 1982)

Watt, D. *Surveying Historic Buildings* (Donhead, 2010)

Wight, J.A. *Brick Building in England from the Middle Ages to 1550* (John Baker, 1972)

Woodforde, J. *Bricks: To Build a House* (Routledge and Kegan Paul Ltd, 1976)

Yorke, T. *British Architectural Styles, An Easy Reference Guide* (Countryside Books, 2009)

Aggregates
Allsand Supplies Ltd
Allsand House
New Hythe Lane
Larkfield
ME20 6FF
01622 662266

Bricks (including rubbers)
Bulmers Brick and Tile Co Ltd
Headingham Road
Sudbury
Suffolk
CO10 7EF
www.bulmerbrickandtile.co.uk
01797 269232

Aggregates, ochres and conservation supplies
Chalk Down Lime Ltd
The Lime Yard
Robertsbridge
East Sussex
TN32 5RP
www.chalkdownlime.com
01580 830092

Art materials
L Cornelisson & Son
105 Great Russell Street
London
WC1B 3RY
www.cornelisson.com
020 7636 1045

British made tools
Harbro Supplies Ltd.
Morland Street
Bishop Auckland
Co. Durham
DL14 6JG
https://www.harbrosupplies.co.uk/contact-us/
01388 605363

Bricks (including rubbers)
Lambs Bricks and Stone
Nyewood Court
Brookers Road
Billingshurst
West Sussex
RH14 9RZ
www.lambsbricks.com
01403 785141

Bricks
H.G. Matthews
The Brickworks
Bellingdon
Buckinghamshire
HP5 2UR
www.hgmatthews.com
01494 758212

Alum
APC Pure
Hyde
SK14 4GX
www.apcpure.com
0161 351 9599

Tuck pointing tools
Speedex Australia
34 Kolora Road
Heidelberg
West Victoria
3081
Australia
www.speedex.com.au
0061 3 9459 3460

Hemp for caulking
Traditional Boat Supplies
Albion Dockside Estate
Hanover Place
Bristol
BS1 6TZ
www.traditionalboatsupplies.com
0117 330 5950

Lime
Tŷ-Mawr Lime Ltd
Unit 12
Brecon Enterprise Park
Brecon
LD3 8BT
www.lime.org.uk
01874 611350

Index